A professional counselor, Mark Bryan has learned many lessons about the complex dynamics of families. The bad news: People often communicate love in code, using words and actions that can be interpreted as love's opposite. The good news: If you decode these messages of affection, you open the door to richer family ties.

There is no way to find authentic love without risking its loss, and this risk may activate your internal skeptic. You may hold back as you read, which is also okay. Just stay in the discussion. Bring your skepticism along and see what happens. You might also find that this whole idea makes you angry, or sad, or brings up memories you might like to put aside forever. Here's an important hint: the more anxiety, resistance, or excitement you feel right now, the more value this book will have for you.

As Murray Bowen, one of the founders of family therapy, once wrote: "The most important process we can undertake in order to mature as adults is to establish a person-to-person relationship with our parents." In a person-to-person relationship you relate in a way that certainly honors your history, but also lets both of you be your fullest selves. To Bowen's assessment I add: Establishing that mature relationship is the most important thing we can do if we want to have love for ourselves, a happy marriage, or intimate friends.

Ultimately this book isn't just about your family; it's about you.

—from the Preface

Also by Mark Bryan

Money Drunk, Money Sober
(with Julia Cameron)

The Artist's Way at Work: Riding the Dragon
(with Julia Cameron and Catherine Allen)

The Prodigal Father: Reuniting Fathers and Their Children

Codes *of* Love

HOW TO RETHINK YOUR FAMILY
AND REMAKE YOUR LIFE

MARK BRYAN

POCKET BOOKS
NEW YORK   LONDON   TORONTO   SYDNEY   SINGAPORE

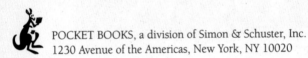

POCKET BOOKS, a division of Simon & Schuster, Inc.
1230 Avenue of the Americas, New York, NY 10020

ISBN: 0-671-03663-7

First Pocket Books trade paperback printing June 2001

10 9 8 7 6 5 4 3 2 1

POCKET and colophon are registered trademarks of Simon & Schuster, Inc.

Cover design by John Vairo, Jr.; front cover photo by PhotoDisc

Printed in the U.S.A.

To my family;
my students, who are my teachers;
the Reverends Peter Gomes, Claudia Highbaugh, and Thomas
Mikelson of the Harvard Divinity School for reminding me that
Spirit and Love are everywhere;
the men and women of Appalachia;
and everyone who longs to love their family.

CONTENTS

I find, where I thought myself poor, there was I most rich.

Ralph Waldo Emerson
"Essay on Character"

Preface
Coming Home

I wrote this book because I used to hate my family.

Yes, I know *hate* is a strong word, but saying I disliked them or that they disappointed me would not reflect the frustrations, anger, or sadness that coursed through my body every holiday season when I picked up the phone to call home from some distant place. Nor could those words describe the shame in my voice each time I described my birthplace in the Appalachian Mountains. If you asked where I was from then, I would have said California. I wrote my family off as too stubborn to change, too different from me, and I exiled myself from the people who knew me and loved me best. I stayed away from them for more than a decade, too lost or pained to visit or speak with them on any regular basis.

How I learned to come back to my family with feelings of love, and how you can come back to yours—no matter how near or far from them you may be—is what this book is about. It is a tale of redemption and forgiveness and, most important, of reconnection: a homecoming in the truest sense of the word.

It is a lie to say that we can't go home again. We *can* go home. In fact, we must go home.

Depending on your circumstances, you may bristle at the idea that your family are the people who know you and love you best.

For some, to even consider returning causes them to flash through a film noir gallery of the defining moments of childhood: scenes of betrayal, of embarrassment, or of violence from years back that still color the ability to love. Journeys home are often journeys through minefields. Simply crossing the threshold into the family home may awaken your youthful self, the person you've been trying all these years to leave behind.

But what if I were to tell you there is something redemptive for you in those stored emotions? What if the very intensity of feeling in those defining moments is not a land mine but a gold mine? What if you could go back home and feel whole and complete? Sometimes the person who feels most unloved is the one that lives closest to home—and has the most difficulty being authentic. My work bringing families together has shown me that anger is often a mask, a cover for fear or for grief. Wherever there are strong emotions there is always something of great value: a lesson of some kind, a joy perhaps forgotten, a grief as yet untangled, a hope not yet expressed.

For the last fifteen years I have worked toward reconnecting fathers with children they may have left or neglected and reforging bonds between a father and mother following a long estrangement. Paradoxically, for much of that time I remained detached from my own extended family. But my experience, first as a counselor and then in healing my own breach, has taught me that even beneath estrangement, deep alienation, grief, or anger, there is nearly always recoverable family affection. This book will guide you through a reconciliation, not in order to eliminate your negative feelings for your family, but to give those feelings their proper weight among the flood of contradictory feelings you may have. Reclaiming those memories with a curious mind and re-framing them with an open heart is a way to make peace with who you are and how you got that way. Only by leaving behind love's shadow side—that gnawing frustration, judgment, and resentment—can we become our best selves.

I know that some resentments are valid, and I am not asking you to forgive the unforgivable. For those of you who come from truly dangerous families, where the threat of violence or emotional mayhem continues to be a real possibility, I add one caveat here: Perhaps this book can help you learn more about yourself and come to peace with a separation that may be imperative. Do not go where angels fear to tread. However, most of us will be able to return home safely.

There is no way to find authentic love without risking its loss, and this risk may activate your internal skeptic. You may hold back as you read, which is also okay. Just stay in the discussion. Bring your skepticism along and see what happens. You might also find that this whole idea makes you angry, or sad, or brings up memories you might like to put aside forever. Here's an important hint: The more anxiety, resistance, or excitement you feel right now, the more value this book will have for you.

As Murray Bowen, one of the founders of family therapy, once wrote: "The most important process we can undertake in order to mature as adults is to establish a person-to-person relationship with our parents." In a person-to-person relationship you relate in a way that certainly honors your history, but also lets both of you be your fullest selves. To Bowen's assessment I add: Establishing that mature relationship is the most important thing we can do if we want to have love for ourselves, a happy marriage, or intimate friends.

Ultimately this book isn't just about your family; it's about you.

Introduction
A Brand-new Past

Many of us wonder if we were ever really loved. I challenge that idea with its opposite: *What if you were loved more than you know?*

The love we want from our parents is clear and easily understood; what we are offered is seldom so. Most people long for closer family connections but don't know what to do to achieve them. We feel we go through the motions of loving family members instead of truly loving them as individuals. We long to appreciate our parents, grandparents, brothers, and sisters as people we *do* love and cherish rather than as people we *should* love and cherish. Often there is a gap in the way love is expressed and how it is received, as if the message were in code. Families, all families, communicate love using words and gestures that not only obscure love but sometimes get interpreted as meaning love's opposite.

Every person has a unique code that he or she uses to express love. Love between parents and grown children is sent, but often it doesn't get through. Code gaps result from generational differences, contrasting emotional styles, gender issues, or a legacy of past misunderstandings. Even some of the ways we hide from pain hurt others; they may not even know that they are loved, that we are scared. For many years, as a counselor and workshop leader, I have been dealing with this struggle between love and fear—fears about our careers, our creativity, and our families.

For some years I have been teaching two distinct sets of skills in my workshops around the country: one is about creativity, and the other is the work I have done for many years as director of the Father Project and author of *The Prodigal Father: Reuniting Fathers and Their Children*. One of the things that comes up consistently in my workshops with children and their parents is the realization that both often feel unappreciated and unloved. This work evolved into *Codes of Love*.

As I began to look more closely at the experience of extended family members, I was forced to examine my own. I saw that the ways I tried to love my parents came across to them as judgmental or condescending. Those same words are often used to describe parental love for adult children. People frequently express their feelings in unconscious languages, using different "dialects" for different people. Family love, often couched in behavior rather than words, is especially subject to misinterpretation. Sometimes it takes us years to understand the true meaning of family gestures, the gestures that comprise a family's Codes of Love.

This book will show you how to decipher those codes. Together, you and I will walk back home with a new understanding and connection to your family, a place you may have never been. In fact, we will walk back to a past that is all brand-new. That is the secret of this work and why we do it. *We can change our past.* Yes, that is what I said. *We can change our past.* We can, because we change the way we experience the past, the way the past affects us, and the way we treat those closest to us who were part of our past—giving them (and ourselves) a new place in our present and our future.

MY STORY

I did not start out life angry and estranged from my family. I was born in a small town in the middle of the Appalachian Mountains in West Virginia, where no one was a stranger to hard work, hard drinking, fighting, or carousing. That kind of hard living went along with a poverty that was even harder. Most of my memories of being home take place at my Grandma Minnie's or Aunt Norma's. At Minnie's, a swinging bridge led over a ravine to her house at the side of a creek bed. I spent many summer days lounging on her porch swing reading as her milk cow grazed nearby and the smells of the ripening garden filled the humid air. She was an open-hearted woman who always kept a pot of pinto beans and a pan of corn bread on the stove to feed whoever happened to stop by.

Clearly I felt different from my family from the start. I was a quiet, thoughtful child who escaped the fighting between my parents by retreating into books. I was drawn to heroic tales—*Johnny Tremain* and the biographies of legendary explorers such as Kit Carson and Madame Curie—because I too was embarked on a hero's quest: I was going to save my family. I was going to stop my parents from fighting by being the best, the brightest, and trying to get everything right: I made great grades, I had a paper route, I worked after school at the grocery store, I made the honor roll, and I was president of my junior class in high school. I took a test my sophomore year that identified me as a possible candidate to be admitted to Princeton, but I was just as interested in Harvard. Either way, I saw the path out of poverty before me, and it was a carpet of ivy. But this was not to be.

What I secretly called my "hillbilly heritage" caught up with me. At sixteen I got my high school girlfriend pregnant. The mothers agreed that we should do the honorable thing and marry, although this meant that as a married couple neither of us would be allowed to finish high school. My dreams of the Ivy League were instantly eliminated. My parents were so ashamed of me that we moved to Columbus, Ohio, to avoid the scandal. The day of my quickie wedding at a justice of the peace, I remember looking at the sorrowful faces of my mother, my sister, my bride, and her mom, and I realized that I had broken the heart of every woman in the room.

This event was the turning point in my development. I had expended so much energy to triumph over what I saw as my family's flaws that when those flaws ended up determining my destiny, I could not help but loathe my heritage even more than I loathed myself. Almost overnight, my idyllic childhood and my brawling-but-loving working-class family transformed in my mind into a horror show of emotional abuse. I no longer remembered the sweet, earthy smells of my grandmother's garden in the summer or her teaching me how to churn butter on the sunlit porch.

I remembered that she didn't have indoor plumbing until I was ten years old, that she had never seen the ocean, that she was virtually uneducated. Instead of recalling her house as the scene of so much warmth and love, I remembered how cold it was in winter—a thin-walled house—and how I repeatedly caught pneumonia there taking my baths in a frigid washtub placed in the middle of the kitchen floor.

My family didn't have to remind me how I'd ruined my life. I felt as though I'd gone from being the hero to being the villain, from being the promise of the future to being the scapegoat for all our dreams deferred. I was so ashamed of what I had become that it didn't take much to set me off. We argued long and often, over the marriage, over the drugs I began to take, over the Vietnam War, and finally over my divorce. In desperation, blame, and grief, I decided they were losers and I needed space.

MY TIME OF ESTRANGEMENT

At age twenty, I moved to Florida, to a lifestyle that was anything but healthy or mature. During what I like to call my lost years, I had a string of menial jobs, disconnected phones, and apartments without furniture, as I tried to hide from my loneliness and anxiety by always moving on. I severed emotional ties with my family, blaming them for my difficulties. At Christmastime I sometimes mustered the courage to phone my family, but those calls usually ended in arguments. My infrequent visits home were themselves acts of rebellion. I'd go just to reinforce how little we had in common and leave carrying a few more bricks to add to the wall between us. My new peer group understood my "victimhood" and joined me in bemoaning our difficult lot in life.

My fractured ability to experience intimacy extended beyond my family to old friends and to lovers. I just couldn't seem to get a handle on friendships deeper than casual or be intimate with a significant other for long. By the time I sought professional help and reentered my family a decade later, one of my younger brothers and my sister both had spouses I had never met and children I had never seen. Years later, even after I became successful and our relationship was civil, my wariness of my family lingered. I still felt I needed to stay away from them because I could not stay around them without being overwhelmed. It seemed that for my own safety I had to leave them behind.

But the one thing you can never truly do is leave your family behind. You carry them with you in that hardened place in your heart you built specifically for them. Despite the miles you put between you, they are always near. Even those who are most angry or resentful at each other are still engaged in a relationship—if only in their minds.

As part of my recovery I, like many of my generation, spent a lot of time in psychotherapy looking for cause and effect, for mistakes to correct, for choices we forgot we ever made. Therapy for many is an important step toward understanding the past and creating the space to become autonomous and ready to play a role in the adult world. Therapists helped me bring significant episodes from the past into sharp focus so that I could, as Freud says, repeat, remember, and work through. While this work is vital, it often leaves our view of the past out of focus, with only the pain in the foreground.

During my time of estrangement, I connected with my peers by reciting the same handful of horrifying stories from childhood. Then they would in turn match me with their renditions of grim pasts, a get-acquainted ritual that all too often made us all reach for another drink. These were the sacred texts of our disaffection with the family and the world. The stories had the hard sheen of oft-told tales recited by rote with very little emotion in our voices. Yet we clung to them as our excuses for our failures, and we were comforted by how they justified our victimhood. We chose these five or six moments from the past not only to define us, but to keep us in place and keep us from change, because we refused to accept our part in the stories we told.

A few years after I resumed the straight and narrow path, I made amends with my ex-wife and got to know my teenage son and acknowledged the pain my absence had caused him. This led to my work in the Father Project, reuniting men with the children they had abandoned or from whom they'd become estranged. The simple exercises I used worked well for those I counseled, because they encouraged forgiveness and eventually love between people who previously could only think of each other with bitterness. Key to breaking the shame-blame paralysis was working with entire families to re-frame their collective view of the actions that led up to the estrangement. The family had to see themselves not as villains and victims but as people who had tried hard at being a family, and now were trying again.

Through this work, I've come to see that memory must not be trusted as gospel. Memory is fluid, changeable, often incomplete or even incoherent. It is not a videotape, not a record. Memories are what we think and feel when we do this thing we call "remembering." The point we want to make through these recollections determines what parts of our past we ignore.

Clinging to these lopsided memories comes at a terrible price. These flawed and unhealed connections deprive us of a major source of comfort and joy and reflect back out to our other relationships as an inability to feel comfortable or be happy. What I saw over and over again in my Father Project work was that for many, there was still an internal resonant space, a haunting gap in the feelings they had for their own parents, which in turn colored their ability to stay emotionally involved and true to themselves within the families they had created as adults.

The same was true in my relationship with my own family. I had worked my way back into my family's daily life. I was again sharing in their struggles in a way I had avoided for more than a decade. But on any deep emotional level I was just going through the motions. I refused to acknowledge the grief and distance I felt when it came to spending time with my parents and siblings.

I used to pity my sister, who was so enmeshed with our mother that she'd never lived away from home and never, in my view, had a chance to stand on her own as an adult. In contrast, I felt superior. At least I had had the courage to leave the scene. What I didn't see until I began the process of true reconciliation was that my distance was simply an expression of the same anxiety that kept my sister close to home. Despite all the miles I'd put between us, I had no real distance, no true perspective, and no deep compassion for the real story of myself in my family.

What I was yearning for was a way not just to love my family but also to love myself. I wanted all of us, every member of my family, to be our biggest and best selves, connected to one another through our shared love, compassionate about all that had come before. In my estrangement, I thought I was wounded by my suspicion that my parents didn't love me. What I was unable to comprehend was my craving to love *them*. I missed the pride I once had in my father and my joy at the humor and impetuousness of my mother despite all that had come between us. I thought all I had to do was fix myself and then I could fix them. What I did not understand is: *You cannot judge someone and love them at the same time.*

CODED EXPRESSIONS

This work came into sharp focus for me one day five years ago when one of my workshop students told me that he'd been invited to his father's eighty-second birthday. "I haven't talked to him in twenty-some years, and we never really had a relationship," Jack said. "Should I go or not?" I was able to place myself in his position easily, but my answer surprised me: "Well, Jack, I think we've reached the point in our lives where it's probably not so important how good a father he was. It's much more important how good a son we can be." There was a stunned silence on the other end of the line. Stunned myself, I thought about how becoming a better son might influence not only my relationship with my father but also my perception of myself.

The idea of being a better son had rarely influenced either my perceptions or my actions. Since I had reconnected with my family, my relations with my father were regular and cordial—although wariness and irritability rumbled underneath the surface. I had to be careful to exercise self-control. In my immaturity I had decided our fundamental failure to connect was inevitable and largely his fault. Despite the great distance we had traveled to get closer, I suspected he was still disappointed in me. I believed he never really understood me and didn't know how to express his love. The simple idea of trying to be a better son turned those perceptions around. I wondered if I ever really understood him. I began to see how much my disappointment around our relationship was based on my not knowing how to receive his expressions of love, or give my own.

Healer, heal thyself. It was time for me to use what I had learned on my fractured memories. I started, oddly enough, with the memory of watching football on television with my father, because for me that act had become a symbol of how my father and I did not connect.

When I was a young boy, my greatest joy was sitting near my father on the old couch in the living room eating junk food and cheering on the Baltimore Colts or Navy against Army. After my early marriage and my subsequent breach with my father, this tradition stopped. I couldn't sit idly in the living room in close proximity, distracted by so much that was going unsaid and the dozens of things I would have liked to blurt out. I would get restless, anxious, and finally bored. I stopped watching sports on television altogether once I left home.

Yet each time I went home to visit my father, we would end up spending our time together in the living room watching sports. We didn't talk much. Although there were many things I was aching to speak with him about, he's never been one to paw over the past. As we would sit watching, Dad would occasionally say something about some player or other, asking if I had seen this play or that game, none of which I had more than a vague interest in. In many ways it annoyed me to participate in what I saw as a hollow ritual of pretend closeness.

Then one Thanksgiving several years ago, my brother Jim showed up. As the three of us watched four football games in a row with my dad, I began to understand what was really going on.

For Jim and my dad, sports talk was a way of connecting.

When they shared an *oohhh* or a *yeahhh* over the game, they reinforced their closeness and shared experience in the present tense. Their shared enthusiasms were coded expressions of love and shared history. After I realized this, I found myself bringing up old football highlights—mentioning things like Johnny Unitas's famous two-minute drill, which we'd all watched together—hoping somehow to wedge my way in. I did. I was able to participate in their dialogue, albeit with a language that was thirty years old. Sharing the game enabled me to hearken back to earlier times, when we were close. I was trying to demonstrate my respect for how long Dad had borne the father role and reestablish that lost camaraderie. I realized that every time I dismissed the way they watched sports, I denigrated one of the chief ways they expressed love. I stayed for the four games and relearned this forgotten language. Only this time, I chose to speak the language without feeling as if I had been forced to speak it. All those years I had been estranged, my father and I had been speaking different languages but trying to say the same thing.

That day together allowed me to look with new eyes at other interactions: My father's referring me to the Weather Channel and picking out my route to the airport took on new significance. I realized that when he points to an incoming storm on the tube and says matter-of-factly, "That snow will probably close Route 7, so take 340 into D.C. and fly out of Washington National instead of Dulles," he is not trying to control me, but saying "I love you" in code. Now, that odd eccentricity of his that had at first annoyed then amused me, took on a sweet significance. I no longer feel *belittled* when Dad offers me the safest routing, for now I know it is one of his Codes of Love, a coded expression of his concern for my safety.

Other memories came streaming back to me: the many days we played basketball at the garage hoop, the nights in the backyard playing football with my friends when my dad was the only grown-up present. I look back now, and it's still hard to believe that for so many years I did not have ready access to those memories. They were such wonderful times. These new memories will probably never erase the terror and abandonment I felt as a child witnessing the conflict between my mother and father, yet these forgotten *good* memories become part of the memory mix. They have their place and are no longer dominated by the darker memories. They are equal and integrated.

When people hear my story about watching sports on television with my father, their eyes light up with understanding. Some people start thinking back immediately, re-framing family events and behavior in a way that renews rather than threatens connection. Many find a way to love their parents through reexamining the very actions that were a source of friction.

A RENEWED PERSPECTIVE

Jenny, an accomplished forty-year-old business executive in Manhattan, for most of her adult life has seen her conservative, successful father as cold and distant. She says, "Every time I had a problem or wanted my dad to comfort me about something, he would take out a sheet of paper and make two columns: PRO and CON. Then he would go down the list of alternative answers for me. It just left me feeling like he didn't give a damn—at least not about my feelings." Before Jenny's father died recently, she had a chance to reconcile with him.

"Now that he is dead, I have to come to terms with his legacy. One of the things I miss about him is his objective viewpoint. He had a singular emphasis on the solution to problems that I can now appreciate. Looking back, I realize that I always wanted him to wallow in sympathy with me, but he never would. His great gift to me was the message, *Focus on the solution, not the problem.*" Jenny has integrated her father's critical perspective into her current life. "I am convinced that his objectivity is a key factor in my becoming successful. He was always there for me, just in his own way," she says.

Through the tools I've developed in my Codes of Love workshops, people find a way to renew their perspective, not only on the past but also on the ways their parents communicate love to them now. You may never know all your family's Codes of Love—some are immediately obvious, some are very subtle—but by working through the exercises in this book, you can develop a renewed perspective on the past in which the negative does not dominate. You cannot use this book to find some simple formula for the Codes of Love. The human experience is a wide and muddy river, too mysterious and deep for such simplistic solutions. The human spirit expresses itself in millions of gestures, great and small, common and unique, that we can, however, learn to appreciate and acknowledge.

Here are just a few of the simpler ways workshop participants have come to understand their families' codes:

- "My father always asks me how my car is running. I used to get mad; I mean, what business of his is it? Then I realized that he just wanted to know I wouldn't get stranded."
- "When I would bring home a report card with all A's and a B, Dad and Mom would shake their heads and say, 'Well, if that's the best you can do, it's the best you can do.' Now I realize that they were joking and pushing me to be the best I could be."
- "My dad always says, 'Let's go over your finances.' I felt that he thought I was inadequate. Now I realize that he just wants to know that I am secure."

- "My dad draws me intricate maps to my grandmother's house every time I go (about once or twice a year). I could save the map or remember the way by now, but I know he loves to do it for me—so we have this ritual where he draws the map, and I say, 'Thanks, Dad.' "
- "My older brother is a successful lawyer. I'm a part-time college teacher and struggling screenwriter. Every time we talk on the phone he gets into this advice-giving mode, going on and on about ways I could really break into the movie biz and I should do this, I should do that. It used to drive me crazy, like I was his head-in-the-clouds little sister. We had a couple of fights over this. But the thing is, he really does love me and care about me, and this was his way of getting that across."

HOW WE WILL GET THERE

In essence the first step in going home to your family is an act of rebellion—for a change this is not an act of rebellion against your parents but a rebellion against your past. You will challenge the beliefs you've held dear, the myths, and the antiquated value judgments. It can be a very disturbing and yet freeing process to view the past as a sacred but mutable text, one that you can reflect upon, talk about, and learn from as you write a more true and complete story of you and your family.

This book is a combination of several disciplines that became part of my own search for answers: family systems theories, cognitive psychology, moral philosophy, and the spiritual traditions. I wanted to know: What do I owe my parents? What are the reasons for my feeling so lonely? Why didn't I get to have a "perfect" family? Why did I hate them (hate myself) so? Why couldn't I feel the love they had for me?

Every family is different, and one's approach to reconnecting has to involve, to be sure, some custom design, so this book is a conversation between you and me. I will tell you about my family, and you will tell me about yours. We will, in effect, change each other as we go.

Although I offer many different exercises to help you see your way home, the basic steps are Remember, Reflect, Re-frame, and Reconnect:

Remember: I want you to reawaken the pleasant memories of your family. The best way to regain a fuller picture is not to use your mind but to use your senses. I will explain why some memories are more dominant than others and help you revive some long-dormant ones. One of the most powerful techniques is to reacquaint yourself with the sights, objects, and scents of childhood. Music, photographs, old toys, and favorite foods help evoke the best parts of your past.

Reflect: In this step we learn how to play with our memories and role-play the various characters in our lives. We often get stuck in a static rendition of our family. In reflecting, we shift forward and backward in time, and practice seeing the events of the past through others' perspectives. In the chapter on this step, we examine the emotionally charged events in the history of our relationship with our family to better understand each member's essential character and our own. Blending our version of the truth with their views affords us a wider vision of the world in which we grew up, and therefore the world in which we now live.

Re-frame: Here we commit to finding the strengths in our family. To understand your family's present and to take stock of your own development, it is a good idea to consider your family's foundation: common traits, heroic acts, legacies, and inheritances. Every family has its legends of triumph over adversity. Exercises in the chapter on this step will help you construct the legends of your family's life and a detailed time line of its past with an eye toward seeing the strong qualities that unite you—and finding their individual Codes of Love. Through this you can gain a broader view of the great chain of generations that shaped your family and gain a better understanding of family dynamics as a whole.

Reconnect: Now comes the real test of our work together. It's easy to talk about changed attitude while in isolation. The real proof of our maturity is in the ability to establish and maintain that person-to-person relationship with family members and friends. In this chapter, we learn the delicate balancing act between the twin forces of togetherness and autonomy. We learn to keep a loving connection without sacrificing our integrity. The keys to this step are acceptance, the use of loving candor, and the cessation of judgment and blame.

The process of reconnecting with your family requires some discipline on your part. The questions and exercises outlined in the Codes of Love process are best responded to and reflected on in solitude, in a quiet place, with no television or other distractions. Some of you will get these answers to your questions immediately; others will want to ponder them for several weeks. While there is no set time limit, I would suggest that you set aside an hour or two each week and count the time as special as you do the work at hand.

Though most of us are not from truly dangerous places, anyone beginning this work would do well to examine the support he or she has. Sometimes those of us who need it most, for instance, those who cannot engage in emotional work without self-destructive or defensive behavior, have the least emotional support. For those of you who are vulnerable to this, I urge you to find a colleague or support group, a mentor, a member of the clergy, a friend, or a therapist with whom to do this work. For some, it may be important to know that there is someone you can call if what comes up for you during these reflections begins to seem overwhelming. This work may call up feelings you have long suppressed—including joy and love and laughter.

At first it may seem hard to find the time and gather the focus, because much of what you are working with has an emotional charge. If you can, begin to look forward to these sessions with anticipation and curiosity. As you cast aside the bitterness and uncover the hidden sweetness in your family life, you will Remember, Reflect, and Re-frame a kinder and more loving view of yourself, one that will enable you to Reconnect to your family and your current relationships. You will free yourself by letting go of preconceived notions of your history that encourage you to hold on to blame or abdicate responsibility. This process will lead you beyond the idea of forgiveness, because the need for forgiveness will lift as you embrace your family and yourself with all your flaws and strengths, and relinquish the judgment of your family and yourself that weighs you down.

Codes of Love Exercise: THE STORY LINE

The story of your life is still unfolding: it is a mystery for which all the chapters have not been written, and some that have are not as they seem. To get a sense of where you are going, use this story line exercise to chart where you have been. This exercise is not as much about what you know about your life as about what you do not remember. Writing down the basics will allow other memories to surface—what I call cooking.

The first step of this work is to piece together the basic history of your life. Let's call it a story line—a generally factual recollection of *your* life as you currently know it. We need just the facts—the who, what, where, and when—of your life. Write down all the significant events. The easy way to get started is to think of your life in five-year increments, speed-writing all the details you can remember for each five-year period.

For instance, for the period from birth to age five, you would write where you were born, who the significant people were in your life during those first five years, whether you moved or stayed put, and so on. What happened to you? To your family? Any major accidents, successes, illnesses, deaths, births, marriages? List everything you can think of. Now do the same thing for the lives of your parents and their parents. *How much* do you know about *their* lives? *Can you answer* these same questions about your parents' story line? How would each of your parent's story line read? Can you call them to fill in the gaps? How much do you really know about their *whole* life?

Now put this into a historical framework. What was going on in the world during this time that was significant to your family: the Vietnam War, the women's movement, the civil rights movement? Who were the politicians, musicians, and movie stars of the period?

Travel right on down the history of your and your parent's lives and list everything you can remember. Take your time with this, but there is no need to make huge multicolored charts or graphs (unless you just like to do that kind of thing). This story line will become a foundation tool, and you will refer back to it at various points in our work together to add items or reflect on them from various points of view.

My story line starts something like this:

I was the firstborn child, arriving in March 1953 at a clinic in Iaeger, West Virginia, to parents Jim and Dorothy. Several of my

*relatives were present at my birth but not my dad, who was at
sea. He arrived a few days later, and I was named Mark Alan,
though my mother had wanted to name me Reginald Elliot
Bryan and call me Reb. I escaped that fate by some unknown
intervention but have always heard about it. My sister, Paula,
was born eleven months later in the same clinic. We all lived in
a trailer beside the Wyandotte River that ran through the nearby mountains. I got pneumonia and almost died when I was
about three. Mom says the doctors told her I might not make it
through the night. We moved to join my dad on different navy
bases from Connecticut to California. My brother Jon was born
in Welch, West Virginia, at the clinic there when I was four. We
moved to Chula Vista then, and I started kindergarten
there. . . .*

This should give you a good start. No need to worry about
grammar or spelling, just get it all down as fast as you can. You
can go over it if you would like and edit it a little (or a lot, depending on your temperament). It will work whether it is beautifully written, done as a detailed flow chart, or scrawled on a
napkin in pencil. Doing the work is what counts. Find out everything you can about your extended family.

Codes of Love Exercise: FAMILY HISTORY: THE PAST AS WE
KNOW IT

All good storytelling has a unique perspective on events, but as
actors in our family dramas we sometimes forget that we are the
narrator and have a unique point of view—and that in many of
our memories, the narrator was someone else, and those memories are secondhand, the as-told-to-us versions that we heard from
our relatives.

This section helps you begin to uncover the different narrators of your life story and the basic temperament and traits that have made you who you are. It is meant to fire up a renewed respect for yourself and the members of your family as evolving personae—the protagonists of your own never-ending story.

It is not uncommon for people to space out when they answer the following questions. You may even get excited or a bit sad. There is no "right" response. Just answer them as best you can, and try to ignore your inner voice should it judge you or your answers.

BEGINNING TO REMEMBER

- Where are you from? Do you ever disguise it? Are you proud of it?
- What socioeconomic class are you from? What signs point to this?
- What three childhood traits are you proudest of?

1.
2.
3.

- What irritated you as a child? Who irritated you? How did you express your irritations?
- Did you ever run away? When? How far?
- What kind of medical problems did you experience growing up?
- What was your temperament as a kid: shy, outgoing, thoughtful, melancholy, upbeat, boisterous, studious, athletic?
- What were some of your special skills as a child? Who noticed them?
- What subjects fascinated you? What television shows?

- List the three happiest moments of your childhood.

    1.
    2.
    3.

- What pets did you have as a child? Did you like them?
- Were you a daydreamer? A go-getter? A reader? Lazy and shiftless? All of these?
- What was your biggest loss? Biggest victory? Biggest embarrassment? Biggest source of pride? Biggest struggle?
- What did you want to be when you grew up? How many times did your aspiration change?

THE FAMILY TAPESTRY

- What three strengths does your family possess?

    1.
    2.
    3.

- What tragedies did your family experience? What successes?
- Who was the most dominant member? How was this person dominant?
- What was your family's medical health profile?
- Which of your relatives were you most like as a child? Which are you like now?
- How would your siblings describe you as a child? How would they describe you now?
- What was the big question you had about your family?
- Did your family have a secret? What was it?

- Does this work make you happy or sad? Why?
- How did your vision of the world differ from that of other members of your family?
- When did this difference start? Who first noticed? How do you think the difference or differences helped shape you?
- What life dreams did you have for yourself that were different from the dreams your family held for you?
- What interests do you share with your siblings? Which do you not share? Are you sure?
- Who influenced you most when you were a child? What events? Who told you this?

THE GOOD-TIMES LIST

- What were your favorite activities to do as a family?
- List three of the happiest moments of your life.

1.
2.
3.

- List five of the nicest things anyone has ever done for you.

1.
2.
3.
4.
5.

- What were five of the kindest things you ever did for someone else?

1.

2.

3.

4.

5.

- Were there any special jokes or nicknames you had with your family?
- What other memories have come into your mind while you were working on these questions? Add those to your family's story line.

CHAPTER 1

From Tragedy to Comedy

In 1983 I had just begun building my life back and was living in the attic of a friend's house in Chicago, when I decided I had better go home for Christmas. Although I said "better" in tones of duty and dread, it is clear to me now that I was the one who wanted to be better for going home. I hadn't been back for the holidays in more than seven years and in that time my parents had split up. My sister, Paula, who now had four kids, and my mother were living in trailers on my grandma Minnie's property. My brothers, Jon and Jimmy, had ended up back in West Virginia, Jon working in the coal mines and Jimmy in high school. My father was living on the other side of the mountain, managing the local hospital. As I packed for the eight-hour trip home, I could picture Minnie's house just as I had seen it so many Christmases before, shabby but solid against the glistening snow and bare trees, warm yellow light glowing from the windows Uncle Bill had installed a few years back.

My feeling of home stopped at the front door of Minnie's house, because once I was inside, my mind went blank. Back then I had virtually no memories of childhood, only flash floods of emotions without the scenes that generated them. My brother Jon—who, like my other brother and sister, says he has few childhood memories—describes going home as "being in the box." Once you're in the box, everything goes dark.

This darkened lens on the family camera includes what I call our culture of suspicion. When family suspicion gets habitual, it can harden into what psychologists call a schema or gestalt: suspicion forms a lens through which we view all our family's actions, past and present. Peering through a suspicious lens, we may keep discovering aggressive and threatening acts, even plots and skulduggery in seemingly ordinary gestures. It's a genre of personal historiography I call family noir.

The twentieth century, as well as psychotherapy in general, has taken its philosophical lead from Freud, Nietzsche, and Marx, not three of the happiest campers in the woods, I sometimes joke. Let's face it, the Freudian picture of family leaves a lot to be desired. Psychology's emphasis on the causality of adult symptoms from childhood experiences has repeatedly had to be modified as the theory has proven limited. This belief that the cause of adult problems is born in childhood parenting has had all of us snooping into the past with a magnifying glass looking for any evidence of wrongdoing by those closest to us.

When revolutionary psychologist James Hillman says that psychology's emphasis on causality disrupts our connection to "the great chain of generations," he is referring to the links to the positive and deeply symbolic aspects of our shared human past. The point here is that too many of us are looking at the world through this filter of suspicion and searching for our victimhood under every childhood bed. I had this same filter as I approached my childhood home.

How would Minnie look? How had the years treated my mom, my siblings? What did their kids look like? Would Minnie remember to make my favorite fudge just as she had all the Christmases before I lost contact with my family? What gap would there be with my father gone? I could see the house, but I couldn't picture the people in it any more than I could imagine myself there. My last memory of that house had been the day many years before when my grandfather Arnie told me that he didn't have a job for me there, that I wasn't welcome: "We don't hire your kind here." My *kind* were the longhaired hippies of the sixties.

Still I better go home, better bring my better self home, the self I had been constructing since I had my moment of grace and woke up. I'd gotten a job as a clerk at the Chicago Board of Trade and remade my wardrobe accordingly. I'd bought a black cashmere coat at a thrift store for eight dollars, which I was always careful to toss just so on the back of a chair so that the one-hundred-percent-cashmere label caught your eye. At the same thrift store I'd uncovered a cache of a rich man's dress shirts with monogrammed cuffs. On my way into work on the El, I adjusted the sleeves of my one-hundred-percent-cashmere facade so someone else's initials peeked over the top. I might be sleeping in a frigid attic on a mattress on the floor straight out of some Appalachian nightmare, but I was determined to disguise my poverty. I was destined for better things. The dream lived on. This was the self I was driving home for Christmas in a rented Lincoln Town Car with a trunk stuffed full of presents I couldn't afford.

I sped through the Midwest in high style with an occasional glance at my sacred garment on the seat next to me. But as I turned off the interstate onto the state road and began my climb up the mountains, my thoughts turned dark. What were they saying about me right now as the women stood in the kitchen preparing Christmas dinner? I bet none of them believed I'd really changed my ways.

The hopelessness of all of it hit me as I passed the increasingly more spindly shacks at the side of the road, the poverty here so deep it practically ran through the veins of coal under the hillside.

Part of what had made me want to come home was my nostalgia for my West Virginia relatives: images of hunting with the other kids for crawdads in the river, shooting BB guns, and running after a wild boar. If I could be that child again—capture just a moment of that playfulness and innocence—maybe I could reclaim my optimism.

Those memories escaped as I climbed the mountain back to Minnie's, noting the abandoned cars hard by the rusting double-wide trailers that dotted the hillsides and the tumble-down general stores that hadn't seen a coat of paint in twenty years. My heart was pounding high in my throat. I hoped they weren't all still expecting me to save them from this, as if they ever had.

The first sight of Minnie's was jarring. Everything the same, everything different. The state had replaced the swinging wooden bridge over the ravine with a sturdy concrete and metal one that forever changed the feel of the place. The good part was I could pull the Lincoln right up to the front of Minnie's for my entrance. As I donned my coat and went to the trunk to gather some presents, my family poured out of the front door to welcome me. I released a huge sigh from my spirit as my mother and I embraced and my brothers' and sister's hands touched me on my back and shoulders as they exclaimed welcomes. That same touch I craved shrunk my soul as I anticipated all that might happen after this loving moment of reunion. I looked over my mother's shoulder at the Lincoln for reassurance. It was mud-splattered and as dreary to me now as the other battered old beaters in the front yard.

POISONOUS SUSPICION

Okay, let's stop the movie right here. Of course, my elaborate preparations for my return home couldn't have made for weaker armor. I was edgy, wary, and hyperalert to any sign my family wasn't fooled by the grand trappings. I suspected they could already see I was an impostor. I suspected they had parts of their own lives they were hiding from me. On top of all that, I suspected that everyone secretly dreaded my return. Ho ho ho. Merry Christmas.

To be wary and mistrustful in a new situation is part of our survival instinct. In more intimate settings suspicion becomes a hunting instinct. Suspicious people are sure to find what they are looking for. If you suspect that your lover is cheating on you, a stray thread or a discarded phone number suddenly becomes a world of hurt. The suspicious person is way past observable doubt, focused only on proving the case: total inference without any evidence.

I think not enough has been written about the poisonous effect of suspicion in the family, mainly because it is mislabeled as guilt or rage, or disguised, as mine was, by grandiosity. Going home brings up at once the differences between you and your family that you have worked so hard to establish and the inevitable similarities that, no matter how much time passes, you can never extinguish. The desire to be seen by your family as better, different, and making something of yourself in life competes with the yearning for connection to the people and places that made you who you are. Yet, the new persona you have constructed for your life in the larger world is naked before your family, people who can at once see you in all your glory and weakness. They can remember you as an early reader, a mischievous child, an A student, a surly adolescent, dumped and despondent about an old lover, ambitious and falsely brave. For some, being among people who have loved you all your life through triumph and through disgrace can feel glorious, the essence of embrace. Others, especially those with issues simmering between themselves and other family members, are rattled by the scrutiny and intimacy. Suspicion becomes a way of ordering the family dynamic that defends our fragile sense of self against history.

There is so much history, so many layers of experience among family members, that the simple act of passing the butter at the breakfast table can be loaded with meaning, if you're of a mind to see it that way. A large part of what makes returning home so excruciating is how quickly our preconscious fears can be triggered by stepping in the front door of the family home. These whiffs of the past jump to the forefront of the mind to shape the suspicious point of view.

For Justine, a magazine publicist from New York, one of the landmark incidents of her childhood is the night her father slapped her so hard across the face during an argument that it was a whole day before his handprint completely faded from her cheek. Now thirty-three years old and standing in that same kitchen on a bright summer day, she sees her father raise that same hand in a similar arc to swat a fly on the stovetop. For an instant, Justine cringes, not quite knowing why. Her body tenses as her mind scans time, snapping through every incident that made her feel like that fly.

Although things between Justine and her father have been stable for years, that single gesture returns her to powerlessness and terror. If she chances to catch him with a dash of that look in his eye, even if he's casting it at the family dog, she suspects without a rational thought to support it that she has misjudged the situation. Memories amplified by emotions are remembered longest, quickest, and with most detail.

Family gatherings, especially those that take place in the family home, are thick with these kinds of reference points, and as James Hillman says, the family home is a metaphor for the family's inner psyches. When I used to visit my family, many of whom are now living in a house in North Carolina, I had to work hard to quell my fears and feel the bond of love that ties them together. My eye saw instead the continuing legacy of chaos in my family. In that house there are interior doors off the hinges, marks in the walls where something went through them. I stepped through the front door with my suspicions intact.

Eliminating your suspicions is an essential step in reuniting with your family. How does it serve my relations with my family to enter the home scanning for evidence to justify my worst fears about my relatives? A guarded, judgmental state of mind keeps us distant from our loved ones and in many ways freezes us in roles that may no longer suit us, particularly during the limited times we spend with them. My suspicious attitude removes me from true connection with my family members and prevents me from giving myself freely to the situation. When I view my family through the lens of suspicion as the cause of my suffering, I give nothing to them but my fears.

Suspicions start early in childhood when there is something in the family's interaction that denies the child's developing sense of self-worth. Cognitive psychologists believe that the self builds a mental model of the world based on the answers to four basic questions:

- Are other people safe or threatening?
- Is the world at large benevolent or malevolent?
- Is life meaningful or meaningless?
- Am I worthy or unworthy?

Our answers to these questions form the basic postulates that, as a whole, become our world view, and govern our expectations and actions.

In some families, especially violent families, the answers to these questions change daily, sometimes hourly, and the child has to be ever on guard.

Another important factor in a child's ability to feel secure and make sense of reality is a child's developmental limitations. Children have a hard time reconciling the multiple identities of the adults around them because their abstract-thinking capacities are still forming. Harvard developmental psychologist Kurt Fisher reframes Sigmund Freud's Oedipus complex, the stage of life when a boy desires his mother and, Freud says, wants to replace his father, as no more than a cognitive problem of role definition. He believes the young boy is unable to distinguish man-dad from man-husband; that is, if I grow up to become a man like Dad, will I also grow up to become my mother's husband? This stage of development disappears as a child's capacity for abstract thinking leaps forward in preadolescence.

Add to a child's limited understanding a misguided search for causality and someone to blame, and our general cultural narcissism, and we have the makings for a potent antifamily cocktail. Whether we use Oedipus, Othello, or any common movie tragedy, the filter of suspicion is very much alive in our culture.

FAMILY NOIR

In my friend Bob's family, his father's frequent accusation against his mother was that she was unfaithful. When this issue came to the fore, his father would tell Bob's mother he was leaving her, grab Bob or one of his brothers, and race off in the family car. All the children remember how it felt to sit in the passenger seat next to their father as he sped through the countryside calling their mother a whore and listing all the men he believed she had slept with. They didn't experience just the terror of being trapped in the car with a raging father or the withering pain of being forced to listen to him shame their mother and hence themselves. The ordeal was an assault on their ability to form a coherent reality.

Those boys loved their mother. She nurtured them and fed them and cared for them—and she was also a lying whore? Bob and his brothers also loved their strong, hardworking father, the very model of a good man, but was he also an uncontrollable maniac? Is the world safe or unsafe? Malevolent or benevolent?

Even in more benign home situations, one of the parents' essential child-rearing methods is to deny reality to protect a child's innocence. Suppose, for example, a child walks into the kitchen shortly after her parents have ended an argument. Her mother storms around furiously wiping down the countertops and tossing dishes into the sink as her father slumps at the kitchen table turning a matchbook over and over in his hand. "Mommy, why are you so mad?" she asks. "I'm not mad," her mother whispers tensely. "Don't upset your mother," her father cautions. The girl leaves the kitchen confused. Mommy was already mad, and the girl sure hadn't caused her anger. What was really going on there? When a child starts to distinguish text from subtext, the mind suspects there may be even more going on than meets the eye.

In the film noir genre of the post–World War II era, suspicion is the operative point of view. Movies like *The Big Sleep, Kiss Me Deadly,* and *Double Indemnity,* through the actions of characters played out against stark interiors, engaged viewers' deepest fears about what people were capable of doing to each other. Nicholas Christopher, in *Somewhere in the Night: Film Noir and the American City,* describes noir films as peopled by "betrayers, dangerous and mysterious strangers, people with double identities, mistaken identities, and those who simply, or subtly, aren't what they seem to be." This too, is the atmosphere of family noir.

When choosing the lighting and soundtrack for your depictions of the turning points in your emotional estrangement from your family, you might find the shadows sharp and the music haunting. People might fling things to the floor, storm out of rooms, or be left crying in the corner. The irony of this frame of reference is that even though the characters in your family noir scenario are mostly victims of their circumstances, suspicion makes them feel powerful. The suspicious mind enters the room assuming that it knows what's really going on underneath the surface. These people you are suspicious of, they are not quite as smart as you. They think they have you fooled, but you're too keen, too aware for them to pull it off. Basically when you enter the family with a suspicious mind, you're spoiling for a fight.

What set you up for this fight is not just the issues between you and your family, but a century of misapplied theories of psychology—the I'm-in-trouble-it-must-be-daddy's-fault school. The twentieth century's initial move in the direction of family suspicion was in fact a progressive step, a step toward enlightenment and away from the false and saccharine images of the nineteenth-century idealized notion of family life. In their version, Mom was happy to scrub floors and let Dad support her, and all was right with the world as long as Dad had control. This view gave us a rosy myth of home that turned a blind eye to the dark side of family and power.

Yet, when misunderstood or misapplied, the Freudian picture of family is not pretty. The Freudian family script includes castration threats, sibling warfare, and devouring mothers. In trying to correct a view of the family that was out of focus, Freud brought to the forefront another myth—the family tragedy. For a century, experts helped us look for family damage without helping us look for the positives and strengths. Worse, they sometimes told us that if we didn't find damage, we simply weren't looking hard enough.

FAMILY COMEDY/BLACK COMEDY

Suspicion also fascinated Shakespeare, who was one of Freud's major influences. Freud read and pondered Shakespeare and clearly owed a large debt to Shakespeare's exploration of the mind. Shakespeare scholar Harold Bloom, author of the recent book *Shakespeare: The Invention of the Human,* believes, as do many, that Shakespeare's psychological insights have never been equaled. Freud found in Shakespeare a focus on the family, especially the tragic family, that emphasized deception and self-delusion. I would like to propose that we overturn that view and focus on what critics call the comic view of the human condition.

This view of the world is often best articulated by philosopher Kenneth Burke, who believed that literary forms reflect general orientations toward life. He found in literary comedy a vision as humane as it is shrewd, as rich in love and humor as it is clear-eyed about the ways human beings may deceive, exploit, or abuse each other. Burke called the comic vision bittersweet: it is neither sentimental, nor suspicious. It knows human darkness but does not dwell there. It works to find human goodness and views our behavior with charity. Burke called his version of this stance, "A Comic Frame of Acceptance." To quote Burke, "The progress of humane enlightenment can go no further than in picturing people not as *vicious,* but as *mistaken.* When you add that all people are necessarily mistaken, and that all people are exposed to situations in which they must act as fools, that every insight contains its own special brand of blindness, you complete the comic circle."

Once in this comic circle, the world changes, because we are released from judgment and blame, without clouding our understanding or steeping us in denial.

Even Freud's contemporaries who later broke with Freud, such as Carl Jung and Alfred Adler, did so based on a much more optimistic assessment of the motivations for human behavior. They believed that humans were essentially social creatures greatly influenced by cultural and historical conditioning, rather than merely victims of their sexual and aggressive impulses. What Freud, despite his brilliance, could not have known during his time, was the tremendous influence of temperament, social context, and genetics that has been discovered in more modern times.

While many psychologists view acts of benevolence and altruism as reactions against their opposite impulses, Erich Fromm first saw them as an example of humanity's innately *positive* impulses. More important for our work, Fromm explored the human motivation to discover our identity through the human need to be active, creative, and connected to others, especially our families.

The way to restore balance to our cultural view of the family isn't to discount the impact that nurture has on our lives, but to focus as much on the positive lessons of childhood as we do on the traumas. As Burke says, "A way of seeing is also a way of not seeing." By viewing the family through a lens obscured by our suspicions, we limit our perceptions at our peril. The first step in the Codes of Love is to reexamine the very memories that we use to justify those suspicions.

Cognitive psychologists, such as Seymour Epstein, believe we have in essence two brains working at once to form our reality: the rational, intellectual brain and the emotional, experiential brain. The rational, intellectual brain operates in the world of facts and logic, while the emotional, experiential brain is not linear in thought or bound by chronology. The rational brain assesses the facts of a situation or a memory, whereas the emotional brain can bring the emotions of a memory into present time. In fact the emotional brain is our oldest brain, anthropologically speaking, and it is also by far the fastest. It accesses its power immediately and often without our conscious awareness.

In the case of Justine, the young woman who was slapped by her father, her rational brain remembers the slap intellectually. It knows the conflict that led up to the slap, the look on her father's face, and the length of time the mark stayed on her cheek. The emotional brain, on the other hand, instantly recalls the flash of pain on her cheek, the terror at her father's rage, the shame at what she interprets as her failure to be his good daughter, the fear of facing his power—all of them linked immediately with her own rage at being belittled.

The more amplified a memory is by attendant emotional pain, particularly pain that includes shame, guilt, embarrassment, or pride, the more weighted a memory is. By this I mean that these memories are more likely to be remembered and therefore will be more accessible than other, less weighted events. The more weight a memory has, the more influence it will wield, even unconsciously, on our mental model of the world—and the more likely it will be accompanied by a visceral physical response. This is what makes our traumatic memories more potent than our everyday pleasant ones.

On the far side of this argument are the extreme cases of combat veterans whose worldview and sense of self have been forever altered by the traumas they faced in war. Their traumatic memories sometimes stay so much in the foreground that they disturb all four of the basic postulates that form our outlook: their sense of the meaning of their lives, the safety of the world, the benevolence of their fellows, and their personal worth, all suffer dramatic shifts toward the negative. Unfortunately for certain vets, these shifts to the negative become part of an ever downward spiral that we now call post-traumatic stress disorder. This state of mind also occurs in some children from especially abusive childhoods. But they are the uncommon exceptions.

In the Freudian worldview the solution would be to help these trauma victims to remember the experience, repeat the details, and work through the pain. The cognitive psychologist wants the patient to extinguish the negative reactions and move toward a renewed sense of meaning, understanding, safety, and through that process return a sense of value to the self.

In *Codes of Love* we want to expand those frames of reference so that they focus on the intergenerational forces that influence our family as a whole, and to view those forces through a framework of acceptance—reflecting on all the historical, structural, genetic, and temperamental elements that have shaped our particular family constellation. These elements make every incident part of an ever unfolding story that has its roots in the distant past and its resolution in future generations.

We will discuss the Codes of Love perspective more in subsequent chapters, but for now let us assume, just for argument, that our suspicious mindset forms a tight band around our brains—both the rational and the emotional—and that this old way of viewing the family has inhibited our ability to reflect on the past. We cannot unstick the problems with our families until we drop the suspicious lens in favor of a much broader perspective.

Paul, a grown man, has had a contentious relationship with his alcoholic father for most of his life. Almost all of Paul's memories from childhood coalesce around images of his father swirling the ice in a glass of scotch with his finger. Once the drug began to take effect, verbal and physical rage resulted. Paul blamed himself for his father's emotions and as a teenager became trapped in a state of violent rebellion against his father. Even now, twenty years later, Paul affects the style of a rock and roller. He has shoulder-length blond hair and a string of earrings rimming his right ear, and he has earned his living through jobs ranging from rock musician to car salesman.

Each family gathering begins in a state of suspicion. Paul doesn't just suspect, he *knows* that his father is bound to express some disappointment at Paul's lack of ambition, to which Paul is bound to answer with defensiveness. Each man arrives at the family event awaiting the inevitable.

I worked with Paul to widen the lens through which he views his dad. Paul's memories were classics of the Family Noir genre, including heated dinner table confrontations, hostile silences, even fistfights and furious exits. I asked him to place his father and his mother in a broader chronological context. Who were his parents' parents? How did his parents meet? What attracted them to each other? What happened in their lives before Paul and his sister were born?

Through this work Paul moved toward a more complete picture of his family, not one defined just by conflict. His father had made his own family proud as a young man by being admitted to a prestigious boarding school and then an Ivy League college. During World War II, he left college in his sophomore year to volunteer, and he served three tours of duty, participating in three invasions of the South Pacific, and won three combat ribbons and a Purple Heart. During the third campaign, Paul's father witnessed the slaughter of all the men under his command and he himself took a grenade and lost an eye. He spent three months in the hospital in Asia recovering from his wound and, upon returning to America, began using alcohol to deal with his memories and his loss. He returned home to a world that was changed forever for him, not only by his experience of war, but also eventually, by his drinking.

In order for Paul to find a way to love his father, he had to see his journey from the promising young man who carried the family's hopes as he went off to prep school to the bitter drinker he became after the horrors of war. It may not be a pretty picture, but it is a comprehensible one. If Paul remains in the emotional field where his memory and judgment are clouded with suspicion, he certainly has the evidence to justify his hatred of his father. Yet if he can also picture his father as an eighteen-year-old boy in the South Pacific watching his entire platoon obliterated in battle, Paul can (and did) move toward understanding and compassion.

As we worked to widen Paul's perspective on his father, other memories came to the foreground that further humanized his father's struggle. Paul recalled how his father, still traumatized by war twenty years later, would scream out at night in his sleep. Paul also remembered how some nights he'd come across his father crying quietly at the dining room table. Instead of seeing his father as simply the inflictor of pain in the family, Paul began to have compassion for the tremendous loneliness and pain that his father carries inside himself.

Through this work Paul has come to honor his father in a different way. He doesn't need to ignore the painful incidents that led to years of conflict between him and his dad. In fact, he should *not* ignore them, as they are true and a part of the whole continuum of experience between these two men. By including more of his father's experience in the framework, Paul no longer has to feel himself unworthy because his father drinks and doesn't act as if he cares for him. By transcending his narrow perception of who his father is, that is, defined only in relation to himself, Paul can drop the suspicious point of view, step outside his family's emotional field, and begin to establish the person-to-person relationship with his father by discovering what about his father he loves and honors.

FAMILY SPIRIT

Many therapies don't do a good enough job with precisely this kind of problem. Through most standard modes of therapy we bring pain to the foreground, and eventually the other, more pleasant memories shrink in power and prominence. What I'm suggesting is that we bring all the memories forward, construct a fuller narrative of the family, one that takes a multigenerational, noncausal view. Paul had been stuck in the pain of his angry history with his father, unable to appreciate the gifts he has been given by his family: their entrepreneurial spirit, intelligence, drive, and heroism. In understanding his father in this broader context, he has actually moved beyond forgiveness into our framework of acceptance.

This process can be described as the difference between family noir and family spirit. Family spirit starts with the moods and feelings cast into our cells through the generations—our animating force—and manifests itself in our loyalty, dedication, and history. Spirit is, in fact, what James Hillman means when he refers to the great chain of generations. In the modern, therapized world we have often become estranged from this legacy of the characters that comprise who we are today. For many, the work before you in *Codes of Love* concerns not so much *creating* the family spirit as *discovering* it. The initial steps involve letting go of preconceptions and accepting limitations. The limitations that we need to understand are first our own, then those of our families.

I remember when I was eight or nine looking around whatever careworn enlisted man's quarters we lived in then, during the nomadic years when my father first joined the Navy, and wondering when my real parents, the Empress of Japan and the Prince of Wales, were going to show up and claim their long lost son. Perhaps at those same moments my parents were casting a doubtful eye on me and wondering if their real son had been switched with another baby at the hospital. I was a bookish geek with thick glasses, unlike anyone else in my handsome working-class family. Where was their football star?

I devoured biographies and heroic tales to escape the ordinariness of daily life. The everyday brush-your-teeth-here's-your-laundry kind of love I got from my family bored me when I compared it to the enduring, powerful love that I was reading about: the love of a country for its returning hero or the honorable love among a family that survived a difficult challenge. I was blind to the love I was getting from my family because I compared them to some vaguely defined, idealized version of family I had conjured to match the grandiosity of my fantasies for my future. I had not even entertained the idea that I might have limitations of my own.

Now I can see how my mother and father sacrificed their lives on so many levels to keep the family together for twenty-eight years despite their occasional marital conflicts and financial struggles. Not until recently did I have the wisdom to see their sacrifices as a kind of heroism, because like most immature people I was, even into my forties, blinded by blame and wondering why my family didn't love me, rather than why I didn't love my family. There's an old Gordon Lightfoot song, "Carefree Highway," in which he sings, "I will never grow so old again, as when I knew I had no one else to blame." Seeking wisdom is the act of maturity. True wisdom comes from accepting our physical, emotional, and intellectual limitations and learning to work within them. To paraphrase Carl Rogers, once I accept myself as I am, then I can change.

LIFE IS SHORT

Another important motivator for change is the realization that our time on earth is finite. We are here for a short time. This acceptance of death—not hiding from the truth by using euphemisms, such as "passed away" or "was lost"—can add to rather than subtract from the quality of life. Our acceptance of death's inevitability creates an imperative to pack meaning, beauty, and joy into the time we have. As psychiatrist Heinz Kohut wrote: "Those who genuinely accept death face it with a quiet pride rather than a sense of resignation and hopelessness. Such people share with

Goethe the insight that the acceptance of death leads to a richer feeling of being alive."

When we insert the idea of transience into our framework, our perspective on our family is immediately transformed. If you knew you or any member of your family had only a year to live, would not most of your conflicts seem tired and trivial? Might you not want to use the time you had left with that person to build the strongest relationship you could? The reality is we never know how much time any of us have. Were your mother or father or sibling to die tomorrow, would you perhaps regret that your relationship died fractured—killed by a handful of incidents that took place long ago?

Carla is a bright young woman in her late twenties who dreads going home to her working-class family because they don't understand her artistic temperament. Carla was a precocious child, always did well in school, and got a nice scholarship to the University of California at Berkeley. Her parents were overjoyed that someone in the family had finally gotten into college and pressured Carla heavily to be a business major so she could make real money in the world. Carla, however, had always wanted to be a writer. She became an English major, focusing her studies on creative writing despite constant hectoring from her family.

Now eight years out of college, Carla works as a housecleaner to keep her time and mind free for writing. She's making progress in her writing and has sold a few stories to literary journals that her parents would never read. In fact her parents don't even know about her publishing successes because she won't show the stories to them. They probably would be hurt if they read them as most concern her family. She tells herself that she doesn't show her published work to her parents because they wouldn't understand, but secretly she knows that they would definitely understand the anger underneath the way she portrays them in the stories.

When she comes home for a visit, the subject of her career is certain to surface. Why, Carla's father always wants to know, did Carla waste all that time and money in college? She could have become a housecleaner right out of high school if that's what she wanted to do. Carla might be able to avoid squabbling with her parents and pouting at the dinner table if she was more secure about her progress as a writer. Her modest success in publishing is nowhere near the dream of the speech she will make when accepting the National Book Award, a fantasy she spins out each day when she sits down at her desk to write. If a family visit is upcoming, she can barely sit down. Once at her desk, her mind is crammed full of the answers she's going to give her father if he dares to bring up the subject of her writing, not focused on the writing project in front of her. Clearly for all of Carla's protestations that she doesn't care what her parents think, she still aches for their approval and fears that what her father says is right. She will never make it as a writer. The family's suspicions that have the most impact on us are the ones we secretly believe are true.

Carla suspects how her choice of supporting herself as a housecleaner plays down at the beauty parlor where her mother has gone to get her hair done every Saturday for twenty-five years. Her mother's beauty parlor buddies cheered Carla on as she went from award to award in high school and then gained admittance to such a prestigious school. They all showed up bearing gifts at Carla's graduation party. Now that she's a housecleaner, they don't know quite how to talk about Carla to her mom. Her mother always says, "Whatever Carla wants to do, as long as she's happy." It is abundantly apparent to her mother that Carla is not happy. She's broke, spends a lot of time alone, and doesn't seem to be going anywhere with this writing thing. Carla's mother wants to be supportive, but she can't see how to do it without making Carla mad. Carla's mother tiptoes on eggshells every time Carla is home for a visit.

If she could drop her suspicions, Carla could see her father's concern for her as not so much lack of faith in her talent and drive but one of her father's Codes of Love. He fears that in her current line of work she will never achieve economic stability or meet the kind of man that could make a decent husband. He doesn't want to leave her that insecure in the world.

Inject the notion of transience into this dynamic and its ripple effect is profound. First of all, Carla must separate from her parents and stand on her own, fully adult and responsible for her own choices rather than in a reactive posture to her parents. If her parents had only a year to live, would Carla want to mar their remaining time together with petty disputes?

Armed with her acceptance of life's transience, Carla could determine to become both a fully autonomous adult and an intimate participant in her family. She could find the strength to not let the fact that they've never supported her writing obscure the many ways in which they have loved and supported her all her life. With this new framework that engenders connection *and* individuality, Carla might be able to convey some of the joy she feels at the way her life is going and hence receive more approval from her parents. She should be able to see her choice to be a housecleaner and a writer not as shameful but as courageous, a manifestation of the spunk that inspired her mother to abandon the security of the small town and the multigenerational extended family in which she was raised and strike out on her own for San Francisco because she wanted a better life. The notion of our transience can help us to focus on our similarities, our spirit, rather than the things that drive us apart.

FAMILY HUMOR

Another powerful tool that can lessen the burden of suspicion in the family is humor. The rigidity of the suspicious point of view takes all playfulness out of the family dynamic. Suppose, for example, that during family gatherings Uncle Steve disappears intermittently to take a swig from a bottle of scotch he's got hidden behind the dryer in Grandma's laundry room. No one ever talks about where Uncle Steve goes even though everyone knows exactly where he is and what he is doing. In fact, during some of the more fractious family events, Uncle Steve has had a lot of company down there amid the bleach and fabric softener. If your suspicious mind is searching for evidence outside yourself of the horrible dysfunction that plagues your family, you need search no further than the laundry room, and the label *alcoholic*.

Say you happen to come across Uncle Steve and his companions standing awkwardly in the dark little alcove in a cloud of cigarette smoke. Uncle Steve quickly hides the bottle behind his back and gives you a conspiratorial hey-get-out-of-here smile. Some family, you think. This family is fundamentally wacked out, and no one here can stand to be together for very long. That must be why they drink.

I'm not advocating sneaking alcohol as a coping mechanism for family gatherings. I'm just suggesting that we need to clear that atmosphere of blame and judgment and see the humorous side. Because not all drinking is alcoholic drinking. Uncle Steve has not had his life marred by alcohol and doesn't return to the family drunk and belligerent. His session in the laundry room is his version, reinforced by identical behavior on his father's part when Steve was a boy, of the time-out walks I take when I need space. In fact, Steve's drinking in the laundry room was an attempt to protect the children, to keep them from "seeing too much."

So, the first step in lightening up the atmosphere is to break the family pattern. Suppose Grandma makes a particularly nasty remark about your brother Mike's former fiancée who left him. Instead of letting the pain of Grandma's bluntness reverberate in the ensuing silence, your brother seizes control of the moment with humor. Mike waits a silent beat, stands up to leave the room, and says, "*Hmm,* I think I'll go see what Uncle Steve is doing."

With that one remark he's done an important form of healing for the family and for himself. He's remained within the family's shared culture by reaching out to the others for support through humor. But Mike has also remained autonomous by refusing to take the bait of Grandma's remark and become embroiled in another debate about his dating choices. If he had reacted with hostility to Grandma's remark, he'd have proven that he was not yet free enough from his family's emotional force field to stand on his own two feet.

When I find myself regularly defending, blaming, or accommodating others, I know that I am still not mature enough to remain connected to the family without judgment, denial, or loss of self—all of which are signs that I have more personal work to do to gain a person-to-person relationship with my family. These signals alert me to the opportunity to relate to my family in a new way—one that allows me to be my biggest self and remain loving. Humor is one of our first tools in helping to lighten the family noir atmosphere.

By refusing to become his smaller, pouting, victim self, Mike has deflected his Grandma's judgment and signaled to the family that he has matured enough not to be baited in the old ways. This behavior is his best hope of changing his grandmother's pattern of relating to him. Because he is detaching *and* allowing the affection to stay in the room. If tense situations do come up, Mike can now handle them without the old need to protect himself or his reputation.

Codes of Love Exercise: THE HOLIDAY SITCOM

Another powerful way to change our perspective about our family is to view it as a comedy of errors. Psychologists view humor as a defense mechanism. I think of it as an acceptance mechanism. With it you can explode the striving and the judgment and connect with others on the commonality of just getting through the day. If you've ever seen a daytime soap opera with the sound turned off, you know there are few things more humorous than bad melodrama. It can't be about right and wrong when everyone in the room is acting like an idiot. Suppose I redid the lighting and gave a new soundtrack for the Christmas that began this chapter. Ah, home for the holidays.

> *Chestnuts roasting on the open fire,*
> *Mama picking on my clothes,*
> *Past transgressions being thrown on the pyre,*
> *And looks that could freeze the Eskimos. . . .*
> *Everybody knows with C-4 and some baling wire,*
> *I could blow the house to bits . . .*
> *Instead I'm forced to let them fill my ears,*
> *With junk I've heard for years and years. . . .*

Viewed with humor, any holiday trip looks more manageable.

Try to recast a family holiday story in a comic light. Look for the humor in every slight, and look for people's foibles instead of their flaws. A hint: How would an alien from another planet react to the strange rituals of your family holiday?

Codes of Love Exercise: THE FAMILY NOIR FILM FESTIVAL

Return to your most emotionally charged family memories with the keen eye of a film director. You know the cast, the characters, and the plot. The questions in this exercise help you play with mood, lighting, and motivation—and to experience both emotional reactions and rational thoughts about these incidents at the same time. This is what I call, living in the paradox. By this I mean to simultaneously entertain the seemingly opposing notions of feelings and thoughts regarding the same events. The ability to do this helps us build an emotional connection to the material while also granting us an observer's distance.

Answer the following questions to see just how dramatic the lighting is in your home movie.

- What subjects are touchy for you in your house? What subjects are touchy for some or all of your family members?
- What phrases do you blurt out that remind you of when you were younger?
- What feelings (rebellious or accommodating) do you have when participating in family functions?
- How do you feel in your parents' home? What do you think about that?
- In what ways are you still reacting to your parents that remind you of how you reacted as a child? What do you think about that?
- Do you pout? What about?
- Do you drink too much at family gatherings? Eat too much? Feel hostile? Why?
- Do you find yourself thinking one thing and saying another?
- When you do not say what you really think, what is the tape that plays in your head?
- Once you leave a family gathering, what do you wish you had said?
- When you are at your parents' house, are you always in a hurry? Why?

- Are you planning your departure from the moment you arrive?
- When loaded topics are discussed, how do you react?

Codes of Love Exercise: THE FAMILY COMEDY SPECIAL

It is funny how we forget to laugh. We sometimes take ourselves so seriously that the world starts to read like the front page of *The Economist*—dry and solid. Here we take a more lighthearted approach.

- What are the five funniest stories about your family?
- Who in your family is viewed as a character?
- Who is the family comic? The drama queen? The tragic hero?
- How do you feel when you are in public with your mother? Father? Sibling?
- What character traits do you exhibit with your family that aren't shown with anyone else?
- How much contact do you have with your family—nuclear and extended—throughout the year? Does that put more pressure on you or less?
- What does your family suspect about you that is true?
- How do you feel about the way you look? Look in the mirror for a full minute. Who do you see there? What about that person do you doubt? Is this the truth or just an old idea? What traits about yourself do you love? What about yourself would you change? Should you change?
- Are you secure in your job? Your love life? Your financial situation?
- Are you able to keep your sense of humor when other people criticize or tease?

- What are the four or five phrases members of your family might say that will set you off? Is there any way you might just laugh it off? Do you have a funny answer for them that is *not* sarcastic?
- What do you look for in family gatherings that you don't get? Is that funny?
- Are you a victim? A victim of circumstance? A victim of love? A victim of the past? A fashion victim? A therapy victim?

CHAPTER 2

Remember

When I was a child, my father's dress white Navy uniform was the most impressive piece of clothing I'd ever seen. I'd watch my father in front of the bedroom mirror as he dressed, his posture straight and elegant as he carefully fastened the gold buttons on the front of the shirt. In his dress whites, sometimes with a gleaming sword strapped to his side, he was someone I honored and respected without a moment of doubt. Our life could be tough at times and the frequent moves caused a lot of stress in our family, but when I saw him in his dress whites the struggle seemed worth it.

By my late teens, that same uniform had become the symbol of every way in which I had failed my father and he had failed me. After our battles over the Vietnam War, I hadn't spoken to my father in years. He was a rigid hard-ass, a tool of the military establishment. I blamed him for the fact that I had no really close friends and had roamed from place to place, unable to get my life together. Our Navy life had ruined my childhood, I can hear my mother saying, by moving us around so much. I saw that uniform as a straitjacket too, part of the reason he often seemed unhappy. I remembered the time my father, who was working two jobs to keep the family going, was getting dressed for an event and discovered a button was missing on the front of his uniform. Furious, he yanked the shirt open. My brother Jon and I both remember the ping of the gold buttons hitting the walls and the floor as he roared with rage.

In rearranging my memories to suit the perspective of an angry teenager what was lost to me was another image of my father in uniform. When we lived in San Francisco in 1961, my sister, Paula, was being harassed by some tough kids at school. My father dressed in his whites and spent a whole day just sitting in her classroom at school. My whole family was incredibly proud of his defense of my sister through that same uniform. She never had trouble with the bullies after that. Also lost to me was the way my mother looked at my father in his dress whites when they left for a function on the base. I wanted no glimmer of what had attracted her to him in the first place to confuse my assessment of their troubled marriage, a marriage that in my mind was the root cause of all my failures and those of my siblings.

As an adult I can see the truth of all of those images of my father in uniform. Viewing them from the eyes of a child, of course, I wanted the certainty of having just one. Either there is no truth or there are several truths, but there's never just one when you look at your history with your family. Memory is malleable. We arrange the past in a way that suits our present. If I am looking to find the reasons why I don't get along with my father, I build my justifications through combing the past to find the incidents that explain the estrangement. These events, when strung together in a narrative, make a convincing case for two people who just were never intended to get along. Ask some therapists, and they will take up your cause, helping you search your childhood for clues, establishing you as a victim and your family to blame.

It takes a skilled and secure therapist to keep your smallest and weakest self from using your parents' failures and missteps as the narrative line of your childhood. There are so many more images and sense memories untapped in your preconscious that with just stretching your mind a bit, you could find that other narrative, the story of your connection to your family. Your bigger, stronger mature self can embrace the dialectic of the past. And any good therapist or clergy member can usually show you this.

In this chapter I will show you how to open your eyes to a different kind of connection to your family, one that casts aside the bitterness in favor of the hidden sweetness underneath. The purpose of these exercises in remembering is to reawaken your senses to all that you were and will be through the love of your family. This new kind of remembering frees you to create a powerful new identity in your family and subsequently the world. First let's explore how we forge our idea of the past and why it is important to free that rigid framework up for a new kind of remembering.

FLASHBULB MEMORIES

Memory is a jumble of seemingly unsorted fragments: the words to the song "Layla," the recipe for your grandma's chocolate sheet cake, what you have to do today, your best friend's birthday, and the way your brother looked after his diving accident in high school, all seem to exist without conflict in your brain. Scientists researching memory have determined that memory is not just sorted randomly. The brain differentiates emotional from factual memories and cues them to different responses from the brain. The most potent memories mix the emotional with the factual.

Justine, the girl in the previous chapter who was slapped hard by her father, would use both rational and emotional memory in trying to make sense of the anxious reaction she experiences when she sees her father raise his hand to swat a fly. The raising of his voice and the arc of his arm stimulate muscle tension and a rise in her heart rate, blood pressure, and perspiration—classic fear responses that happen beyond consciousness. If, when she scans the past for a reference for this body reaction and uncovers that day her father slapped her, she brings the rational memory and the emotional memory into present time. That remembering of the slap becomes part of her contemporary experience, taking emotional meaning from the past and using it to give meaning to the present, thereby reinforcing the power of that incident from the past to influence her today. Each time she makes this triangular connection between the facts and the emotions of the past and the present-day cue, she brings that memory in the foreground.

You may have these same kinds of conditioned anxiety responses in your memory bank, a response that psychologists call signal anxiety. Anxiety is the response to real or imagined threat. Chronic anxiety becomes a state of being—and is the key component of your family's emotional force field.

My friend Elaine, for instance, begins to get anxious when she's in a car with an aggressive driver. She becomes flushed, her heart races, and if it goes on too long she starts fiddling with the door handle. This response never made much sense to her as she's a demon when she's behind the wheel.

In searching for a memory to give meaning to this response, she recalled a time when she was five years old. It was a crisp fall day late in October and her father had just bought a new Triumph sports car, a convertible. He picked Elaine and her older brother up after school and tore around town in his new car. He drove to the local cemetery because it had a series of traffic circles good for demonstrating how well the car handled.

It was dusk as they sped around a big circle and Elaine's father said he was going to leave the kids in the cemetery for the Halloween spooks to find. Elaine screamed, but her father was too taken with his idea to acknowledge her. He dropped the kids off at a gruesome mausoleum and dashed off. He was probably only gone for a moment or two, but in Elaine's five-year-old mind, he seemed to be gone for hours. She screamed and clung to her brother.

This memory came back to Elaine as a single image, what memory researchers call a flashbulb memory, a memory made especially clear by its emotional resonance. This single snapshot of Elaine shivering next to her brother at the mausoleum was enough to fill in the half-hour scene that preceded it.

Memory researchers have found that flashbulb memories are rooted in the body with a surge of adrenaline. The amygdala—the primitive emotional brain—detects an adverse situation in memory and turns on the bodily systems. That surge of bodily energy seems to improve the quality of the memory, which makes empirical sense. Certainly if you look back at all the things that happened to you today, the ones that will be the most detailed in your mind will be those mixed with emotion. You will remember the lunchtime romantic confession of a coworker in more detail than you will recall the exchange you had with the clerk at the grocery store because both emotional and rational memory systems have responded to the coworker's situation. However, while emotional memories may be more vivid, they are not necessarily more accurate, and though memory can be very accurate, its accuracy is not consistent. No memory is a carbon copy of the experience that formed it.

When we do this thing we call remembering, we are on a mission. We shift our focus from the stimulus of the present and scan the historical landscape for a fragment of the past that shaped the person we are today. Through this we shape our past. Sociologist George Herbert Mead says: "The past is an expression of the present." The need to remember—to reconcile your understanding of your self with your inner feelings—can distort history in the service of those feelings. The malleable stuff of memories is manipulated by the person you are today—your perspective, biases, and defenses—from information gathered by a child.

With that in mind let's reexamine Elaine's horrific memory from the cemetery. As Elaine was five when it happened, her sense of how recklessly her father drove could be completely off as could her sense of time spent at the mausoleum. Temperament is also among the factors that limit the accuracy of our memories. Elaine's brother, Howard, who is three years older, remembers the incident with affection—a rare moment of unbridled joy with their chronically depressed father. Her brother is more adventurous generally and hence remembers wishing her father would go faster, really make the tires sing. Not for a single moment did Howard feel unsafe. He even dug the macho dare of being left in the graveyard with his silly, squealing sister.

Another element that makes this incident vivid in Elaine's mind is the perspective she has on her father today. In the intervening years, her father abandoned the family and cast them into poverty. Elaine's mother doesn't have a good thing to say about her former husband and has never shielded her children from her opinions. The stories she tells about him portray his destructive, maniacal side. When Elaine shared her cemetery memory with her mother, her mom was horrified and gratified simultaneously. It had been a long time since she'd had fresh evidence for her twenty-five-year-old anger toward her ex. Elaine and her mother felt closer through Elaine's uncovering this bit of the past.

I'm not relating this story to discredit Elaine's rendition of the past, only to demonstrate how the person we are in the present determines how we view our past. When I was marginally employed in Florida and hadn't spoken to my family in years, my peers would not have been receptive to a positive view of any of our dads, because we all needed someone to blame so that we did not have to look at ourselves. When I thought or spoke of my father, I, perhaps unconsciously chose the memories that justified my distance. Those who have no communication with their family convince themselves that they have no relationship with them, that they left all that behind. The truth is that they are just as enmeshed with their family as they would be had they never left, because their entire personae is a reaction to the family caused by their denial of a continued emotional connection. These emotions, regardless of the physical distance, are still a strong motivating force in their lives.

RETHINKING EMOTIONAL MEMORIES

When people explain why they don't get along with their family, there is a numbing predictability about the stories they tell. Each memory trudges glumly forward, building a narrative that justifies the estrangement. If you ask the narrator a question to break up the monotony of the story, the flash of defensive anger lets you know right away you've breached etiquette. Ask, for example, "What was the moment when your parents felt the most proud of you?" The narrator will most likely respond, "My parents never told me they were proud of me." This version of the past, in most cases, is as extreme a form of denial as the version told by those people who remember their childhood as nothing but joyful. Whenever you hear the words *never* or *always,* there is usually a framework of suspicion or denial lurking behind them.

Christy is a successful thirty-four-year-old department store buyer who can hardly deign to spend time with her father at all. She can readily explain the reason she and her father barely talk. She believes that the trouble started with her gender. Her father always wanted a son and was disappointed that she was a girl. She frames all her past on that premise and has uncovered a lot of evidence to support her thesis.

"From the time I was born, I was always Daddy's girl," she says. "I hung on his every word, sat on his lap whenever he was home, and followed him everywhere. Some of the best moments of my early years were the anticipation of Daddy coming home from work. I'd be looking out the window as his car pulled into the driveway and he came out with his briefcase slung over his shoulder, looking so strong, so worldly and confident in his beautifully tailored suit.

"Our relationship started to change when I was six. He wanted me to play softball instead of soccer, and I had to, even though I didn't like softball at all. I quit halfway through the season, and for the rest of my life he's called me a quitter, someone who can't commit. Of course it's total hypocrisy on his part. He had a hard time with commitments himself except the ones he had to his law practice. He was always too busy working to show up at any of my band performances. He never could just sit and talk with me. He always had to be teaching me something around the house when we were together, always the kinds of things he would be teaching a son if he had one. I know basic plumbing, electricity, and car repair, although they're not skills I need very often in the fashion world in New York City.

"He was livid when I got into an East Coast school, even though it was prestigious and Ivy League, because he didn't want me to leave Seattle. I went anyway, and then his criticism focused on the boys I brought home from school. None of them were good enough for me, in his eyes. The fact that I didn't want to follow in his footsteps and go into law irked him. He thinks fashion is frivolous, which means he thinks I'm wasting my life, and I just don't want to hear it anymore. But the real problem is he just never wanted me to be who I am. He always wanted me to be him. Really, I think he wished I'd been a son because a son would make a better carbon copy."

Christy's story is more legal brief than memoir. She's got a case to prove about the past, and all the evidence fits. If you step back from the narrow focus of the narrative and examine the voice of the narrator, it's a story told from the perspective of a child rather than the mature viewpoint of a successful woman at the top of her career who has established a person-to-person relationship with her family. When assessing her relationship with her father, Christy is still the powerless child, the victim of his whims and willfulness. She'll never be able to please him. With this as her framework, it's not surprising Christy cringes at the idea of spending time with her father. No matter how much joy and love may now pour from his eyes when he sees her, Christy's narrative shows she sees herself as a disappointment.

It might be true that Christy's father was disappointed she didn't carry on the family law practice. At this point, however, the decision has been made and Christy needs to put that issue to rest and stand up as her full adult self in the family context. She's still thinking of herself as someone who can't stand up to her father, when in fact she has for years. Essential to her finally becoming her authentic self within the family is Christy's being able to remember the many ways that her father had an impact on her life, not just the age-old battle that is rooted in her emotional memory.

Christy remembers quite vividly the two weeks she and her father fought over which college she would attend. What she can't see is how once she convinced her father to let her go east; he helped her prepare for the drive with incredible attention to detail, especially about the car she was driving. She remembers how he picked on her boyfriends and sees it as an expression of a lack of respect for her judgment, but she forgets that she eventually decided all those men were bad choices anyway. To admit that her father might actually have been kind or right seems like an excruciating assault on her attempt to build a self that is autonomous from the family. What she doesn't realize is that admitting her father's intentions were loving is a necessary step in the development of her autonomy.

Once you begin to blast away the suspicious mind-set that frames your childhood, your memories may suddenly seem less potent. Without suspicion to create drama, chart fears, and ascribe blame, your narrative will begin to lose its drive. Gone will be the moral to the story. Those same five or six stories that you use to justify your inability to get along with your family will be stripped of their power to enrage you when, in the absence of suspicion, you no longer cast the players as victims, villains, and heroes. In fact, in most landmark incidents, you will come to understand that the damage you experienced came, not from your family members' willfully wanting to cause one another harm, but from a more fundamental human weakness, an inability to stop harm from occurring.

This realization will quickly be replaced with terror. The anxiety you may now feel arises from even considering the notion that there is a different way to look at the past. Over time, our memories become our identity. Giving up our version of the past, our perspective, shakes our view of ourselves. *Who I am is no longer true without these stories to support me. And who I think others are is in doubt as well.* Suddenly you will be a stranger in a familiar place, floating free in time and history, untethered to the world, which creates a crisis of emptiness. *Without my mental movie, and the emotions that it raises, what is left to me, to my family? Who am I? Who are they?*

Love, history, genetics, and an ache for a closer connection are the reasons you bought this book. To become a full adult—confident of your strengths and aware of your weaknesses—requires a training ground that teaches a more confident footing in the world at large. The incidences of conflict that comprise the story of your life with your family takes up only a small percentage of the time you have on earth, yet the meaning and importance you give them influence how you see yourself in the world—as neglected or a victim, as struggling *or* successful.

THE TRIUMPH OF CONNECTION

Although Stacey is a respected lawyer legendary for her tough stance in negotiations, when she visits her mother, she is meek, indecisive, and accommodating. While Charles has made many friends in his construction job because of his go-along-get-along unflappability, with his dad he is, even at thirty-five years old, the very picture of a surly, pouting adolescent.

For Stacey and Charles the contrast between their two selves is so dramatic it's no wonder neither of them views going home with excitement. The person they are in their family is the person they've erased with nearly every choice they've made in adulthood. In each context Stacey and Charles are living a narrow part of who they are, with the full range of their qualities and experiences closed off by this bifurcated view of the past. Could Charles's relationship with his father benefit from his being more easygoing? Yes, and his candidacy for supervisor at the job site might pick up momentum if he had more of an attitude of entitlement at work. Stacey, on the other hand, needs a broader canvas for her emotions. They're all coming out in her negotiating postures. If she could display more of her canniness and humor with her mother and her boyfriend and mix up negotiations with unexpected softness, Stacey might feel more alive, more integrated, more fully herself, everywhere in the world.

This new kind of remembering doesn't try to dislodge your stories from their role as tools for interpreting the past. The following exercises are designed, not to make you deny the past, but rather to help you see that your memories may be limited, not only by the perceptions of the child or teenager that observed the incidents, but by the person you are today—a person whose identity is shaped by attachment to these memories. Although the past can be used to explain the present, who we are today limits the narrative we weave from the past. Yet, we are the storytellers. And we can choose a different moral for the story, one that details the triumph of connection over isolation.

I'm not asking you to be false or to deny the reality of your home life. I'm asking you to enhance it. So often I find that when people talk about their family, their emotional color palette is limited to black for depression, red for anger, and perhaps a garish yellow of false feeling reflecting a grandiose hope for a flawless reconnection with the family. Falling in love and staying in love with your family is less a goal than a process. The exercises that follow are designed to help you introduce new colors to the emotional palette: a quiet yellow of contentment, a sepia tone of warmth and nostalgia, a rich green of renewal of spirit. You can use as many colors as you find when you open your mind up to a fuller picture of the past.

Just as Proust used the scent of a madeleine to reach back to his past, you can use your childhood senses to remember the good times with your family. It might take a while to reclaim those moments and gain balance in your new perspective. When you first start trying to love your family, pictures of the past may fade or be replaced by new brighter ones. Little by little, your senses will adjust to the new view of life and family. The stimuli will come from the oddest or most unexpected places: for me, one day the taste of a Dr Pepper brought back the world of my aunt Norma and our kitchen talks.

I've always thought of Aunt Norma as my nearest relative, be-

cause as a kid I thought that was what "nearest relative" meant—
the one who was the most like me. She was tall and lean, with
dark dramatic features and thick long black hair, with an air of intelligent sadness. She glided around the kitchen like some ethereal
spirit in a long housecoat: light, waiflike, and wrapped in a cloud
of cigarette smoke. Her feet seemed to barely touch the ground.
More than her dramatic appearance, I loved the atmosphere of intimacy in the kitchen, her command center, from which she sent
us, her faithful minions, out into the world to retrieve more Marl-
boros and Dr Pepper. She was always curious about people, interested in their opinions. Conversations moved quickly from life in
the mountains to television shows to what was going on at school.
It seemed that no topic was off limits at Aunt Norma's, and she
treated everyone with the same mixture of humor, curiosity, and
respect.

When I was working on developing a more complete memory
of my family, I often experimented with assigning my students to
eat a favorite childhood food and report back to me. One day in
class a student mentioned Kraft macaroni and cheese and Dr Pepper and the memory of Aunt Norma's kitchen rushed back. The
difficulty in holding on to that memory was that it had no place
holder in my time line. Nothing dramatic ever happened in that
kitchen except talk. No crisis earned it a regular place in the story
of me and my family. Yet, it was a significant memory, because lost
with it were other evocative or sweet moments from my past: my
first crush on a cousin, the sound of a panther's scream from the
woods, and the uncensored discussions of grown-up life that
every preteen craves.

For this book I tried to develop a relative scale of value between the good and the bad memories. But I could not make it
simple. And perhaps that is the point. Over time, does thirty afternoons with Aunt Norma equal one nasty fight at dinner be-

tween my mother and father? Do one hundred afternoons on Grandma Minnie's porch swing have the same relative historic value as the screaming debates my father and I had about the Vietnam War? I was never able to weight that scale to my satisfaction, but understanding that there is some heavenly scale of value that weights those pleasant memories, even if en masse, to offset or perhaps cancel out the difficult ones, is comforting. As light is to shadow, night is to day. The contrast between these bitter scenes and sweet ones gives life depth and meaning. The exercises that follow will help you balance your more potent, dramatic memories with the sensory pleasures of your childhood.

Codes of Love Exercise: RECOLLECTIONS

With the following questions or excursions, I ask you to search for more sensory clues to the past. Moving from just the mental images of memory to the emotional and the tactile, we are looking to enrich your experience of your story in concrete ways. Working to awaken these sensate memories is the next important step toward becoming more aware of the positive qualities and strong bonds that are an essential element of any family.

BACK TO THE FUTURE

Remember the movie *Back to the Future?* At the end of the film, Michael J. Fox's character returns to present time to find that by changing one thing in the past, he has transformed the present, and particularly his parents. Instead of the slobs he left behind, his parents have changed into the ultracool, perfect, tennis-playing parents. Here we travel backward with a view to what our past tells us about our present and the forces that shaped us. What might you want to change about your future?

- If you can, pay a visit to your childhood hometown or your elementary school. If you can't, write down all you can remember about them. Can you remember what they look like? Whom you knew there?
- Who was your favorite teacher? Why?
- Make one of your favorite childhood foods.
- What was your father's favorite music? Your mother's? Is there a type of music or specific song that you especially remember? Hunt at a record store for music from your childhood home. Yes, the hunt can be fun.
- Did your family dance? To what? When was the last time you went dancing? GO.
- What were your favorite family outings? Think of as many as you can.
- What photographs do you have of your family? Where are they? Which ones do you most remember? Put them up in the house for a while. What do they tell you?
- What was your favorite birthday party?
- Do you remember any Halloween costumes?
- Is there a movie or television show that you remember watching with your family? Can you watch it now? What cartoons did you watch?
- Is there a movie that reminds you of your childhood? Will you watch it?

THE TIME MACHINE

Imagine that you have a machine that can travel back and forth through time.

- What would you go back in time to change? Why? Are you sure?
- What pleasant moments from your past would you revisit?

- What would you like to change in your own behavior?
- Is there anything you might want to say to someone from your past? List three things.

    1.
    2.
    3.

- What might you do differently? How would your life be different?

THE BUDDY LIST

- What did your favorite childhood house look like? Where was it? What was your room like? What did you have on the walls?
- What movie star did you have a crush on? Which band did you worship?
- Who were your friends then? How were their houses different from your house?
- What was your favorite shopping trip? What were your fashion symbols of your teenage wardrobe?
- What were Sundays like when you were a child? What are they like for your parents now?
- Who in your family really listened to you?
- Did your mother ever save anything you wrote for her?
- What kind of memorabilia do your parents have of you?
- Did your parents ever bail you out of a jam? How?
- What did your parents hope for you concerning a spiritual life?
- What did your father and mother (or other relative) protect you from?
- What kind of kid were you? Shy? Boisterous? Daydreamy?

- Did your father brag about you or your siblings to his friends? What did he say?
- Did your mother and father love each other? How do you know?
- Did your parents ever catch you in a very big lie? How big?

CHAPTER 3

Reflect

There are some memories, some crisis points in my life, that I recall as if they were being played out under water. My time sense is skewed by the agony of what transpired, and it seems as if the entire episode plays in slow motion, each moment building inevitably to the next. The day I found out that my high school girlfriend, Betsy, was pregnant is one of those memories, slowed to a glacial pace by the intense shame I felt at the time and which I subsequently carried for so many years.

We were in Virginia, in October 1969, when the phone on the wall behind my father rang just as my family was sitting down to dinner. As my father reached back to answer the phone, my stomach clenched. We hardly ever received phone calls at dinnertime, and I had known for days that Betsy might be pregnant.

"It's Betsy's mom," my father said with a quizzical look on his face as he handed me the phone. "What's she calling for?"

When I put the phone to my ear, I heard Betsy sobbing in the background.

"Mark, I think Betsy's pregnant," her mother said in a voice that barely contained her anger. "I think that you and your father should come over here right now."

"We're having dinner," I said, stalling like a madman.

"I think you had better come over," she repeated.

Two or three times I avoided agreeing to come until she asked to speak to my father, which I wouldn't allow. When I hung up the phone, everyone in the family was staring at me. Most likely they already knew what was going on.

"She wants to talk to us," I said with as calm a manner as I could muster.

"She wants to talk to *us?*" my father asked. "What does she want to talk to *us* for?"

"She just wants to visit," I said. "She thought it would be nice if we came over for a visit."

"She wants *me* to come over for a visit?" Dad said.

I was buying time, but for what I don't know. I suppose I was hoping that I could stall things long enough so that by the time we got to Betsy's she wouldn't be pregnant anymore.

We got into the car to drive to Betsy's, even though it was only a five-minute walk from the house. My father was direct.

"Is Betsy pregnant?"

"No! What the hell?" I said. "What are you talking about?" I asked indignantly. Denial makes you mad, and I was livid. "What are you, crazy?"

"Did you use a rubber?" he asked.

"What do you mean, did I use a rubber?" I said. "I told you I didn't have sex with Betsy."

I was sixteen years old, my girlfriend was pregnant, and my navy lieutenant commander father was driving me over to her house to face what we both knew was coming. I wanted to die. I imagined that my father would take me out back and shoot me if Betsy's warrant-officer father didn't get emergency shore leave and get to me first. I was going out of my mind and I was lying, lying, lying as fast as I could.

The atmosphere at Betsy's was so thick that I truly did feel underwater. I was certainly in over my head. Betsy was sobbing on one side of the living room, and I didn't even try to comfort her. I thought that someone would slug me if I so much as touched her. I sat hunched over with my knees locked together, my elbows tight at my sides, trying to become as small as possible. Every light in the house was on, and everything moved in slow motion. The adults paced in their separate orbits, smoking menthol cigarettes, and taking turns berating me. My life crashed down around me as I shriveled in the glare.

The families agreed we would marry. Abortion was illegal and—with two religious families—unthinkable, as was putting Betsy in a home for unwed mothers. I trudged through the weeks leading up to my marriage in a comatose state. My parents had to keep reminding me to get out of bed, go to school, do my paper route, things that had been automatic just a few days before.

The flashbulb memories from that time are still clear to me: resigning my class presidency, as Betsy and her friends sobbed in the front row of the school auditorium; the grim-faced principal telling me I had to drop out because school policy forbade married people from attending regular high school; enduring my long night of the soul with my father, who spent an entire eight-hour shift of his night auditor job chiding me for how I'd ruined my life; finally packing up my stuff as my family plus our newest member, Betsy, fled to Columbus, Ohio.

While I wish that the night we found out Betsy was pregnant was the worst we had to endure, it got worse. In nearly photographic detail, I can recall the many ways I eventually became irresponsible and neglectful of both my wife and child. As I've written in my book *The Prodigal Father,* Betsy eventually fell in love with another man and remarried. He adopted my son, Scott. I was no longer legally responsible for him, and we lost contact. It took me years to make amends and reestablish my relationship with my son, something I wish I had done years earlier.

In the more than ten years between the time my marriage

ended and when I finally sought professional help to get my life on track, I grew so ashamed of what I had done and how it had played out that I could only blame others. The amount of blame you heap on others is equal to the amount of shame you carry inside. It was my family's fault for making me get married. It was the school system's fault for having such antiquated rules about married couples, which forced me into night school. If we hadn't moved to Columbus, I wouldn't have fallen in with such a bad crowd and started my downward spiral. I was stuck in this anger and memory, thrashing around for an exit. For ten years, my perspective on it remained that of the frightened high school junior stalling and lying as he hoped it would all just go away.

The remembering exercises in chapter 2 worked to reawaken your sense memories and bring the pleasant images of your life with your family to sit alongside the painful ones. Now the task is for you to set aside your painful or angry memories and become willing to get lost in the familiar. Allow yourself to accept the possibility that what you think of as the truth is only part of the picture. If the idea of challenging your story of your life with your family makes you apprehensive and angry, that is understandable. That story has become an important part of how you make meaning in the world, both as part of your self-image and as how you position yourself in the family context. That anger is an important signal of the primal power family relationships have over our everyday lives. The more anger you hold about your past, the more benefit doing this work can provide.

The problem with potent memories is that we view them as gospel—accept them as unquestionably true—and the more emotion they rouse in us, the more we cling to them. Here we shift perspective on those episodes so that we can appreciate these memories as sacred texts, whose full meaning can only be discovered upon reflection. Each religion has its sacred text, symbolic stories whose meaning can be interpreted and reinterpreted from different perspectives across the generations by those seeking hope, salvation, faith. Important moments in your family's history can have this same kind of depth of interpretation if you are willing to explore them with the better angels of your nature—with an open heart and mind.

Philosopher Otto Scharmer has said that reflection is the opposite of blame. Reflection also allows you to transcend blame. If you are searching through your memories for someone to blame, you are not yet in a state of receptivity. Reflection starts when you give up searching to prove yourself right in favor of finding a deeper meaning. Growth comes from understanding and acceptance, attitudes that are closed off to someone looking for causality.

REFLECT, RE-COGNIZE, AND RE-KNOW

After I began to rebuild my life, I made my first consistent efforts to find my son and build a relationship with him. In fact, my yearning for him and my desire to be the kind of man of whom he could be proud were my major motivations for looking for the deeper meaning of my past. Yet, each time I sat down in present time to write a letter to Betsy to apologize and to ask to see Scott, my feelings of anger and blame from the past would seep in, no matter how hard I tried to clear them from my mind and my words. I would find myself spacing out or swamped with feelings of self-loathing, unable to write.

Although I had been in therapy and attended support groups, I was still too ashamed of my actions to be able to face Betsy and Scott. The shame I carried created a barrier to reconnection. Because my sense of self was so wounded by the early failure, I could not cease projecting my low self-worth onto them in the form of resentment and blame. This kept me locked in the past.

Upon reflection, I realized I had not forgiven them because I had not forgiven myself. That forgiveness seemed impossible, stuck as I was in my weakness.

Many of you may be carrying the pain of a similar story. After a major loss or failure somehow the world never seems the same again, nor does your image of who you are. My friend Phyllis calls this kind of an event the Big Hurt. It takes the foreground in the landscape of our lives, so that it looms over everything that comes after it. In order to open up my perspective on the past, I gave myself a reflection assignment: I went back to high school.

The building felt small around me as I mounted the steps to Lincoln High School in Chicago, but my compassion grew as I recalled how scrawny I had been then. My real growth spurt didn't begin until after I dropped out and sprouted to my full six foot one inch height. Looking back, marriage and father-hood must have been a lot to carry on those slender teenage shoulders. As I stood in the doorway watching the boys clown-ing around, trying out their version of adult swagger, I looked in amazement. How quickly they went from boy to man and back again. One look at a passing girl and they'd have the leer-ing face of a twenty-year-old bachelor on the make, and a few seconds later they were shoving and punching each other like third-graders.

They were so cocky, so full of piss and vinegar, and so heart-breakingly unprepared for the price of that false sense of matu-rity. I saw in the faces of these boys my own reflection. My heart went out to them in their hubris and ineptitude and then reflected back, to forgive me for mine.

When you are young, the world around you shows you little except your limitations, while your spirit soars out into the larger world, where your possibilities seem limitless. Upon reflection, I could see that I *was* telling the truth when I said I loved Betsy and wanted to marry her. I loved her to the limits of my understanding of love. I vowed to love, honor, and obey with all my sixteen-year-old heart and with only the slightest understanding of how those words are put into practice. Surveying the boys in the high school corridor, I tried to imagine any child of that age being able to fulfill the vows I broke.

With all this stacked against us, Betsy and I were courageous to try to do the right thing even if we failed. Although to this day I have regrets for my actions during my marriage, in that moment in the high school doorway, I discovered compassion for my teenage self for the first time in fifteen years. That compassion allowed me to step outside the emotional field of that event and explore the reality of the forces at play around me. Compassion allowed me to come to a realistic acceptance of who I was at that time, in that place. Compassion is the way to begin healing the Big Hurt.

For many people the words *compassion* and *family* don't fit in the same sentence. One of my students once described going home to his family as entering a battlefield where the floor of the house was seeded with emotional land mines. The intensity of the feelings he carries into that house creates, as I've said, not a land mine, but a gold mine.

The gold lies underneath the grief, the sadness, the anger, the betrayal, and the slowly smoldering resentment of past conflict. Mature connection with our family comes from not just the sweet moments remembered with nostalgia but also from the survival of our struggles. None of us is perfect, and through compassionate reflection on landmark events we see that cliché demonstrated without dispute: Not only is no one perfect, but all people fail.

In conflict, people demonstrate character, not always their

best character traits but character nonetheless. If you are searching to develop new insight and understanding about your family, the place to look for those insights is *within the moments of conflict.*

Here we reflect, thinking quietly and calmly, so that we might *re-cognize,* in other words, *re-know* our past and present in a new light. This new light allows us to drop the burden of blame. We reflect on the same memories from different points in order to transform them. The more mature we become, the more able we are to see others' points of view and move beyond our limited perspective. With less blame, judgment, or emotion, we gain a higher vantage point and are able to see a wider truth.

You must start reflecting on your past with this exhilarating leap of faith: *Much of what you know is wrong.* You must say to yourself: "I have certain memories and constructions of meaning around those memories that I have to be willing to entertain as untrue." That's the leap of faith. We want to hold on to our versions of the truth because we are afraid of what will happen to us if we release them. We tend to believe a memory is true simply because we remember it. We instantly attach causality: "It happened, so someone must have caused it, and that someone cannot be me. It must be my father, my mother, my grandparents, *someone.* It all started there, on that one afternoon when my father said . . ."

If that is not the reaction, then this is: "Everything is *my* fault. It happened, so I must have caused it." While this might make us feel powerful in the short run, in the marathon of life, we begin to hate ourselves as the inevitable failures of life accumulate. Always believing ourselves to be to blame is no more true than always shifting the blame to everyone else.

Blame is a heavy burden to carry, but for many blaming themselves is so familiar it has an air of comfort about it. It seems like home. But although it may seem like home, it is by no means a comfortable place to live. By remaining barricaded in by blame, by labeling members of your family based on their past actions, or by being too frightened by the legacy of the past to speak your true feelings with your family, you can't feel good no matter how familiar it seems. Yet you may be clinging to this view of the world because it's one you've been constructing for most of your life. This is why attempting to see familiar episodes without the blinders of blame can lead to the promise that all the spiritual traditions have: the moment of clarity in which the world is transformed.

In the previous chapter you introduced a richer color palette to paint the past through reviving and exploring nonthreatening sensual memories of your youth. You may have noticed a rise in your spirits, a freeing up of energy through doing these exercises as you realized how limited and limiting your view of the world had become. In reflecting, we introduce this same playful spirit to liberate your view of yourself. This is when the real excitement begins.

WORKING WITH SIGNAL ANXIETY

The process of exploring the past for pleasant memories often enlivens not only the time you set aside for this work but other times during your day as well. Being able to say, "I haven't thought of that in years," reminds you of the simpler aspects of the longstanding connection you've had to your family. However, when you turn your mind to exploring the hidden nature of moments of conflict, something in the body starts to go awry.

The process can have powerful effects on you physically as well as psychologically. You may find yourself fidgety. Your efforts to mentally enter your childhood home may be blocked by sudden desires to overeat, to sleep, to buy something you don't need, to bite your nails, to get a drink. For many, having the desire and acting on it occurs so rapidly that the behavior becomes compulsive: before you have made a conscious decision to do so, you find yourself in the kitchen eating whatever comes into view or on the phone to someone you haven't spoken to in years. Or you may be overcome with fatigue and be back in bed minutes after beginning one of these exercises. Television may also become an irresistible distraction; once it's on, the effort required to turn it off may seem immense, and an entire day can slip by in a haze.

These are all manifestations of what psychologists call signal anxiety, a sign that beginning to consider a different perspective on the past disturbs something fundamental within. We all want to hold on to our version of the truth. These fits of desire you may be experiencing are simply the mind's way of distracting you from the work before you. Just connecting those two—the work and the anxiety that it generates—is the beginning of reflection.

Anxiety is powerful energy. Directed to good use, it can be a force for internal change. Misdirected, it can turn into self-destructive behavior. While working on this chapter try to impose the five-minute rule. *If you are overcome with the desire to eat or drink or any other distracting or self-destructive behavior, allow that urge to surface and examine it. Write down the impulse and tell yourself you can do whatever it is, if you still want to do it, in five minutes.* In five minutes that urge will most likely have evaporated. In a lot of cases it will be replaced by another urge, which needs its own five-minute waiting period.

When you write these down, you will have a record of exactly how fidgety the process of reflecting makes you. The anxiety comes from entertaining the idea of letting go of your version of the past. Somewhere inside, you understand that it will be difficult to describe who you are and fix your place in the world if you are exploring the idea that these familiar tales could be, at times, exaggerated, incomplete, or just plain wrong.

OUR FALSE SELVES

For years I held on to my recollection of the drama and aftermath of my teenage fatherhood. Blaming everyone around me justified my role as a victim of the forces of nature and circumstances beyond my control. With that as my supposition, life was meaningless. I was unworthy, and the sheer malevolence of the world had made it unsafe. It was only when I had the maturity to accept my part in what happened that I was able first to have compassion for myself, then to move forward and sincerely apologize for my actions, and start to build a life I could be proud of. I had to let go of my false self to become mature enough to accept my part in what went on and move forward toward my real self.

The false self is the part of us that is invested in our limited view of the past. Changing this view is a process, and new understanding does not come quickly, so there is no need to rush. You will have to suffer through the anxiety of examining your past with your family, whether it was tempestuous or just boring. Your version of the past won't want to die and it will grip on to any distraction it can to prevent you from making this transformation. Change this fundamental can be threatening on an unconscious level, so our false self latches on to various distractions in a desperate attempt to keep us from the ultimately gratifying process of becoming more honest with our family and subsequently the world.

Few people are comfortable enough with who they are to be their truest self with their family. Before a visit with the family, many people prepare as if going into battle. You may recall the false self I constructed for my first Christmas reunion with my family. I was decked out in my thrift store finery and driving an expensive rented car. I'd even paid extra for the cell phone, which I knew wouldn't work in the mountains of West Virginia, because it made me feel so prosperous. We each prepare our false selves differently, depending on our family and on our temperament—it doesn't matter whether your family was rich or poor.

In an effort to defend ourselves from others knowing our vulnerability, we often create a false self that is powerful, unflawed, and perfect, someone without weakness and therefore without humanity. This persona is not someone with whom anyone in the family can be intimate, because there is no common point of connection, no vulnerability. This false self is the one who will neither test nor experiment, especially with the past, because his hold on his self-esteem is in reality so tenuous that he can't take the risk of endangering it. For all his grandiosity, this false self, therefore, is weak and must stay at an emotional distance from the family to preserve the facade.

Another false self we create is infantile, someone who is unable to own their feelings, live up to their full potential in life. This hiding is just another way of avoiding conflict and pain. This quiet version of the false self is enmeshed with the family through timidity. For example, Sheila is always the dutiful daughter, helping with the chores and keeping everyone informed about her husband's advancing career. She would never dream of talking about herself—her interests, her feelings—these are too risky. The pain of abandonment she feels when he works out of town several months of the year is never mentioned. Sheila would be the last to complain.

Staying small in the family, not letting the others know what you are thinking and feeling, is a no-self position. Those hemmed in by fear of family conflict become the accommodators, never giving their real opinion, placating the others in the family, quietly going about the business of being present physically while being mentally somewhere else. The quiet false self is often the more insidious, since the grand false self is often a transparent jokester whose balloon is begging to be punctured. The quiet victim, how-ever, when suffering in the extreme, can justify anything. As my brother Jim says, "Dogs that don't bark, bite."

Both versions of the false self keep us victims. The grandiose false self often externalizes her victimhood with rages, defensive accusations, or obvious self-destructive behavior disguised as re-bellious fun—all defenses against facing the responsibility for change. In an attempt to hide, the quiet false self has turned in-ward. This false self internalizes the anger, or defensiveness, and may be in a hidden depression or withdrawn in a fantasy world. This side of his false self can be hard to spot because he is the for-gotten one, present but not seen. The old adage that children should be seen and not heard is only too painfully true in a family that fosters the quiet false self.

When our false selves are in control, we are incapable of a person-to-person relationship with anyone in the family. The grand false self breezes through the family offering advice and promising to help, imagining she can rescue everyone. However, it is not uncommon that this grand self is incapable of fulfilling any of these promises, because she has promised more than anyone can deliver. The quiet false self often hides close to home, serving others, while sniping behind people's backs, neglecting to say what he really thinks, or withdrawing from emotional contact or creative expression in order to protect himself from the judgment of others. The sad thing for this false self is that because he is too intimidated to ask for what he really needs or strive for what he really wants, he almost never gets it.

Even contemplating reengaging with our families can activate either of our false selves. Looking back over the history of our families, most of us can see how we have at times played any number of variations on these basic false selves. The mask we choose is often based on a combination of factors including: our inborn temperament, our mental capacities, and the specific dynamics within the family as well as external circumstances.

Recognizing that we have false selves that appear to greater or lesser degrees when we are under stress is a fundamental step toward being a more accurate and engaged observer of ourselves. Through the mask of the false self we cannot see the family as it truly is, nor can the family see or feel us. The mask is the barrier to human vulnerability and authenticity.

PERMEABLE BOUNDARIES VERSUS IMPENETRABLE BARRIERS

Within the family, no doubt it is important to keep a boundary between you and the other members in order to keep yourself sharply defined: boundaries will help you not to lose your sense of self, your identity. But there is a difference between boundaries and barriers. Permeable boundaries are the tools of the authentic self because they allow self-definition while still permitting the love and respect between family members to pass through.

In contrast, barriers are rigid and heavily defended with emotions real and false. They seem to protect us but, in fact, often isolate us because we fortify them with anger or physical distance. This degree of familial isolation is unnatural for such a social species as we, and so barriers are often breached for the simple reason that no one can stand being so alone. When these barriers get breached, we resort to the false self as our last line of defense—either relying on too little emotional distance or too much.

Jeff, a thirty-five-year-old musician, traveled frequently and, despite an active spiritual life, was not able to remain faithful to his wife. During one road trip, he had a brief affair. After discovering his dalliance, his wife filed for separation and left with their two daughters. Jeff refused to accept responsibility for his actions. He blamed his wife for her disloyalty, and raged at how "she took the first chance she could to leave." He cut off all contact with her, though she tried to remain civil for the children's sake. Jeff's blame and anger erected a barrier around him, a wall through which neither light nor love could pass. He refused to form a new relationship with his estranged wife and because of it he missed the love of his daughters and caused them to miss the love he had for them.

The impulse to erect a barrier is often a wise one for a time—a limited time—the time necessary to protect us from overwhelming emotions. A barrier can provide breathing room during a crisis: a time-out in which to reflect and to refocus energy for a new approach to the problem. However, once in place, barriers are often left up too long. The most destructive myth in America is that time heals all wounds. This is not true. *Time heals nothing.* There are many families who have lost years of love and connection waiting for time to heal the rifts between them. The longer a barrier is allowed to remain in place the more likely it is to become a *wall*, something seemingly impossible to get over. Walls form prisons. For Jeff, the impenetrability of his barrier kept him from his daughters and kept his emotional life trapped.

Jeff's withdrawal, for instance, is an act of vengeance. For Jeff, his attempt to punish his wife reminds me of the old Chinese proverb about revenge that states: "Before one seeks revenge, one must first dig *two* graves." Vengeance always backfires. Jeff lost his wife and his daughters as well as the ability to be trusted by new lovers. Once women found out that he was still angry at his now ex-wife and had no relationship with his children, they saw that attitude as a barrier to intimacy with them. As a result, Jeff's barrier became a grave for his own emotions as well as one for the love of his children.

A barrier has a hot feeling to it—it is angrily defended and is often heatedly denied by its maker. We fortify these barriers with distractions from our true feelings. We might eat too much, be slothful, act out sexually, procrastinate on the job, or become a workaholic in order to keep the barrier impermeable. These barriers are energetic—made up of emotions, not bricks and mortar, though they might as well be. As the woman said about talking to her husband: "It's like talking to a wall." Her words, her love, her concern, bounce off the barrier and never reach the intended person, leaving both partners isolated. This is also true of the barriers we erect between ourselves and our families.

Boundaries, on the other hand, are lower in temperature, cooler. They protect the authentic self, allow us to remain calm, whole, and lovingly detached in the face of conflict. Boundaries are in many ways stronger than barriers because they adapt to meet any crisis. They allow us to remain fully expressive and receptive at the same time—achieving a necessary balance between individuality and togetherness. This use of temperature as a gauge of our emotional intensity can alert us to how well our boundaries are holding. The cooler we remain in conflict, the better.

Stephanie's interactions with her mother had been heated since she was a teenager. Stephanie was a quiet, studious young woman who was appalled by her mother's flamboyance and numerous exploits. Her mother's depression and loneliness had made Stephanie's mom very needy and no matter how much love Stephanie expressed it could never satisfy her mother's craving for a kind of intimacy without boundaries. As a young woman Stephanie had erected a necessary barrier between herself and her mother in order to become autonomous and protect herself from her mother's unquenchable thirst for affection.

One year, when her mother called to ask Stephanie to drive four hundred miles with her small children to visit her for Easter,

Stephanie felt the old sense of entrapment and duty and of guilt, which quickly rushed in to accompany them. She understood how little she wanted to go, not just intellectually but viscerally. Her heart started racing, her voice went up an octave, and she became flushed. Barriers often announce themselves through physical reactions in the body and simultaneous emotional reactions that seem out of context or proportion—given that it's just an invitation for dinner, for example.

Stephanie told her mother she had to discuss Easter plans with her husband before she could make a commitment. In fact, Stephanie listened to her body and read its signs that told her that her mother had rubbed up against her barrier. Stephanie took a moment to reflect.

Now a mother herself, Stephanie could empathize with the desire to have the family together on a holiday. Previously, in an attempt to understand her mother better, she had reflected on her mother's childhood. She could appreciate how her mother's unquenchable thirst for attention stemmed from the neglect her mother had endured from her own mother. Remembering this reflection inspired a moment of clarity that removed Stephanie from the emotional field. Her old resentment lifted enough that she could express her love to her mother without the old feeling that she was going to be smothered. In this breakthrough moment of empathy, Stephanie shifted her defense from a barrier to a boundary—and was simultaneously able to take care of herself and communicate her love to her mother when she called her back.

"Mom, I love you and I'd really like to see you for Easter, but it's been a difficult month and the drive would be a lot for us right now," Stephanie said.

"You know, Stephanie, I may not have that many Easters left," her mother responded, trying to draw her in through guilt.

"Well, Mom, that guilt might work if I thought we had a bad

relationship, but you know I love you and I need you," Stephanie said. "I'm looking forward to seeing you on Mother's Day."

Although Stephanie's mother's behavior did not change, Stephanie's actions and reactions were no longer defined by her mother's neediness. With her barrier down and a healthy boundary in its place, Stephanie was able to appreciate the many positive aspects of her mother that she did love: her mother's sense of style, her love of life, her razor-sharp perceptions about others, and her amazing hostess skills. Many times her mother had hurt Stephanie's feelings by saying, "You'll never love me as much as I love you."

For years Stephanie had interpreted this statement as an attack and felt saddened and guilty for not being able to return her mother's love as fully as she needed. As an adult with appropriate boundaries, Stephanie was able to see the truth of that statement and what it meant for her as well as for her mother. What that statement meant for her mother was that Stephanie may never comprehend how much she was loved. Perhaps Stephanie would never love her mother in the same way that her mother loved her. And maybe Stephanie has no desire to be that enmeshed. Stephanie understood, however, that she definitely did love her mother deeply and as fully as she could and she always would.

Moving from using barriers to using boundaries can also make us feel as if the ground is shifting beneath our feet. The guilt may still be present at first, even though the anger and need for physical distance are gone. But more important, the communication of love is *real*. As a result of her fuller understanding of the love she had for her mother, Stephanie felt proud of the way she had handled the invitation to Easter. Had Stephanie reacted as she often had in the past—with immediate anger and rejection—her mother would not have heard the love and would not have dropped the issue, as she did after the above exchange. In fact, as Stephanie says, her mother never brought the issue up again. Stephanie's change in behavior—creating a permeable boundary instead of an impenetrable barrier—forever changed her interactions with her mother because it was a fundamental step toward Stephanie's being her loving authentic self in the family.

Now a year after her mother's death, Stephanie is more than grateful for the inspiration that showed her how to switch from barriers to boundaries, and allowed the love to flow again between mother and daughter.

Boundaries are a necessary element of the authentic self. To fall in love with your family, you need only find a way to be lovingly who you are while you are with them. This is not to say that you have to tell the family everything about your life or that you throw in their faces information about the way you conduct your personal business you'd rather they not know, information they'd rather not hear—this can indicate that you lack boundaries.

The false self always has something to prove to the family: either that the family was right about them or that the family was wrong. The false self has not yet emotionally separated itself from the family, a process psychologists call differentiation. As a result it can not grow and mature. The real self has a healthy boundary between itself and the family and knows when to assert itself, how to step back without anger, and when to keep its mouth shut, allowing others their successes or failures.

We as individuals evolve throughout our lives, just as our species evolved throughout the ages. As we evolve personally, we shed a series of affected selves, which is similar to the process of "going through a phase," such as the time you streaked your hair orange for a few months or scandalized your grandmother by getting a nose ring. These are often referred to as acts of rebellion, but they are actually external ways of differentiating from the rules and strictures of the family, a practice run at becoming your real self.

Establishing a real separation from the family is an internalized process that can't be purchased at a tattoo shop. Through these outward manifestations we say, "I am. I am unique." The false self says, "I am superior" or "I am inferior." The real self is not threatened by similarities to the family, nor empowered by differences. The real self not only says, "I am me and I am unique," it also says, "I am like you."

The real self can say, "I am and I love," without reciting a litany of incidents that created or forced a distance. The real self has a sense of continuity and recognizes that throughout all these different phases of personal evolution, a special someone persists in space and time and endures, as psychiatrist James Masterson says. This real self, is able to engage fully with the family, confident and proud of that essential continuity of self. This self is so *real* that she is able to be physically and emotionally present with her family, and is so aware of life's transience that, like Stephanie, she is aware that we must act quickly. Our real self is disengaged enough to maintain its integrity without being trapped in the family's emotional field, and honest enough to stay engaged as an equal and express and receive love. Turning barriers into boundaries always takes practice and negotiation.

BRINGING IT HOME

While many of us have learned to have adequate real selves in the world at large, we reach a point at which the skills we have learned outside of the family must be brought home. It is an important piece of personal evolution as we increase our ability to maintain an emotional equilibrium in more intense and intimate interactions. As we continue the process of shedding our false selves in favor of becoming real within our families, we often let go of the false self gradually so that the process is not too terrifying. The exercises that follow will help you in this step-by-step process of differentiation and help you to recognize and strengthen your authentic self. Before we start, here are the intellectual underpinnings of those exercises.

First, nearly everyone in a family has a label. For instance, one sister will play the good girl while another may play the slattern. One cousin is the loser while Uncle Joe is the alcoholic and Aunt Sara is a big phony. This poisonous combination of suspicion and misplaced therapy language diminishes our family members by creating intrafamily stereotypes that become difficult for the labeled person to rise above or dispute. Our authentic selves are not strengthened by diminishing others through labels or blame, nor are they accurately described by a single word.

To call Jeff a deadbeat dad does not sufficiently describe the man. He is a great comic, a volunteer in his community, goes through his struggles at work, and is an ardent fan of the New York Yankees. To label Stephanie's mom a neurotic, a sex addict, a codependent, whatever, doesn't acknowledge her full humanity. Sure she wears grand clothes and exaggerates her financial success, but she is a loving and generous grandmother, a great cook, and one of the most loyal friends Stephanie had ever seen. Labels keep us from expecting change.

Labels limit family members to a two-dimensional portrait without depth or compassion. They also serve to make the person who is applying the label feel superior. In an ironic twist of human nature, the person in the family that we are often quickest to label or most judgmental of is the person most similar to disowned parts of ourselves. If I label Aunt Sara as a phony, it may be because she's got the money and the nice clothes I wish I had—or the attitude of entitlement that I wish I possessed. If I loathe my sister for being the favorite who gets everything she wants, I may be avoiding my problem with asking my family for what I need.

Blame is another tool of the false self. Our real self gradually gains mastery over our different expressions of anxiety that arise in present time. Yet, sometimes our real self somehow goes missing when we review the past.

Many of us remain hidden from our families behind the barriers of blame and labels attached to old identities that we forged from the perspective of the child. The child did not understand the pressures of being a parent, nor of earning a living, nor of maintaining a marriage, nor the speed of our century's changes. The child receives the effect of the pressures without the capacity to comprehend them.

FEELINGS VERSUS FELTS

The final step in preparing our minds to freely reflect on the past is to train ourselves to stop reacting to it. In many cases you've stopped reacting, but you may not appreciate it yet. Physicist David Bohm delineated the difference between a feeling and a "felt." When you tell stories about why you are estranged from your family, you bring with them the *memory* of a feeling. These memories Bohm calls "felts," because the attendant emotion is not being caused in present time. Your pulse may quicken and your face may flush, but *you are now causing it.* Because of these "felts," we remain in a reactive state when our authentic present-day self might much rather move on.

What, you may ask, do we do about the felts that still feel like feelings?

For a long time Beau carried resentment toward his mother. When his father left, she depended on Beau as the father figure, although he was only eight years old at the time. Many a night, his distraught mom would come into Beau's room and sit on the edge of his bed, not so much to kiss him good night but to unload her worries. She'd sometimes lay all the bills out on the empty side of the double bed and say, "These are the bills and this is how much money we have. I don't know what we are going to do."

As his mother tried to fight back her tears, Beau would feel inadequate. He couldn't help his mother. He was too young to get a job and contribute to the family, nor could he help his mother handle the family finances. His overwhelmed mother was reaching out to the wrong person for support, but Beau was the only person she had.

After a few years of being single, Beau's mother remarried and the family's finances took a turn for the better. Nevertheless, Beau's feeling of inadequacy both with money and women dog him to this day. He's the kind of guy who never breaks up with a woman. He stays passive as things decay so he can be the victim when the woman finally dumps him. The passivity is similar in his career. He's now in his thirties and has wandered from job to job. His finances are shaky. In many ways he's still that eight-year-old child blinking dumbfounded at the adult world.

After a few months of therapy (which he had to quit because he ran out of money), Beau recalled these bedside sessions with his mother as an explanation for the plight he finds himself in today. At the first rush of recollection, Beau's memory carried with it a powerful surge of emotion—rage even—at the poor judgment of his mother in dumping adult problems on him. In returning to his childhood bedroom, Beau understands intellectually that his mother's actions may have contributed to his feeling of inadequacy. Beau's emotions related to his mother's ill-advised dependence are most definitely "felts," but dwelling on them only keeps him in a state of blaming and therefore hampers him from taking action in present time to engage more fully in life or with his mother.

Upon reflection, Beau was able to free that incident from blame. He widened his view of the past to include the possibility that his parents' years of hostility and his father's abandonment of the family may have contributed to his feeling of inadequacy too. The real progress isn't just to spread the blame around, however, but to see into that incident to understand what was happening to everyone in the family at that time and that place. His mother, who had been raised to depend on a man for stability, had her world turned upside down when her husband left. Beau began to understand, and in turning blame to compassion, he could leave the weak childhood self in that bedroom and begin the process of pursuing a more mature position in the world and with his mother. Through this, he left behind the felts and was able to have his own real feelings. By the time he was called upon to speak at his mother's funeral, he was able to use the same story of his mother laying the bills on his bed as an example of how, in her own perhaps misdirected way, she was trying to teach him how to be a man.

By dropping the blame and the labels and distinguishing the real feelings from the felts, we gradually clear away the cobwebs that surround the past. This is all part of true reflection, because reflection looks for connection. Focus in on whatever member of your family has caused you the most grief—or rage—and explore the incidents that have come to define the conflict between you, keeping an eye out for the barriers to connection. Watch for blame, labels, feelings, and felts—they define the frame of your old ideas. Through reflection on these old ideas, we build our new past.

For Pamela, for instance, the long-standing issue with her mother has always been her weight. Even as a small child, Pamela's mother was concerned that she would become a chubby adult. Her mother had been a model and struggled with her weight all her life.

From Pamela's infancy her mother tried to control Pamela's

food intake, putting her on skim milk instead of regular milk from the time she was a small child. In elementary school, Pamela spent every summer at weight-loss camps only to regain the weight by Christmas. As a teenager, her mother took her to diet doctor after diet doctor and enrolled her in modeling schools, trying to get Pamela to see what a beauty she would be if she only dropped the weight.

At the height of her adolescent rebellion, Pamela gained a tremendous amount of weight partially to demonstrate to her mother that she couldn't control her anymore. As an obese adult, she dreaded the visits home because she knew that the subject of her weight would be sure to come up and that her mother would scrutinize every morsel she placed in her mouth, whether it be a "good" salad or a "bad" dip into the candy dish.

Although Pamela was unhappy with her size, it was her last defense. Fat was the major barrier to being engulfed by her mother and being made to answer for the dreams she projected on to Pamela. From time to time, Pamela attempted to diet but never told her mother. She didn't want to get her mother's hopes up or to have to answer for another failure if she couldn't stick to the plan. Both Pamela and her mother were locked in a relationship of unhappiness despite their many common tastes and values.

In order to step outside the emotional field, Pamela reflected on the love her mother expressed in other ways. Although Pamela's weight dismayed her mother, she always made sure Pamela looked her best. They shopped together, her mother carefully looking for the best large-size clothes. Her mother's eye for what looked good on her was acute. Even though when Pamela looked in the mirror she saw nothing but fat and self-disgust, her mother was far kinder. She always found something to compliment and gave Pamela carefully chosen accessories to enhance her looks without bringing up the issue of size.

By examining whether these were feelings or felts, Pamela uncovered that her mother was concerned more for Pamela's health and happiness than for her mother's dream of Pamela becoming a model. After all, at the age of thirty-four, Pamela had missed the opportunity in any case. Still, Pamela's felts kept her back. When her mother complimented a scarf she was wearing, Pamela took it as an insult. She believed her mother was, in fact, hunting desperately for something nice to say to cover up her shame at how Pamela hadn't measured up to her expectations. Pamela discovered it was she who was stuck on her inability to fulfill that maternal dream; her mother had moved on long before. By accepting the present-time feeling of love from her mother, instead of the felts of the old past, Pamela was more free to love herself and her mother in present time. Many issues between family members can be brought into present time through this kind of reflection.

TEMPERED STRENGTH

People who suffered through especially painful or threatening childhoods tend to find reflection on their pasts difficult. However, there is much to be gained by escaping from the prison of our felts and working through our feelings in the here and now. Sometimes the worst episodes and traits of your family life may have forged some of your most tempered strengths as you learn to turn lemons into lemonade.

Nora is a writer and can spin a gut-wrenching tale of neglect and abuse taken from her often horrifying past. As a ten-year-old, Nora frequently felt as if she were the adult in charge because the actual adults were too drunk to care for her and her brothers and sisters. While she suffered from the obvious difficulties caused by alcoholism, Nora's writing ability actually benefited. She has an amazing gift for storytelling. She analyzes each situation in terms of the power dynamic: Who is in charge? Who is at risk? What does each person want? This is a technique that was forged in the fire of her past, and one she uses every day in her work, at which she is very successful.

Josh provides another example and was raised in a substantially less threatening situation. Josh is the product of hippie parents whose unstructured lives and antiauthoritarian attitude has marginalized them and made them financially insecure in their old age. Josh blamed them for the five years he lost to excessive marijuana use and, once he became a successful stockbroker, refused to speak to them for years.

Now in his early forties, Josh has made peace with his parents and even helped them build a retirement fund. He understands that his rebellion against their values honed his financial skills. He brings to his work an agility and a determination absent in those trained in more sedate business schools. Josh's analytic tools include a Marxist perspective on capital as well as a firsthand sense of market economy, which he developed from his parents' perspective on their failed homegrown business attempts. As an adult, Josh has been able to differentiate himself from his family. He has learned through reflection that what he originally viewed as a detriment came to have a decidedly profitable effect on his adult life.

Reflect on your own life with this same filter. What strengths of yours were tempered in the fire of adversity? Does your amazing knack for organization come from your disgust at the slovenly house your parents kept? Are you an excellent cook not because you come from a long line of accomplished home chefs but because your mother's cooking was horrible and you learned to cope? This shift in perspective is not an attempt to put too sunny a light on the past but is instead an attempt to allow you to hold both ideas simultaneously: our fundamental strengths can often be generated by our family's weaknesses.

Codes of Love Exercise: REFLECTING

As this chapter concerns reflecting, let's take a moment to reflect on how you are doing and what is happening to you physically and emotionally as you work toward this new perspective on yourself and your family. What thoughts come up for you? What feelings? Then let's look at how your family's self-definitions—feelings, felts, blame, labels—have influenced your interactions.

Codes of Love Exercise: TAKE YOUR TEMPERATURE

- What happens for you as you read this book? Do you get bored? Sleepy? Notice your mind wandering? Feel restless? What do you think is happening? Is it signal anxiety?

- How long did this book sit on your bedside table before you picked it up? What do you think that is about?

- Are you taking good care of yourself: exercising, eating well, getting enough sleep?

- Do you look forward to this work? What do you hope to gain? What are you afraid to lose?

- Are you checking in with your support person? Have you shared this work with any member of your family? If so, what happened?

- What feelings are present in your body as you focus on this work? What desires come up? Eating? Sex? Drinking? Phone-stalling?

- How much quiet time do you give yourself? Do you feel you need more space now to be in solitude?

- What are your dreams like lately?
- Are you more or less volatile at home lately? At work?
- Are you keeping up your exercise or leisure routine? (We often do not take care of our bodies when our feelings threaten to overwhelm us—since feelings occur in the body, we often stop exercising to avoid them.)

Codes of Love Exercise: *WALKING INTO SACRED SPACE*

Go alone to spend an hour in a sacred space. It might be a church, temple, mosque, beach, or the like. The more deserted it is, the better. Let the space infuse you.

Codes of Love Exercise: *FEELINGS VERSUS FELTS*

- Can you tell when you are thinking versus when you are feeling? Can you distinguish between feelings (emotions in present time) and felts (memories of feelings)?
- How many felts from the past do you still keep as feelings?
- How do felts continue to shape how you make many of the four postulates?

  - Life is meaningful? Meaningless?
  - People are safe? Threatening?
  - The world is benevolent? Malevolent?
  - You are worthy? Unworthy?

- Have you identified any feelings that are really felts? How have your feelings changed?
- Are you willing to look at your relationships with new eyes? How would that change the way you view past relationships? Current relationships?

Codes of Love Exercise: THE BLAME GAME

Many times we unconsciously blame others for our dilemmas. Spreading the blame to others keeps us from acting to solve the problem. These exercises are designed to help you identify your problems and who besides yourself is taking the blame for them.

- Complete each of the following two sentences (five times for both):
  - I am angry that . . .
  - I am angry that . . .
  - I am angry that . . .
  - I am angry that . . .
  - I am angry that . . .
  - I am sad that . . .
  - I am sad that . . .
  - I am sad that . . .
  - I am sad that . . .
  - I am sad that . . .

- If I'd had a perfect childhood, I would have . . .
- Whom do you blame for how your life turned out?
- Whose blame list are you on? For what?
- What do you usually accuse people of? Where does this pattern come from?
- Make a list of how you wish your life were different. What action could you take toward those goals?
- Have you been labeled by your family? Are you willing to ask them how you have been labeled?
- Reflect on the accuracy of those labels.

Codes of Love Exercise: WILL THE REAL ME PLEASE STAND UP?

Labels are not just for others. Sometimes our identity is composed of the labels we give ourselves, rather than the true elements of our character. In these exercises work to name the traits and characteristics that collectively identify you and examine which describe the real you.

- When you are not true to yourself, which false self do you use?
- Has this changed over time?
- What are your identity groups? Poor, urban, country, northerner, southerner, gay, straight, rich, old, young, alcoholic, fat, thin, bright, forgetful, arrogant, conceited, patsy, chump, successful, loser, . . . ? List the words you associate with yourself. How do these affect how you portray yourself to others?
- Are there character traits or behaviors of yours that you disown? For example, bitchiness, kindness, meanness, aggression, . . . ? Is there any part of them that is a strength?
- Which false selves do you use outside the family? At work? In your marriage or intimate relationship?
- What do you fear would happen if you said what you really felt? Really thought? How are they different?
- What selves do you keep hidden from your family? Which do they hide from you? Which do they not hide that you don't acknowledge?

Codes of Love Exercise: COLOR ME BLUES

Temperament is an aspect of identity, but few people are aware of the color of the lens with which they view the world. Your taste in things such as music and movies can help you better understand your fundamental perspective on reality. Are you basically happy or sad? Pessimistic or optimistic? Shy or outgoing?

- What kind of music do you listen to? Happy? Sad? Has this changed over time?
- What kind of movies do you like? Tearjerkers? Those with happy endings? Comedies? Escapist?
- What do these movie choices have in common with how you *feel* about the world? How you *felt* the world?
- Are you able to reflect on your emotional states? On your moods? On those of your family?

Codes of Love Exercise: NEW IDEAS ON OLD THEMES

Understanding the forces that shaped your family in present time and your role in these outcomes can make a profound change in the way that you view the past. These questions are designed to help you liberate your perspective from the old meanings and entertain new ones.

- Can you see the relationship between stressors on the family and family members' reactions? What kind of emotional shock waves have rocked your family over the years? Can you trace the effects through the extended family, as with the damage from an earthquake?
- The true self: When have you risked telling someone what you really thought? How did it feel? How did they react? What was the aftereffect?
- How do you deal with rumors? How much do you inquire versus advocate? How much can you inquire about yourself in the presence of others? Are you open to their

insights? Can you give up your version? Be open to the mystery by admiring your problems for a time.

- What would a spiritual master say about your current relationships? About you?
- If you loved everyone in your life more than you can now imagine, how would that change your life? Are you able to receive love? What does that mean?
- Are you finding yourself triggered into reminiscing about a specific time or place or event? Can you view it differently now that you are older?
- List five memories you had lost but have now recovered since we started this work.

1.
2.
3.
4.
5.

CHAPTER 4

Re-frame

I don't know how I scraped up the money to go back home for Grandma Minnie's funeral in 1988. Mostly I remember a sense of urgency about getting there mixed with a deep sense of regret. I had not been home for my grandpa Arnie's funeral, nor my grandma Elizabeth's. Just as important to me, I'd missed Aunt Norma's. As I'd begun to rebuild my life, I'd grown to see how vital it is for us to show up for the big moments in our family's history—the weddings, the funerals, and the births—so that we can witness and participate in life's important transitions. In going home for Minnie's, I wanted to honor the role she had in my life and face this loss with the only people in the world who could understand how deep it was.

Minnie had made no secret of the fact that I was her favorite. No matter what I'd done or how long I'd been away from home, she always made me feel special. As a child confused by the conflict in my family, Minnie's house had been a refuge for me, a place where I felt unconditional love. I was determined to make it back for Minnie's funeral no matter the financial or psychological cost.

James Hillman describes the apprehension about going home as the sensation that "we're all going down the drain together." Certainly I felt that in my body as the tiny propeller plane circled down through the mountains to the Charleston airport. My memory of Minnie had gone through therapy with me: despite the love I always held for her, therapy had given me an intellectual, even judgmental perspective on her role in the family, one that focused on her losses, her fears, and her compromises. Part of the psychological price I knew I was going to pay for returning home was not just facing the loss of the bond Minnie and I had shared but experiencing firsthand the dysfunction in her life that I'd discovered underneath. The suspicious framework stood between my memory of her and the love of a young boy for his grandmother.

RE-FRAMING GRANDMA MINNIE

Something seemed to me to have gone wrong in Minnie's marriage to Grandpa Arnie way back when. Perhaps the deaths of two of the five children she bore him broke the marriage into a before and after. Whatever had caused the break, for my entire life Grandpa Arnie had lived upstairs and she down. I never saw them so much as exchange a hug. This aspect of her life went on year after year without comment from the family. It was just Grandma and Grandpa's way.

So, too, was her isolation. She grew up in the house in which she had been born, never journeying far from the homestead. As I bounced around the country from Florida to Illinois to New Mexico, the world of the West Virginia hills looked limited to me. Minnie herself rarely left her property in her later years. Through my heightened analysis, I saw this as a sign of her pathology, which I could have labeled in therapy-speak as agoraphobic, depressed, codependent. None of those labels would have captured who she had been.

Once I arrived in West Virginia, I found my family fraught with tension. The funeral was a rare public ceremony for us. We wanted to be at our best, so, of course, everyone was behaving at their worst. There were arguments about who was going to pay for the casket and predictions that we wouldn't be able to afford the nice walnut one—and would Minnie want it if we could? My mother was agitated about trying to find the money for an appropriately somber dress. I was sad and withdrawn because I hadn't the money to solve any of these problems. Each decision about how the funeral would be conducted produced an argument, and the tone was less one of mourning than of anxiety expressed as petty sniping. Every adult had a very firm idea of what Minnie would have wanted, and none of these ideas matched.

One thing I knew I could do was help the great-grandchildren—my nieces and nephews—deal with their loss. I asked each of them to write a letter to Grandma Minnie expressing what she had meant to them. As people filed into the funeral parlor for the service, the great-grandchildren and I sat outside the entrance sobbing as we wrote heartfelt letters to Minnie. I collected them shortly before the service was about to begin, intending to place these messages of love in the casket so she could carry them with her on her journey. Even in this simple gesture, I was thwarted. As I entered the funeral home, my mother snatched the letters out of my hand, refusing to allow them in the casket. She thought they were sacrilegious.

After the service, we went somberly back to Grandma Minnie's not knowing quite what to do next. The house seemed small and lifeless without her. As I sat on the porch swing lost in my memories, I looked up to see dozens of people coming across the bridge over the creek carrying baked chicken, pies, and casseroles. This impromptu observance lifted me out of the gloom that was overwhelming me.

In the end, nearly fifty townspeople showed up to mark Grandma Minnie's death, people I'd never have expected to care that she was gone. Neighbor after neighbor told stories about how she always welcomed a visitor, always had beans on the stove and corn bread in the skillet. They memorialized her biscuits, famous throughout the town for their unique flavor. She'd only use Hudson Cream flour and buttermilk in her biscuits, each with a swirl of bacon drippings on the top. Even when Uncle Bill bought her an electric stove, she kept the coal stove working, because, as she said, "That electric just doesn't do no good for my biscuits." No matter what she thought of her husband, she was up every morning making him biscuits before he went to work. Grandma Minnie's Code of Love was food.

Food and shelter, actually. Many came to recall how, when they had no place else to stay, Grandma Minnie had a room for them until they got back on their feet. Buck, now one of the richest men in the state, was there too. He reminded everyone of how, when he and his brother were hungry, Minnie fed them. As one person reminded me, she was a cornerstone for the town. Her father owned the first store and ran the first post office. Minnie not only knew your father, she knew your grandfather and your great-grandfather. When she died, so much history died with her.

These moving testimonials to Grandma Minnie smashed up against my therapizing. This dissonance between my superior therapeutic posture and the intimate and loving appreciation of my grandmother by her peers, helped me get out of myself. I came to see how the landscape in which I'd placed Grandma Minnie was one with me at the center. Through listening to those who spoke at her house after the funeral, I saw her in her own world, a context bigger than mine and one that honored her position in the community instead of just her importance in my development. Lengthening the time frame beyond the few years I'd been on the earth and taking a panoramic view that encompassed not only her role in my generation but in generations of my family stretching back to the turn of the century allowed me to re-frame each one of my judgments of her.

Minnie's view of the world was one where home came first and the women made the home. She was rooted in the community in a way that was hard for a nomad such as myself to imagine, except in a kind of romanticized postcard vision. For Minnie the essence of home was to maintain continuity: simply to be there for the family, for the community, for whoever happened to stop by needing a meal or someone to listen. As a young man, I couldn't perceive differences in temperament. I saw Minnie as sadly resigned to a small life, housebound and, I believed, defeated by her lack of imagination and ambition, traits that I had to an excessive degree. My judgment of her was exceedingly egocentric. I was projecting on to her how I would feel if I had spent all my eighty-one years in the same small town, in the same aging house in West Virginia.

In addition to being blind due to immaturity and temperament, I'd ignored the social forces that shaped a woman's place at the turn of the century. When Minnie was born, women were quite literally the homemakers. Through their cleverness and industry, they kept the family fed and clothed even when times were lean. It is a role that I can see being passed down through the female line in my family to this day in the way my mother and sister always manage to keep food on the table. In fact, by re-framing Grandma Minnie's life to include factors outside my limited perspective about her, I found in her life qualities I have grown to value: a sense of continuity through time, and connection to home and to community. In re-framing Grandma Minnie, I found a personal definition of "family values" that goes beyond the moralistic and the political.

A VIEW ACROSS TIME

The remembering and reflecting exercises in the previous chapter were really acts of willpower. To accomplish them, we had to detach from our idea of the truth and augment the memories and judgments we've carried with us for years to find compassion for those in the family who have caused us the most trouble. After liberating the past from our idiosyncratic suppositions, values, and justifications, we reflected on the idea that there are other equally valid perspectives on the same situations. Now, in re-framing, we take the final step toward unlocking the mystery at the heart of our own story.

Through re-framing we strengthen our identities by recognizing the elements at play in those incidents that weren't apparent: the social, historical, and genetic forces that influence the choices we make on a daily basis. Re-framing is the most powerful tool— and in many ways the most liberating one—you can use to reconnect with your family. Through re-framing you explore the past with a new perspective; in other words, *not all the situations in which our families found themselves were completely of their own making.*

The term *re-framing* comes from the world of psychology. But in this work it refers to the act of composing or framing a photograph. As with many of our potent memories, a photograph captures a single moment in time. The photographer has tremendous power to shape the viewer's emotional reaction to the subject through the way he or she frames the picture. How you frame that picture frequently has more to say about who you are and what expectations you bring to the person whose image you are trying to capture than it does about the person in the frame.

You focus first on the primary subject; in this case let's say it's your mother. Just as snapping a photo of you today at your workplace captures only a portion of who you are, seeing your mother in relationship to only yourself reveals only a part of her. If you view her close up and snap the shutter at a pensive moment or an angry one, you capture a totally different view of her than if you had waited for a smile. You could frame her in isolation looking directly at you or you could widen the frame to include her interacting with your father and siblings with the house in which she raised you in the background. Your perspective on your mother and her role in your life influences when you take the picture and who you include.

Emily's efforts to make a photographic memorial to her mother are a good illustration of framing and re-framing. She assembled the photographs for the program for her mother's memorial service with great care, including images from her mother's childhood and pictures of her with the most significant people across the seventy years of her life. Emily's relatives were very complimentary of the selection, but Emily's aunt wanted to know why she hadn't included her favorite photo, one of Emily's mother at a Fourth of July celebration ten years earlier with a big grin on her face and two sparklers in her hand. Emily said that she had been unable to lay her hands on that photograph at the time she was choosing what she would use for the program, but the truth was that Emily had decided specifically against that photograph. To Emily, this Fourth of July photo was an image that was atypical of her mother because it was too carefree and happy a depiction of a woman she saw as judgmental and pessimistic. To Emily's aunt, however, this was the quintessential image of her sister, one of joy, humor, and hope. Re-framing can help you gain a wider perspective than just your own .

Picture a Christmas: the dinner table with everyone gathered round for the meal; the excitement of wrapping a present you are happy to give; the false smile of opening a present you didn't want; the joy of the elder members surrounded by their legacy; the dejection of the rebellious adolescent slumped by the fireplace. None of these moods alone describes the *true* holiday picture. Only by including all of these images can you get a complete perspective on the family holiday.

To capture a true picture of you among your family, envision an especially powerful lens, one that not only frames each individual in their wider current-day context but also sweeps back across the past to include the preceding generations. This lens across time can help you understand your family's actions in terms of all the forces that influenced them. These influences course through the generations to shape the way you live your life today.

As a young girl, my mother wanted desperately to leave the confines of West Virginia. She married my father, and for twenty-eight years they traveled around the country as my father rose through the ranks as a naval enlisted man and then officer. Yet, when their marriage ended, my mother found herself living in a trailer back on Grandma Minnie's property, bickering with her mother but close to her until the day Grandma Minnie died.

My sister, Paula, swore she wouldn't live that kind of life. She married and had four children—exactly the same number that my mother bore—and, after Paula's husband died, she found herself moving in with my mom. My sister and mother's relationship now mirrors my mother's relationship with Grandma Minnie. They share a house and find ways to make do with what they have, laughing and bickering in the fashion of mothers and daughters across countless generations. Using re-framing, you begin to see that to some degree or another, we are all playing out dramas that are influenced by our family's past, our genetics, our temperaments, and the time and culture in which we live.

Sometimes when I talk to my father on the phone, I can hear behind his firm, controlled voice a deep yearning for his children. I can also hear a yearning for his father. It is something that I understand from my hunger for closeness with my father and with my son. Yet on a fundamental cellular level and by virtue of our culture of masculinity, many men today remain detached. The role of provider often keeps us at arm's length from our loved ones.

My brothers, Jim and Jon, and I are playing out this family drama in our own particular ways. Jim is a plant manager who gets up at four-thirty AM and drives an hour to work, not returning most days until after dark. Jon's family lives in northern California, but his job is in Los Angeles and so he stays with me during the week and journeys home every weekend. I didn't have contact with my son for years, and though now we have a great relationship, speaking frequently by phone, he lives on the East Coast. Jim, Jon, and I are not bad men neglecting our families: we are trying to provide for them. Like so many parents who must work long hours or travel out of town, we are each trying to keep the separations from wounding our children.

Knowing about these unseen forces that shape our actions deepens our understanding of those actions and enables us to see them as elemental forces of life and not just personal choices. If these factors are at play for you, so too must they have influenced the lives of your parents and your grandparents, your sisters and your brothers. Your whole chain of generations is connected by a fundamental spirit of family. Re-framing your perspective on your family to include these undercurrents gives you a picture with more texture and more depth. Through re-framing you can untangle one of life's fundamental mysteries: *How can it be that I can do seemingly everything in my power to be different from my family—I can make conscious decisions not to repeat their patterns—and still find myself in a life eerily similar to the one I tried to discard?* This never hit me harder than when I realized I was in graduate school at age forty, the same age my father was when he attended.

Simone was appalled by her mother's lack of resources after her parents got divorced. She and her mother and older brother lived from hand to mouth, paying the electric bill one month and the phone bill the next. Finally, her mother married a malleable but comfortably well-off man who gave the family economic stability, but fell far short of being her mother's ideal man. Simone was disgusted by her mother's numerous affairs, with which her mother tried to avoid the pain of isolation and boredom in a loveless marriage. Simone's mother's depression, combined with other health problems, caused her mother's death at age sixty.

Simone swore she would never end up uneducated like her mom. She went to medical school and married for love, but, as the years wore on, Simone began to see her husband as weak and malleable and lost respect for him. Infidelity broke up her marriage to her architect husband, and Simone found herself at age thirty-five in a situation identical to the one her mother had faced, albeit with better finances. She was a single mother of two, an older boy and a younger girl, and battling a serious depression.

How these patterns repeat over time is uncanny. Is it nature or nurture? Genetics or environment? Psychologists and genetics researchers have not definitively answered those questions. For our work here, the fact of this phenomenon is more important than its cause. The family system perpetuates our finest qualities as well as our essential flaws and predispositions. You may run to a foreign country to put as many miles as you can between yourself and your family, but as the saying goes, wherever you go, there you are. Rather than throw yourself into despair about this inevitability, you can use this information to re-frame a more complex and compassionate understanding of how you and your family ended up the way you are.

AUTONOMY VERSUS FUSION

Pioneering family therapist Murray Bowen was one of the first to treat the whole family as a system. Bowen's multigenerational view of the family as a system had its inspiration in biology. In fact, he viewed the extended family as a single organism, each of the members playing parts and influencing each other in specific ways across the generations. As such, he saw the roots of family emotional turmoil as much deeper, stretching backward and forward across the generations. Psychodynamic therapy explains emotional illness in terms of the individual and assesses family members based on analysis of suppressed feelings, poor communication, and maternal deprivation within a single generation. This didn't make sense to Bowen, who was puzzled as to how severe emotional problems, such as schizophrenia, could suddenly arise in an apparently normal family.

Bowen believed that the level of anxiety in the family system replicated the patterns of past generations and was a result of the ability or inability of family members to separate from each other and the family as a whole, in other words, to be authentic—to be able to make your own decisions, act on your own interests, say what you think, feel what you feel, while remaining emotionally engaged with your family.

A child is born into the world in a natural state of fusion with his mother. As he matures and begins to do more for himself, the child draws away from this fused state. Depending on how independent his parents are from their own families, he will separate in much the same way and to more or less the same extent that his parents separated from their parents. Often as a child matures and begins to individuate, the anxiety on the part of his parents for his safety can translate itself into an attempt to rein him in, thereby fusing him with his parents. This anxiety in the system is generated by the tension between the twin forces of togetherness and individuality for the family as a unit.

Bowen's research showed most people are attracted to mates who have achieved a similar level of autonomy within their own families of origin. As a result, according to Bowen, the family system perpetuates similar levels of autonomy within families in subsequent generations. Over time, influenced by nature, nurture, and fate, families either move toward more autonomy and therefore more flexibility or they move toward fusion, which raises the level of general anxiety, decreases flexibility, and makes the family more susceptible to outside stressors. In the systems context, anxiety acts much like a virus, generally present among the group but not always causing symptoms, like many of the physical viruses we carry. In the Freudian notion of anxiety, it emanates from within an individual, not the system as a whole.

In Bowen's systems framework, a family system is working well, operates in balance, when the relationships and the stressors are in equilibrium. As the stress of change occurs within a well-balanced family system—stress from children leaving the nest, from illness, from deaths, or even from sudden prosperity—the family is able to adapt to the losses and deal with the increased anxiety with minimal disruption. However, when the stress of change occurs within a more fused family unit—meaning a family in which there is more pressure to remain together and not differentiate as individuals—the family is unable to adapt to the change, which results in anger, resentment, and schisms.

In a fused family, there are fewer boundaries between individual members, and the system must withstand more anxiety: "your feelings" become "my feelings," and vice versa. There is an increased pressure for togetherness at the expense of autonomy. The increased anxiety of stressful events is not dealt with by the family unit but contained by it and passed around between different family members. In a suffocating cycle, the force for togetherness increases in response to that anxiety, ultimately preventing family members from working toward the real solution to their problems.

NEGATIVE INTIMACY

In February 1972, the Pittston Coal Company's refuse pile dam collapsed and dumped millions of gallons of coal sludge on sixteen small communities near my hometown in West Virginia. More than 125 people were killed and thousands more were left homeless. Families awakened by the sounds of screams and roaring water did not have time to escape from the deadly black waters, which lifted houses, cars, and everything else in its path. Families were scattered all over the Midwest, living with relatives and friends.

As in any disaster, natural or otherwise, to the degree that family members were autonomous, they were better able to rebuild their lives together with a minimum of disruption. The more enmeshed they were, however, the more likely the family members were to "act out" or fall into depression or flee without reflection. Factors such as inborn temperament, intelligence, and physical strength (nature) combined with finances, education, and support systems (nurture) determined how well or how poorly they dealt with such a blow.

We can see this theory at work in our own families in less dramatic situations. As a teenager attempts to extricate herself from a more fused family system, the more likely she is to do some acting out—drinking, taking drugs, becoming promiscuous—as an expression of the anxiety that her desire for independence creates within the system. The teenager is then often labeled "the problem child." Some theorists call the person on whom the family focuses its anxiety the "designated patient." Her parents, therefore, though they may have their own emotional problems, bring their daughter in for psychological treatment to "get her fixed."

In the family systems approach, the daughter would be considered to be carrying the anxiety for the family system itself, and a systems therapist would more likely treat one or both of her parents, not the teenager, in effect working closer to the source. The goal of the therapy would probably focus on guiding the parents to focus on themselves and work toward their own individuation, thereby creating the space in the system for the teenager to do the same.

This "acting out" by the teenager is one of three basic ways that Bowen says a family system expresses anxiety. Parental conflict is the second way the family system balances the twin forces of togetherness and individuality. Conflict grants both of the spouses emotional distance and thereby a form of temporary autonomy. This distance, however, is "negative intimacy." They are still the focus of each other's world, though now in a negative framework.

Sophie, a successful journalist, marries Bill, a junior law partner, and they have their first child. Life is good. Sophie decides to quit her job and freelance magazine articles from home. Life is better. As Bill's career begins to take off, they have another child. Without them acknowledging it, the second child substantially raises the level of anxiety in the system. This is not uncommon, and it is rarely seen for what it is.

Feeling a need to make more money and ensure his growing family's financial security, Bill begins to work longer and longer hours. Sophie feels guilty about taking time for herself away from the children because Bill works so much. Sophie has less and less time to write, has a hard time losing her pregnancy weight, and adds more weight. The growing physical distance between them becomes an emotional distance as well. Bowen calls this loss of contact "an emotional cutoff."

Soon Sophie is never happy and neither is Bill, with daily arguments and violent and escapist fantasies filling their thoughts. Sophie is sitting in the passenger seat in the driveway one day with the two kids in the back in their car seats. As her beloved husband, the father of her children, closes the gate to the backyard and walks toward the car, she imagines his head exploding and reforming and exploding again. These homicidal fantasies are another common indication of the need for more autonomy.

Bill, meanwhile, tries to deal with his escalating tension by working out at the gym. While he is on the treadmill, his mind is clouded with emotions and sexual fantasies about the women he sees working out on the weights and in the aerobics room. Both Sophie and Bill become caught in a vicious cycle of shame and blame that alternately fuses them with guilt and separates them with conflict. Each loses sight of the person they married. In fact, the person they married is no longer there, hidden by a curtain of anxiety.

"What do you want to do for New Year's, Sophie?" Bill asks.

"I don't know. I don't have a single idea," Sophie replies, thinking the one thing she would like to do is be alone.

"I'll do anything to make you happy," Bill says, which only infuriates Sophie. She hates to see him demeaning himself and wishes the strong man she married would return. She is expressing unconsciously the one power she still has, the power to say no.

"I don't know," she says, in that low voice spoken into her chest. "I can't think of a single thing that would make me happy."

Neither of them was able to see that their disappointment with each other was a consequence of the increasing anxiety and pressure created by a growing family. Instead they separately decided they had made a terrible mistake. They blamed each other and themselves, they continued to fight more and more frequently, and eventually they retreated from the marriage.

If they had been able to re-frame their conflict from a family systems perspective, they might have been able to see the twin forces of togetherness and individuality at work. They would, perhaps, have been able to compensate for them and save their marriage. These twin forces influence our need for approval and our need for emotional or physical distance. They also affect our tendency to incite conflict through blame and withdrawal. When we look at the interplay between these forces and these needs, it becomes easier to step outside the emotional field and gain a fresh perspective on the actions of those close to us as well as on our own.

Another way a family deals with anxiety in the system is to unbalance a couple, granting one an overfunctioning autonomy, while the other takes the role of the underfunctioning dependent.

Nancy, a thirty-five-year-old photographer and former athlete, was interested in doing the Codes of Love work to discover why she had trouble with intimate relationships. She felt that she always seemed to "stay too long or leave too fast" in her love affairs. Nancy attributed much of this behavior to the drama and denial that shrouded her family's secret.

When Nancy was sixteen, she discovered an old photograph in her grandmother's wallet and asked her who the woman in the picture was. Her grandmother revealed that the woman was Nancy's biological mother, a woman who had died when Nancy was eleven months old. While Nancy dearly loved her stepmother, Gloria, the shock of being misled all these years instantly put up a barrier of mistrust between her and her family, especially between her and her older brother, John. He had been four when their mother died and had kept that secret along with the adults. Why had they kept this important information from her for so long? Why did they let her be the last one to know?

With re-framing exercises, Nancy explored her birth parents' relationship as the starting point to purge her lifelong feelings of alienation. When Nancy's biological mother, Charlotte, and her father, Barry, met, her father was a hero cop, a leader in youth groups in Chicago, and a successful boxer. In short, he was a man in the prime of his life fulfilling his dreams. He met Charlotte, who was a beautiful, innocent Iowa farm girl working as a waitress in a coffee shop. When they married, they moved to Arizona and began a new life. A few months after Nancy was born, Barry's hand was nearly severed by a saw blade in a home construction mishap.

The shock wave of the accident rippled through the family for months. They returned to Chicago to live with Barry's mother, Geraldine, because they believed the medical care there was better than that available in Arizona at that time. Barry was shell-shocked, reduced from the powerful man who had been so confident and controlled in his body and secure and supported in his marriage to a cripple who could neither provide for his family nor defend them. For a few tense months the entire family was crammed into Geraldine's one-bedroom apartment as Barry's hand was on the mend, pinned together but rehabilitating. When he improved, the family decided to rent a motor home and take a spring vacation in Florida.

During their first week in Florida, while Barry watched the children on the beach, his mother and Charlotte, who had been a champion swimmer, took a dip in the ocean. Try as they might to struggle against the current, Charlotte and Geraldine were drawn out to sea by a riptide. At first it wasn't clear to Barry what was happening out on the water as his mother and wife splashed about in the surf. When he finally realized what was going on, it was too late. While Geraldine survived, the lifeguards dragged Charlotte out of the water, and Barry sobbed beside the lifeless form of the beloved and beautiful wife he was unable to save.

Within a year after the tragedy, Barry met Gloria at divinity school, where he'd gone looking for answers to the crisis of faith this series of events created. Gloria had only recently left a convent to enter law school. She was charmed by Barry and the two children—especially precocious Nancy, an adorable, spirited little girl who was a year and a half old by then—as well as being drawn to Barry because of their shared faith and idealism.

In the early years of their marriage they were true equals—she working in public interest law, and he helping to organize the farm labor movement. Though both Gloria and Barry were sustained throughout their marriage by a strong faith in God, soon Gloria would need all the strength God could provide her. After Gloria and Barry married, he left to take a six-month job in Africa, establishing early on a pattern of long absences and episodic single motherhood for Gloria that would become a fixture of the marriage.

Over the years, Gloria became the one who held the family together, often providing the emotional and financial continuity for the family during Barry's absences. The stronger Gloria became, the smaller Barry seemed. Over the years, he medicated his isolation from the family with drinking. After a fire destroyed their home and the loss ruined their finances, Barry was never the same, drinking more and working less because of health problems exacerbated by his drinking. By that time, it was nearly impossible for Barry and Gloria to start over with seven children in tow, but they managed, although Barry died within a few years.

From the perspective of Bowen's theory, as Barry began to withdraw and underfunction, his wife grew and filled in the gap so that the family could survive. These changes happened gradually over the years, the power shifting subtly from Barry to Gloria in an attempt to keep the family system balanced. Clearly Gloria rose to the occasion, becoming the overfunctioning adult whose competence and self-sacrifice allowed the rest of the family to flourish. Gloria became a partner in a law firm and successfully raised gifted children; her five children with Barry graduated from high school with honors and attended prestigious colleges, and Barry's two children from his first marriage became star athletes.

During her Codes of Love work, Nancy began to see the multigenerational patterns behind Gloria and Barry's dynamic of overfunctioning and underfunctioning, as well as the long-term effect that the tragedy of her mother's death had, not only on Barry, but on the family system as a whole.

Nancy's grandmother Geraldine had essentially raised Barry and her other children alone, learning early the need to overfunction in order to compensate for her husband Louis's long hours away from home and many hours after work spent "decompressing" in bars. Barry once confessed to Nancy that he had very few memories of his father, who was essentially out of the family picture due to his drinking by the time Barry was a teenager.

For Nancy, understanding how her father and stepmother had adjusted their relationship to deal with the anxiety in the family system removed the escalation of Barry's drinking and underfunctioning from the realm of moral judgment. The anxiety still present in the system that stemmed from the early death of Nancy and John's biological mother, Charlotte, became the elephant in the room: the secret that drove everyone's anxiety but was never acknowledged. Secrets are a sign of family fusion: they are often rationalized as necessary because the truth is thought to be "too much to bear." Barry felt he could not tell Nancy about her mother's death because "it would upset her," but the more likely truth was that dealing with his daughter's grief would force him to face his own.

At the time of Charlotte's death, Barry was already feeling reduced as a man because of his injury. He was further shamed by his inability to help his wife and mother during the tragedy. The anxiety created by his profound grief fueled his need for long periods of solitude and contributed to his drinking. In Bowen's terminology, drinking is one of several potential negative outlets for anxiety within the family system—what he called "the social dysfunctions." The particular social dysfunction a family uses is often multigenerational, as patterns repeat themselves in a seesaw fashion.

The "emotional shock wave" created by Charlotte's tragic death placed too much anxiety in the family system, resulting in Barry's flights of emotional and physical withdrawal. The absence of the father was a pattern he had seen in his own childhood with his father. By re-framing her family story, Nancy came to understand that her father was an improvement on his own: at least he kept coming back.

By looking deeper into that day at the beach when her mother drowned, Nancy also found empathy for her brother John's estrangement from the family. At the age of three, a time when his mother is the entire world for a little boy, John watched his mother drown. Understanding that allowed Nancy to see why her brother had never really felt close to Gloria, never really felt close to anyone. Another way that family's contain anxiety is by emotional withdrawal by one or more of its members, in this case, John.

Nancy also had always felt like an outsider within the growing family. Although she was close to Gloria, she was so different from her stepmom and her younger siblings that she often wondered where her true tribe was. Those years of living in the secret caused Nancy to feel like the odd woman out, different from her mother and sisters, who excelled at academics but were physically awkward, while Nancy was a champion athlete with tremendous physical prowess and beauty—just as her biological mother had been. Until Nancy learned the family secret, she had no idea that her temperamental and intellectual differences were genetic.

The benefit of this work to her intimate relationships is three-fold: One, by accepting her family as they are, she is now able to accept *herself,* without the pervasive feeling that she needs to be "fixed." Second, she is now able to see her attachment to a man who spends most of the week out of town as the echo of past generations. Finally, she can understand why she has often felt that she doesn't really fit in: in a career, in a group of friends, or in an intimate relationship.

This knowledge leads to a better understanding of the forces that create difficulties in families. Through that knowledge, Nancy found a way to have compassion for her father and, in turn, a better understanding of herself. After re-framing her past, Nancy was even able to reach out to her brother, John, whom she had not spoken to in five years.

Holding family secrets, as this story illustrates, has a powerful long-term effect on the family system. An analysis of the destructive power of secrets, as Edwin Friedman discusses in his great book *Generation to Generation,* reveals how a family secret creates false alliances and unnecessary estrangements. For those without the key piece of information contained in the family secret, commonplace events become indecipherable puzzles leading them to feel crazy as the unknown (the secret) makes their version of the world seem incomplete. As a result of these gaps in information, the family functions at a generally higher level of anxiety. A secret has a ripple effect on all communications within the family, not just between those involved in keeping the secret. Once the secret is revealed, the change in the family system is more profound than the content of the secret, as communication about ALL things becomes more open.

Some of your present-day relationships may still be influenced by ways your family system handled difficult information when you were a child—choosing when and what to tell others—in effect attempting to "manage" the truth. Using re-framing, the pictures of your family once described in narrowly focused terms begin to expand to include many generations in all their dimensions and to reveal patterns in the way they communicated that still influence you today.

Most of the past was *not* personal—it was the result of the confluence of forces bigger than any of us. Nancy re-framed her father's many absences as a reaction to the anxiety created by his first love's untimely death. An untimely death that affected all four of his basic postulates, the meaningfulness of life, the safety of the home, the benevolence of others, and his own feelings of self-worth. These thoughts are what drove his global search for his lost self-esteem. Nancy saw her father's travels away from home as mirroring his own father's long hours away—the search for the enormous paycheck that would somehow redeem him in his own, and perhaps Charlotte's, eyes, just as his father had once hoped that earning power would make up for absence.

The hurt Nancy felt was real, the isolation painful, but now it all had a context, and within that context, understanding. Now, armed with that understanding, Nancy is ready to see the intimate relationships in her own life in a new light, a light that illuminates why she "stayed too long, or left too fast."

TRIANGLES

In the family systems world, the basic building block of these intergenerational forces is the triangle. Triangles are the common denominator of human interactions, whether in the family or in the business world: the secret kept from others, the sides taken during conflict, the search for enemies and allies. Knowledge of how triangles work and how they can be used to our advantage to gain authenticity for ourselves and our families is one of the most powerful lessons in human psychology.

Describing relationships merely in terms of the interactions between two people is inadequate. Inevitably both people in an intimate relationship are linked to many others, and both attempt to draw these other people into the relationship, particularly when under stress. When a relationship between two people is calm, the triangle is almost imperceptible. But when conflict occurs and anxiety increases, a third person is inevitably drawn into the twosome as an ally or an enemy in an attempt to alleviate the increased anxiety in the system. Understanding the triangles at work in our intimate relationships can allow us to step back from the powerful forces that threaten to involve us in dynamics that would be better solved by the other two people in the triangle.

For example, when Sophie and Bill were having difficulties in their marriage, their daughter started making trouble at school, being disobedient and neglecting her homework. The couple united to focus on their daughter's problems, and for a time the conflict in their marriage diminished because of their shared concern for their child. Once the daughter's problem was solved, their conflict returned.

Later, Sophie reached out to her mother to complain that Bill was neglecting her and the children. Sophie's mother was sympathetic because Sophie's father, who had been dead for five years, neglected their family while working long hours. Sophie thereby distributed the anxiety around the extended family circle by drawing her mother into an alliance that forms the strong side of the triangle, which put Bill on the opposing corner. Her mother unwittingly accelerated Sophie's departure from the marriage by choosing sides within the triangle.

Some triangles outlive the original participants. Just as people choose spouses with a similar level of autonomy from their families of origin, they also tend to be drawn into similar kinds of conflicts. Sophie was able to triangulate her mother (which often seems like support) and put Bill on the outside corner (which often feels like betrayal) because her mother resonated with a situation that was familiar in her own life—that of a husband who seemed to have lost interest. Had Sophie's mother been aware that she was exacerbating the problem instead of solving it, she might have acted as a more positive force in the marriage, questioning Sophie's role in keeping Bill distant or reminding her how much Bill loved her. Either of these responses would have removed Sophie's mom from the triangle and placed the anxiety back where it belonged—between Sophie and Bill—so they could solve it together. This might have helped Sophie to focus her energies inside the marriage instead of looking outside it for justifications.

Michael E. Kerr, M.D., head of the Georgetown Family Center, and a major contributor to both Bowen's work and to family therapy, says that the way to know when you are being drawn into the emotional force field of a triangle is to monitor your allegiances. You have been drawn into a triangle when you are sympathetic with one person over the other, when you feel anger or frustration at one of the persons involved, when you believe that the two are better off keeping their distance, when you feel that one of them is a victim, or when you feel sorry or guilty for one of them.

Whenever anyone tries to get us to validate his or her emotional position of "I am good and the other person is bad," the person is trying to triangulate us by excluding the other person. A hallmark of emotional and intellectual maturity is the ability to understand both sides of any argument. Similarly, many well-intentioned attempts to get someone else to "express his feelings" or to "get help" make us lose our effectiveness as an agent for change. The desire to change someone can draw us into that person's emotional field. The only way we can help anyone is by learning to keep our independence of thought and feeling.

ROSE AND MAX'S TRIANGLE

For Rose, the tension in her relationship with her older brother, Max, stretches back more than thirty years, to when she was ten and he was fifteen. The two of them have been acting out a triangle with their mother even though their mother has been dead for many years. Back in childhood, when Rose was first experimenting with her looks, her brother would deliberately sabotage her sense of self. For example, he'd recommend that she get her hair cut short. "You'd look so cute with short hair," he'd say. "You should give it a try." When Rose arrived home with her new short haircut, Max would snort with contempt. "You look so ugly," he'd say.

This dynamic between them played out repeatedly over the years until it became very difficult for Rose to trust Max or accept compliments from anyone. The wariness between them calcified their relationship and made each family event a tense occasion, with Rose always looking for the hidden insult underneath everything her brother said and sometimes finding slights where none were, in fact, offered.

Now an adult in her forties with both of their parents dead, Rose wanted to try to find a way to have a loving relationship with her brother. He was the only living family member she had (other than her son), and she could remember a time when they were close. Instead of challenging her brother on their past, Rose chose to remember, reflect on, and re-frame the family as a whole. As part of this work, she explored their relationship with their mother.

Rose's mother had been sick ever since Max was born, with an increasingly debilitating case of arthritis. The anxiety caused by her illness increased the pressure in the family. The entire family had to treat her gently; "Don't upset your mother," their father would always warn. This was something that as a teenager Max became increasingly unwilling to do. He responded by treating his mother and Rose less and less gently, placing himself on the outside of their triangle.

From his earliest memory as a child, the only thing Max wanted to do in life was to play the piano. Their mother had been a professional violinist and so this was encouraged. When Max was thirteen, their mother discovered Max was smoking cigarettes. She punished him saying that if she ever caught him smoking again, she would take away his piano lessons. In her infirm state, she was trying to keep her son close by controlling him with the most powerful weapon she had—his beloved piano. This technique rarely works and often backfires.

Her threat just infuriated Max and brought up feelings of rebellion as he struggled with his desire for autonomy in the face of his mother's pressure to conform. Unable to focus his anger on his invalid mother, he transmitted that anger to his sister, who was positioned as the family favorite. This was the beginning of their negative triangle—Mom and Rose forming the strong side, Max at the opposing point. Being angry at Rose, expressed as his undercutting her sense of self, was an unconscious attempt to lessen his own anxiety—yet it just cemented the bond between Rose and her mother.

This tension in the family system escalated as Rose's mother, who had been a younger sister herself, defended Rose against Max, regardless of the specifics of the conflict between them. Triangles can be more or less active, depending on the anxiety that exists within the family. The force of Max's teen desire to separate from the family ratcheted up the anxiety in the family system and further ensured a bonding between Rose and his mother. Up until his father's death Max was often in the opposing corner of an interlocking triangle between his father, mother, and himself. The mother's illness gave an intensity to her relationship with her husband that made it difficult for them to focus on either of the children. When their father died, when Max was twenty-two, there was no other person in the system to turn to—and Max became increasingly locked in the opposing position in the family triangle, particularly after he left for college. Rose and their mother got closer, and Max got more distant. While the whole system is carrying the emotional shock wave from their father's death, Max increasingly withdraws and Rose and her mother increasingly fuse. Max is angry at his mother, so he passes that anger to Rose. Mom defends Rose and chastises Max, who later perpetuates the humiliation of Rose when Mom is out of earshot, unconsciously embedding the pattern deeper and deeper in his relationship with Rose.

This pattern is one more way that family anxiety moves around the system. Mom is sick and frightened that she's losing control of her children. When Max starts to need more autonomy from the family, Mom grabs him back—or Max withdraws. Max is increasingly anxious about his role as the outsider and feels his mother has hampered his attempt to stay connected as he ventures into the world. His attempts to displace his sister on the strong side of the triangle do not work. He cannot win his mother over by denouncing Rose or form an alliance with Rose by criticizing their mother. In frustration, he emotionally checks out of the family.

It is now almost thirty years after their mother's death, and the same triangle continues, though Rose has been trying to reconcile with her brother for the past eight years. Max, who is a successful professional and has no children, offered financial help for Rose's son, Zack, when he got into college. Rose, who has been a single mom for most of Zack's life, had been comforted by this promise. After Zack got into a prestigious and expensive private college, she approached Max, expecting the help he had discussed with her. Max acted as if Rose were suggesting something absurd, just as he had reacted to her teenage hairdos. Rose was deeply hurt by her brother's rejection. In effect, Max and Rose are reviving the triangle that existed between them and their mother by substituting Zack for Mom. This alignment keeps Zack and Rose bonded closely and Max still on the outside.

In the past, Rose had found ways to angrily blame him for his past transgressions toward her (and her mother) so many years ago, a tactic that encouraged her brother to withdraw, just as he had in childhood. She could now understand the larger forces at play for her brother and herself, and her own part in them.

Though Rose finds it difficult to accept her brother's decision to withdraw his offer of assistance, re-framing helped her find the strength to step outside the emotional field of this disappointment. Rose re-framed her attempts to reconcile with her brother by trying to view him from a non-emotionally-reactive place.

Instead, Rose stepped outside the triangle by telling Max in a nonemotional way, "If you have decided not to help Zack with school, then please tell Zack yourself so he can make other arrangements." This leaves Max to wrestle with his conscience about disappointing his nephew. By doing this, Rose stands up for herself and places the anxiety in the system where it should be— on Max.

By de-triangling herself from Max, Rose has taken a step toward her own autonomy. Her move to a higher level of differentiation is the only real chance for a lasting change in behavior for all members of the triangle.

Once we understand the nature of emotional triangles, the tendency for patterns to persist across generations, and the impersonal way that anxiety moves through the extended family organism, we gain a new vision of our interactions with our family members. Now we can see, for instance, that Barry (Nancy's father) was essentially in a triangle not only with Nancy and Gloria, her stepmother, but with Nancy and Charlotte's ghost as well. It seems that his travels and his returns may, in fact, be explained by his conflicted loyalties to his two wives—not a saint-and-sinner dichotomy between Barry and Gloria.

As we re-frame our family's past in multigenerational-system terms, we gain a powerful new perspective on significant events and even on specific family character traits, such as Max's tendency to criticize Rose or Gloria's spirit of self-sacrifice. This new frame establishes an entirely new place to stand from which we can more fully comprehend not only our family members but many of the otherwise painful events that have developed huge significance for us over time. Even something as difficult as physical violence becomes at least comprehensible.

For example, Justine, the woman who was slapped hard by her father in a previous chapter, asked her brother, who was also in the room when she was slapped, how he remembered the event. Her brother remembered thinking what a pain Justine was being that day, how irritating and confrontational she was with everyone in the family and how much she was provoking her father. He was thinking she needed to be slapped, thinking he'd like to do it himself, just at the moment when her father did the deed. While it doesn't excuse her father's loss of control, it re-framed the incident for Justine. She wasn't simply the victim of her father's rage; she was an adolescent trying to separate from her family and causing friction in the process.

To understand the forces that drove my mother and father to argue so violently, I had to step outside my own family's emotional field and look beyond the automatic emotional responses I have always had to the memory of their battles. I had to ask myself the kind of questions that would never have occurred to me as a child watching my parents fight:

- What kind of stressors were present that contributed to their anxiety?

- How old were they when the fighting began?
- What were their expectations in contrast to the kind of life they lived?
- What differences in temperament were there between the two of them?
- What emotional shock wave had they suffered as a couple?

To aid in re-framing, I asked both my mother and father to write me a letter describing their courtship and early years of marriage. My father's first response was as I expected: he wrote that the past was the past and we should put it behind us. Yet, some months later, I received his eloquent reply. My mother, however, immediately wrote a beautiful ten-page letter that depicted how it felt to receive a call from her Navy boyfriend when she was in the dorm at college studying to be a teacher. She described her hopes for an adventurous life with my father and the family that they would have. Even though much of that sweetness seemed to vanish in the ensuing struggle between them, the voice of her letter brought tears to my eyes. More than forty years since their courtship, she still had the romanticism of a young girl as she recalled herself at that time.

My mother was a feisty, independent young woman in her twenties with a hunger for life. She imagined my father and herself in glamorous ports exploring foreign lands. The reality of being a military wife—often alone, with three small children underfoot—must have seemed far removed from that dream.

Sadly, just like Bill and Sophie, my parents expressed their anxiety with marital conflict. Both my mother and father wanted to leave West Virginia and see the world, but neither of them knew that the cost would be the loss of their social and familial supports and eventually, their romance. Lonely in Connecticut or

San Diego, the family became an island where each partner became suspicious of the other's actions—she feeling abandoned and he feeling disrespected—and, over time, conflict became the norm. This anxiety was the result of an "emotional shock wave," as Bowen would have called it, that rolled over my parents as they dealt with the reality of being alone in a new city without their previous emotional supports.

When anxiety is unrecognized for the difficult houseguest that it is, it throws a family back into a suspicious framework, just as it did with my mother and father: If Dad was not happy, it had to be Mom's fault, and vice versa.

I always thought that my mother and father's fighting was a sign that they were both crazy or somehow flawed or even that it was *my* fault. As the pressure within the family increases, everyone becomes mistrustful of each other and they begin a downward spiral toward disillusionment. The growing emotional distance caused by seemingly innocent white lies results in the loss of true communication. Gradually this dynamic becomes more insidious and the spouses' inner worlds no longer match. Each begins to edit their feelings, fantasies, hopes, and insecurities to avoid the conflict they know will ensue. Sides are taken, blame is laid, and patterns are established (or repeated) for generations. By understanding the effects of this emotional shock wave, amplified by the twin forces of togetherness and autonomy in my isolated family, I was able to re-frame my parent's marital conflict and have compassion for what they must have suffered instead of for only what we kids experienced. I was also able to see them as less crazy and diffuse my adolescent feeling that their problems were "my fault."

Now that I see their anxiety for what it is, my parents battles no longer make me feel like I grew up in "dysfunction junction," as I used to joke. I now realize that my father's frustrations were expressions of his own anxiety and that Mom's problems with Dad were probably expressions of her anxiety and not some moral flaw. I can come to understand their relationship through the forces that shaped it. I no longer have to judge it and them as somehow mistaken or cruel, since through re-framing I realize that their actions were not personal and that if they had known better ways to resolve their conflicts, they would have used them. Understanding this allows me to stop *blaming* them for who I am. It also enables me to stop their patterns by remembering my autonomy and keeping my communication with them, and others, open, and by finding better ways to resolve conflict myself.

There's no better place to start than with our own families.

Codes of Love Exercise: RE-FRAMING

The basic purpose of these exercises is to help you gain a new perspective on the impersonal forces that forged your family history. Events that engender potent memories are often caused by emotional shock waves that reverberate throughout the extended family and forward into time. The disruptions caused by these shock waves can have far-reaching effects in our family without our knowing the true source of our problem. A death of a parent can contribute to a divorce two years later; the major illness of a child can ruin a career; an economic upheaval—caused by either a firing or a promotion—can trigger stress among friends. Often these interrelated events have a long-term impact. Yet, shock waves are hardly ever understood as contributing to our traumas.

Look back at your story line and the story line of your extended family:

- What were the major events of your youth?
- What were the major events of your parents' youth?

135

- Can you remember any emotional shock waves in your extended family that preceded major changes?
- Any divorces that followed deaths?
- Any marital conflicts that followed a cross-country move?
- Any illness that preceded or followed divorce or separation?

Look for the links in the system; many may be elusive.

Codes of Love Exercise: MORE THAN ONE WORLD

In my example with my grandmother Minnie, I had opinions I was sure of in MY world, where I am the center. But Minnie had her own world. List the five people who are most dear to you. Remember, these do not have to be people that you are currently in contact with. They could be dead or estranged.

1.
2.
3.
4.
5.

- How do you look from their world?
- Are you able to see that you have a world?
- How loving is your world?
- How lonely is your world?
- Are you able to receive as well as give?

Codes of Love Exercise: FEELING VERSUS THINKING

In order to stand outside of our own world, it is necessary that we learn to separate our feeling from our thinking. Observe your actions over the next several days and see when you are feeling and when you are thinking. Take a walk or do some kind of physical exercise that causes you to sweat profusely. This will often release emotions by centering us in the body. Then answer these questions:

- What are you feeling right now?
- What are you thinking?
- What signals does your body give you when you are emotional? How do you "work through" these feelings?
- Remember signal anxiety? Listen to your body for signs of disturbance or calm.
- Do you tap your feet? Jiggle? Squirm in your seat?
- Do you flush with excitement or anger?

Codes of Love Exercise: TWIN FORCES

The twin forces of individuality and togetherness are always at work. Emotions serve to control the balance between contact and separateness in a relationship.

- Are you able to notice or feel when you are being drawn either closer or further away by the interplay of these forces?
  - Within your family of origin? With your parents? With your siblings?
  - With your significant other? In the workplace?

- Are you feeling smothered?
- Do you feel abandoned or forgotten? Why?
- Do you feel guilty? About what? About whom?
- Are you able to express your needs within your family? Do you know what you need?

- Do you have violent fantasies about those closest to you? This is often a sign of a need for more autonomy.
- What kind of dreams have you had lately? Flying? Drowning? Revenge? Fleeing? Hiding? Sexual? Being far away in solitude? Is there a pattern?
- Are you financing your own life?
- Do you still live at home?
- Are you crashed on someone's couch?
- Do you blame others for how you feel?
- Do you speak in "I" statements or in "you" statements?
- Do you avoid others because they will push your buttons?

Codes of Love Exercise: SIGNAL ANXIETY REVISITED

There are many ways that we attempt to manage anxiety. What are your favorites?

- Overeating?
- Undereating?
- Overachieving?
- Underachieving?
- Excessive alcohol or drug use?
- Sexual compulsivity?
- Violence, emotional or physical?
- Withdrawal?
- Marital conflict?
- Bitchiness or being overly critical?

Codes of Love Exercise: THE POSITIVE SIDE OF STRESS

Not all the ways we deal with anxiety are negative. Anxiety is a powerful motive force for change once we learn how to channel it. Are you able to use your "energy" in positive ways?

- Do you work and play well with others?
- Do you have an exercise routine?
- Do you have a sense of humor? Do you use it?
- Do you do anything for charity or to serve your community?
- Do you do anything to serve your family? Your elders?

Codes of Love Exercise: TWO TO TANGO

The person in a relationship who seems indifferent is just as dependent on and influenced by the relationship as the person who seems preoccupied with it. The typical scenario goes like this: When one person pressures for closeness, the other often dances away. We always have a part in whatever is happening in our lives. It is important to step outside ourselves and see each interaction with others as part of an ongoing dance.

- Which dances do you find yourself repeating?
- Are you able to see yourself as a dancer?
- Are you willing to learn new steps?

Codes of Love Exercise: MY WAY OR THE HIGHWAY

As Michael Kerr says, "the phrase 'emotional separation' is not to be equated with people avoiding each other. The urge to avoid others is a function of a lack of emotional separation. Efforts to get people to open up or express their feelings reflect the inability of the helper to tolerate his own anxiety about those feelings."

- How invested are you in being right?
- List three times when you were sure recently that you knew the only right way.

1.
2.
3.

- If the response to the above task was "never," why aren't you ever right?
- Are you always placating or accommodating others?
- Can you allow for the possibility that you may be right and someone else may be right?
- What would it feel like not to be right?
- Is being right a burden?

Codes of Love Exercise: FEEDING THE LIONHEARTED

We make mental choices constantly about how to view life and whether to view our future with optimism or pessimism, whether to whine about the thorn in our paw or ask for help. We make choices in our everyday language when we describe our lives, both to others and in our inner dialogues. These choices both reflect and shape our attitude. Choosing our words carefully can make the world a different place very quickly. For instance, "I got to go to work" can become "I get to go to work."

- Can you change what you communicate from expectation of the worst to anticipation of something better?
- Are you able to deal with uncertainty?
- Do you call every pleasant incident a "fluke"? Every setback a "nightmare"?
- Are you never "hungry" but always "starving"? Not "full" but "stuffed"?
- When was the last time you used "should," "ought," "must," "rejection," or "overloaded"?

Codes of Love Exercise: TRIANGLES

Murray Bowen says that the third element in a triangle doesn't have to be a person. It can be a fantasy, a memory, an object, an old behavior or a current one, such as drinking or gambling. These elements can disturb the equilibrium of a relationship as much as a third person. These activities can also be positive, such as a hobby or a sport or an exercise regime.

There are many negative responses to the fear of being triangled. Some of the most common are

- Physical distance.
- Denial.
- Projection of your feelings and attitudes onto others, which relieves anxiety by allowing you to view other people as the problem.

- Which of the above do you use? Which do you use when under stress?
- Do you accommodate to achieve peace at any price?
- Do you rebel to thwart the perceived wishes of others?
- Do you attempt to dominate, fix, or scapegoat others?
- Do you think you've outgrown someone?
- Are you able to observe this from a systems perspective now?
- Can you keep your head while those about you are losing theirs and blaming it on you?

Codes of Love Exercise: TRIGGERS

Triggers are words or gestures that habitually draw you into your family's emotional field to the point that you lose your objectivity and begin to take action to relieve your anxiety. For some it is their parent saying something like, "Have you gone to church?" or "Are you still shacked up with that woman?" For others it might be "Are you ever going to get another boyfriend?" "When are you going to lose some weight?" "Why can't you get a decent job?" "Have you paid those bills yet?" "How can you live in that dump?"

Triggers can also be gestures.

- Rolling of eyes.
- The sneer.
- The dismissal.
- The *tsk tsk* of disapproval.
- The once-over that says, "Take a look at you!"

Take a few minutes and go over the above list.

- What triggers from your own family come to mind?
- What makes you see red?
- What do they say that make you blush or squirm?
- What subjects do you hope will not come up?
- Do you notice when you make others squirm? About what? About whom?

Codes of Love Exercise: RESENTMENTS

Triangles are not necessarily between three living people. They can include someone who's deceased. They can exist with someone who's alive but whom you never talk to. They can exist with a person you "hate"; in other words, resentments are a way to continue to have a relationship with someone—they are a form of negative intimacy. Anger is often a sign of the inability to let go. We can also have triangles with processes, as Bowen says, with alcoholism, sex addiction, workaholism, overspending, gambling, or hoarding money. One of the most insidious of these is the idealized version of our life—our idealized mate, job, house, self.

- Is there a fantasy or a memory of a perfect something that is disturbing your current life?
- Does your family accuse you of being selfish?
- When you are angry, what do you do to calm yourself?
- When you are lonely, what do you do to calm yourself?
- When you are sad, what do you do to calm yourself?
- When you are excited or happy, what do you do to calm yourself?

Codes of Love Exercise: BUILDING THE TRIANGLE

We all build triangles as buffers for our anxiety during crisis. Have you drawn someone into a triangle recently? How? For instance, is there someone to whom you tell all the particulars of your intimate relationship? Explore the following questions:

- Does this person know more about your thoughts and feelings than your mate?
- Do you keep a rain check—someone you flirt with or who flirts with you?
- Do you chronically adapt your thoughts, feelings, or behavior to reduce the tension of others? Who?
- Are you able to see that you can be drawn into a reactive state by facial expressions, tones of voice, or changes in body posture?
- Can you usually see both sides of an issue or an argument?

Codes of Love Exercise: LEARNING TO DISENGAGE

There is an old Zen question: How do you clear muddy water? The answer: Do nothing.

- What muddy water have you tried to clear lately?
- What did you do?
- Did it work?
- Do you have the self-control to do nothing? The patience to wait for events to take their course?

Codes of Love Exercise: IT IS NO ONE'S FAULT

One of the most important concepts of this chapter is that we drop the idea of linear cause and effect. List three current issues between you and your family.

1.
2.
3.

- How would you feel if it was no one's fault—not yours *and* not theirs?
- What action would you take?
- How often do you attempt to defend your position? Explain? Justify?
- What do people say to you that is blaming, judgmental, or proves that they are convinced of their righteousness?
- What have you said to others recently that is blaming, judgmental, or proves that you are convinced of your own righteousness?

Codes of Love Exercise: VICIOUS OR VIRTUOUS CYCLES

We often forget that behavior is on a continuum, *always*. In our modern world we tend to try to analyze human interactions in terms of black and white—which distorts the real story. There are vicious cycles and things that we do that are negative and spawn more negative actions: my eating unhealthy food makes me feel bloated, which makes me feel low, which makes me sedentary, which makes me feel fat, which makes me stay out of the gym, which adds to my anxiety, which causes me to eat more.

Let us not forget that there are also virtuous cycles: I work out, which relieves my anxiety, so I am tempted to eat less, which helps me lose weight, which makes me feel better about myself, which gives me energy so I work out more, which relieves yet more anxiety . . .

I like to think of these cycles as spirals, going either up toward a fuller, more realized life, or down, toward pessimism and depression. The good news is that we can turn the spiral upward from any point.

- When have you been involved in a vicious cycle?
- When have you been involved in a virtuous cycle?
- How could re-framing your family change a vicious cycle into a virtuous one?
- What action could you take to start a new virtuous cycle in your life?

CHAPTER 5

Reconnect

The other day I was at a coffee shop nursing a double espresso trying to write about reconnecting with your family, but I couldn't concentrate because I couldn't take my eyes off the table adjacent to mine. It was late in the afternoon, and two sisters and their four squirming toddlers had come to the coffee shop looking for a respite, but the kids were too revved up and having none of it. They climbed all over the double stroller, tussled over their toys and spilled cup after cup of water.

Part of what held my attention was the patience and vigilance of the two moms: covering the corners of the table with their hands as one boy careened by nearly bumping his head, steadying the chair as the two little girls reared it onto its back legs, snatching a straw from a little fist seconds before it ended up in an eye. Their instinct to block danger was automatic, and the continual rescues were fluid responses, transpiring without comment.

Their instructions to the children came from the universal well of maternal wisdom. To the child banging with all his might on his little brother's fist: "Be gentle. Gentle. Gentle." When the little girl yanked her cousin's hair, her mother admonished, "Be kind to each other." The biggest boy, who grabbed the teething ring out of the mouth of the infant in the stroller, had his own hand grabbed by his mother as the baby escalated from silent shock to wailing, hands waving furiously in the air as he reached for his mom. "Ezra," she said firmly to the biggest boy, locking her eyes on his. "How could you be so mean?"

It occurred to me that these three simple admonitions, which barely registered at all on the minds of the marauding toddlers, are central to the core of the Codes of Love: Be gentle. Be kind. How could you be so mean?

But what made the encounter even more significant was that while these two women—they were sisters—demonstrated their enlightened mothering skills, performing effortless rescues and dispensing sage advice, they were trashing their mother, just ripping her to shreds. The older of the two had recently come to her mother with a crisis. "You know what the first words out of her mouth were?" the elder sister said. " 'You don't know how this makes me feel.' " The younger sister nodded while the older continued, "Hello! Perhaps this is the one situation in the entire world that is not actually about *you,* Mother."

The younger sister followed with her own litany of maternal slights: She'd invited their mother over for coffee the previous week. From the moment Mom walked in the door, she did nothing but criticize, the younger sister said. "Do you really think midnight blue was a good choice for kitchen curtains?" their mother had asked, observing that the sun cast a strange light through that dark a blue. Their mother asked, "Do you really think it's safe to be giving the children organic apple juice? They don't really pasteurize that stuff and it's *so* cloudy. How do you really know it's okay?" The final question the younger daughter noted was more personal: "Have you put on a little weight? You need to watch that," their mother offered. "You start to let yourself go and pretty soon there's trouble in the marriage."

That last comment was the clincher. Silence fell between the two sisters as they let the remark rest between them.

"You know, I love Mom," the elder sister said, "but I don't have to like her."

That paradox haunted me for hours after my espresso was only dregs at the bottom of a cup. *I love Mom, but I don't have to like her.* Is that even possible?

In just the brief time I spent observing these two women, I could see what an excellent mother they had. They had obviously learned the graceful way they kept their children out of danger without hysteria or anger, all the while maintaining focus on their adult conversation, from the loving and attentive way their mother had raised them without sacrificing all of herself to the task. They didn't appreciate that their mother was *still* treating them that way, still trying to protect them from mistakes, still trying to shield them from danger, both the small ones of odd-colored kitchen curtains and the larger ones of neglecting yourself and your marriage. Somewhere along the line, probably when they were adolescents, their mother's expressions of concern began to deliver a different message—one of control and disapproval. Their teenage need to differentiate from their mother probably joined them in an alliance against her, each getting support from the other for their escape into adulthood. The sad fact was they were still acting like the teenagers they once were.

Mom's statement that so offended her daughter, "You don't know how that makes me feel," is one I've heard many women complain about. It is, in fact, the previous generation's version of a popular therapeutic characterization of empathy that has been corrupted through use by politicians: "I feel your pain." In their mother's case, it is also an apology, in some ways, for being unable to continue to protect her daughter from harm, an instinct that parents carry no matter how old their children become, no matter how independent their children want to be.

Mom's questions, suggestions, and exclamations of dismay

were the adult form of that hand placed on the corner of the table to save the boy from hitting his head. Yet for whatever reason—the sisters' leftover teenage rebellion or the failure of their mother to balance her concern with acknowledgment and approval—these well-meaning warnings were deciphered as attacks.

I imagined Grandma sitting in the kitchen that morning at her daughter's house, playing with the grandchildren and enjoying the coffee and the bond they all shared. She was most likely unaware that what her daughter would take away from this morning was not the joy of their continued connection, but the three questions she saw as attacks.

In some sense both the daughter and the mother got what they were looking for in the meeting: Grandma got to see her grandchildren and offer some support and advice to her daughter. The daughter got to show that she was doing things differently and demonstrate her independence. She got to create some distance for herself from her mom. The grandmother found the love she was seeking, while the daughter found evidence of a love that never really was, thereby freeing herself from the obligation of loving her mother.

CONTACT VERSUS CONNECTION

These two daughters would probably disagree with this analysis of them. If you questioned them about their family, they would probably say, "I have a great family," referring to their husband and children. Only on further questioning would their denial of their true feelings for their mother surface. Most likely they have regular contact with her. They remember all the important occasions; they are civil, often even affectionate, giving their mom a hug when she really needs it. Each daughter speaks with their mother on the phone, but the conversation is more often about the antics of the grandchildren than the relationship between the women and their mom.

Contact is not connection, and connection is what we truly long for in our relationships. Connection is the process of allowing someone to see through our defenses to who we really are. Connection requires also that we be able to engage someone else with our truth—to say the difficult things in ways that can be heard and discussed—instead of having them become part of our cynical repertoire of disregard, like the sisters' list of complaints about their mother.

Our critical adult voice, our cynic's voice, is the one that punctures these exchanges with such questions. There was a time for all of us when we were those children in the café—joyful in the moment, running gleefully or playing quietly, unaware of the ways that our mothers were constantly rescuing us. In that blissfully ignorant state, we trusted. We were unafraid to pour our feelings out into the world and innocent of the idea that criticism might be malevolent. Yet, here were these two grown women, still ignorant on some level of the debt they owe their mother, unable to appreciate the constant vigilance she still demonstrates today.

Undefended as we were as kids, we had no expectation of anything other than a genuine exchange with our parents. Now we focus on their faults and talk about them behind their back, logging all the misconnections instead of the ones we make.

The assumption of bad intentions on the part of these two sisters recalls the suspicious framework described in Chapter Two. Perhaps by commenting on her daughter's curtains, choice of apple juice, and physical appearance, the mother wasn't really saying, "I don't love you." Perhaps she was really saying, "I *do* love you. I am still concerned with what is best for you." Luckily, she is not too intimidated to tell her daughters what she really thinks. This is a much more difficult and loving act than ignoring or denying important changes or risks. Saying the unsayable, the difficult, or the embarrassing with love and concern is a great skill. Hearing it takes even greater skill. What made the exchanges between mother and daughter, and sister and sister, painful was not so much the mother's critical nature as it was the daughters' inability to stay engaged with their mother on the various points she raised and the triangling both sisters do to keep their mother at a distance.

If the daughter had either explained that she didn't care about the light the curtains cast because she never closed them or admitted that she thought her mother was right and that she had made a mistake, her mother's comments would not have been criticisms but opportunities for connection. The daughter had an opportunity to honor her mother, acknowledge her concern, and advance her connection by explaining why she decided as she had. If she were able to discuss with her mother her struggles with weight, she would be able to ask her mother if it had ever been an issue in her own marriage, and if so how she had dealt with it. She could have gathered useful information, not just for herself but about her mother.

The daughter assessed her interaction with her mother by the standards of a child: Is she praising me? Is she approving of my choices? These questions add up to Is she loving me? In fact, the more loving a mother is, the more involved she is. It is only the depressed or emotionally stunted mother or father who withdraws from the child and ignores its needs. The withdrawn parent causes as much harm as the overprotective one. It is often the child who has been most loved that feels unloved as an adult, because that adult still longs for the same kind of profound connection of borderless involvement and acceptance as they received in childhood.

DEFENSE MECHANISMS

For all of us, to some degree, when the inner reality of what we feel and what we need doesn't match up with our outer reality of what we can get in response to those needs, we develop defenses to protect our sense of self: A self that is vulnerable to abandonment, shame, anger, sorrow, and a host of other threatening emotional conditions. Over time these defenses can become automatic responses that are meant to shield our maturing self from pain. These automatic defenses are organized attempts to make meaning of the world and, as such, often distort reality in the service of social equilibrium. Understanding the form and force of your defenses, as well as those of your other family members, is essential to finding a way to reconnect with your family with love.

In his passionate book *The Wisdom of the Ego,* Harvard psychiatry professor Dr. George Vaillant describes human defense mechanisms as "wise, creative, essential, and essentially unconscious." Defenses, according to Vaillant, are our emotional shock absorbers, buffering us from the fear of engulfment or the isolation of total autonomy. These shock absorbers keep our emotional balance in our present-time dealings with the family and the larger world. Vaillant describes defense mechanisms on a continuum that begins with defenses that are immature and evolves to more mature ones. He believes that, over time, our immature defenses can mature. This is the heart of the evolving self, and what Vaillant feels is an important key to understanding one another. The defense mechanisms are: immature defenses, such as projection, fantasy, hypochondria, passive aggression, acting out, and dissociation; intermediate (neurotic) defenses, such as displacement, intellectualization, repression, and reaction formation; and mature defenses, such as altruism, sublimation, suppression, anticipation, and humor.

For my part, at the immature end of the scale, when I was a teenager and was overwhelmed by the anxiety within my family system, I "modified reality" with the defense of projection. In the first line of this book I said that I used to hate my family. At the time that I felt this I was actually projecting my own unacceptable feelings of self-loathing onto the nearest and most important emotional connection that I had—my father, mother, and extended family. Instead of facing the deep sense of failure I was feeling, I made them the *object* of blame and let my fragile ego off the hook. This is one of the ways in which immature defenses work. There are many others.

Less mature defenses include:

- Hypochondria, such as deciding we have stomach cancer just because we were nauseous for a day or two.
- Fantasy, such as living in our dreams like Walter Mitty or fantasizing about the perfect lover instead of being with the one we have.
- Passive aggression, such as telling someone that we would be "happy to do that," then waiting past the deadline to start the project.
- Dissociation, such as dodging painful reality with a drunken spree or "leaving our body" rather than endure physical abuse.

These are unconscious mechanisms that help us escape from the pain of our limitations into a more protected but unreal world.

Our immature defenses protect us from being overwhelmed by a painful reality, but they keep us from adapting to the truth we don't want to face. Crises may not be gifts, but they can be opportunities to see a larger truth about ourselves—though they may often feel more like punishment. Denial, the drug of choice for many of us, is the defense we use to ignore external reality: a husband believes that his wife really does love him, even though she will not stop sleeping with other people and is rarely home. In his immature state, this husband must deny the truth to protect his wounded sense of self, which cannot afford to grasp the truth of her absence. If he acknowledged the truth, he would be forced to change: he would have to work on himself and the relationship or he would have to leave. His denial protects him from a change he may feel too weak to undertake and creates a false reality in which he can remain in the marriage.

Many of us spend a good part of our teens "acting out"—experimenting with drugs, alcohol, school failure, shoplifting, or promiscuity—only to mature out of them as we grew older. For many, however, this same acting out can become a way of life, well into old age, unless some kind of outside assistance is sought. This is what the joke "How come self-realization is always bad news?" refers to—our ability to hide from painful reality. If you want to stop acting out and begin to set and achieve goals, you can not do so until you stop responding to your anxiety with the short-term methods of relieving these painful emotions—drinking, drugs, procrastination, and so on.

The more able I am to function in reality—that is the more my inner and outer worlds match—the more likely I am to depend upon more mature defense mechanisms in times of trouble. These intermediate defenses, ones that are simply "neurotic" as Vaillant says are:

- displacement
- intellectualization
- repression
- reaction formation

When I use displacement, I may come home angry at the boss but I kick the dog instead—displacing my emotions onto a third object. If I use intellectualization, I hide from my anger with my boss, but I discuss with others his failure to understand capitalist management techniques, thereby dodging my feelings by discussing them in cerebral terms. If I use repression, I may claim to myself and others to have no problems with my job while developing an ulcer. If I use reaction formation, I hate the thing I desire or love the thing I say I hate, in other words, I may say to other coworkers, "I love the boss; he's a great boss," denying my anger at him to my coworkers and to myself.

The good news is defenses can mature. Those of us who have been able to establish solid levels of autonomy within our families of origin and have a defined and authentic sense of self learn to employ the more mature defenses:

- altruism
- sublimation
- suppression
- anticipation
- humor

It is on these defenses that the sanest of us usually rely. These mature defenses are, for the most part, healthy ways to adapt, although they can be overused.

Playwright David Mamet jokes that if actors had not wanted to be actors, they shouldn't have had such terrible childhoods. The same could be said for painters, sculptors, writers, or athletes, anyone who "struts and frets" their childhood pain on a stage. It can also be said for the rest of us in one way or another. Sublimation, certainly the most celebrated of the defense mechanisms, allows us to transform our anxiety, whether sexual or aggressive, into some sort of creative outlet.

Altruism, the emphasis on service that so many of the support groups and religious orders advocate, is an age-old practice and a healing mature defense. Although it is possible to neglect yourself in service to others, focusing on serving the larger family or community can, through the power of altruism, connect and ground us, returning our efforts to us, as the old biblical expression goes, tenfold.

Suppression is best defined as the delaying of gratification. If my goal is losing weight, I learn to suppress my desire for fatty foods while I am attempting to learn better eating and exercise habits. Anticipation, another mature defense, may also be at play here as the "anticipated" feelings about weighing less and looking great add to our resolve to keep the compulsion to overeat to a minimum. This can lead to the virtuous cycle described in the last chapter. The mature defense of humor helps me to "take myself less seriously" when I lapse from my diet and make jokes about wanting to buy a condo above Baskin-Robbins. Humor teaches an important lesson about humanity and demonstrates the evolving nature of my "self."

All defense mechanisms are by definition unconscious and rarely used alone. Knowledge of them can be very important when we are trying to reconnect with our families. Knowing that some painful or irrational behaviors are merely defense mechanisms helps us to take a lot of what goes on in the family less personally.

Vaillant says that defenses arise to protect us whenever there is a dramatic change in our desires, conscience, peers, or reality. For example, an employee who is "downsized" might run through a series of defenses in a six-week period to cope with the change in her reality: First, she might use *reaction formation*—hating the thing you love or vice versa—by starting to hate her much-loved boss because he couldn't protect her. This could temporarily help her deal with her loss and protect her from the notion that she can't trust anyone. She may go on a spree to Las Vegas, deep in *denial* of her changed economic situation and *acting out* through gambling as a distraction from her pain.

Sometime in Las Vegas, her denial may break, and she would then come home in a state of urgency. Her desire for a stable life and a moment to reflect would motivate a change to more mature defenses: She would now *suppress* her gambling desire by living frugally, *sublimate* her anxiety into a rigorous job search, and *anticipate* the way she will be able to live when she gets the job she's after by planning carefully for her future.

This quick cycle through a series of defense mechanisms is evidence of a fairly healthy coping strategy during stress. Her initial defenses distracted her from the assault on her ego that the loss of this job had caused her, keeping her busy and keeping her pain at bay until she found the strength to make positive changes. Had she gotten stuck in any one of those defenses, she'd have caused herself and those who depend on her a lot of heartache.

The hallmark of an immature defense is that it often hooks the person it is used on, making it hard for that person to see the relationship clearly. For example, reaction formation may initially protect a woman for a time from the pain of separation. Yet, the intensity of her new hatred for her former beloved may attract the man she loved yesterday but now despises, as he tries to fathom her anger. She is freed and he is hooked. The intensity of the loss may be managed differently by each member of the former couple—she by hating him, he by fantasy and denial, as he struggles to avoid the pain and confusion over her change of heart. In its more extreme cases, he may get lost in obsessional fantasy (driving by her house at night), or she may slander him and their former relationship to her friends and even the authorities.

After a time, defenses can become less protective and more constricting than is necessary for survival. When our defenses barricade us or freeze us in time, we may close off from emotional growth and true connection with the family. Understanding that many of the actions others take are done to defend themselves—

and are not necessarily conscious or personal—is an important step in not being drawn into their emotional field. Understanding this allows us to stay connected to their fundamental humanity as well as our own, without overreacting.

RUTH'S EVOLVING DEFENSES

Ruth is a good example of how defense mechanisms can evolve over time. Ruth was raised in a working-class multigenerational household where there was a strong pressure for togetherness despite the tremendous amount of conflict and neglect. As a small child she escaped into fantasy as a defense.

When she reached school age and began to interact with peers, she moved from fantasy into denial. The tensions in her household were so difficult for her that she wouldn't bring any friends home to play. Unconsciously she was defending herself against the opinions and reactions of her school friends to her family, which could disturb the equilibrium she had established at home by ignoring the conflict. If she brought friends home, they would see what she didn't want to see. She hardly ever talked about life at home with her friends except to describe the basic facts of where her mother, grandmother, and grandfather worked or what the family had done over the weekend.

As she progressed in school, Ruth showed she was an extraordinarily gifted student. Encouraged by the praise and support she got from her teachers, she sublimated her anxiety about her home life into superb performance in school, an arena where the stable structure and continual rewards were satisfying to her. This external validation gave Ruth an enhanced sense of self, an identity independent from that of a small child in a house full of people with immature defenses. She was her shy, withdrawn self at home and a boisterous extrovert at school. She shared her family's extroverted character but was afraid to unbalance the dynamic at home by asserting herself, so she channeled that energy into the outside world.

During college she defended herself against the anxiety the separation caused with three defense mechanisms—reaction formation, projection, and acting out. Through reaction formation, Ruth became convinced she hated her mother even though they had been very close. She blamed her family for the difficulties she was having adapting to the rigorous standards at college, projecting onto them her feelings of insecurity and inadequacy.

In isolation from her family, she began acting out sexually and denying this reality to herself and her family. She chose psychology as a major in college and studied to become a therapist. Engrossing herself in her studies, she stopped acting out and moved from her former immature defenses to intellectualization and suppression. Ruth's analysis of her family dynamic created a safe place for her to stand in the family context, but not an emotionally authentic one. Her sense of duty and responsibility compelled her to stay in contact with her family, but she was mentally and emotionally distant from the family.

In the closed world of a family home, the defenses you build to protect yourself generate the need for other family members to defend themselves as well. When Ruth was a small child, lost in her own fantasies, she could not grasp how uncomfortable her withdrawal made her family of extroverts. They saw her as a loner, lost in her own world, and shy. Her lack of interest in the world, her lack of friends, also made her family wary of her. They couldn't figure out what made her tick.

In studies of families, psychologists find that parents' assessment of their children matches the assessment by trained outside observers only about fifty percent of the time. Parents are part of the system at work and are therefore less able to accurately comprehend their children. Each parent filters his or her view through a mix of his or her own history, hope, temperament, and skills, as well as defense mechanisms. This is why I often ask parents to let the child's school performance and teacher assessment aid them in making sure their children are doing well. School failure is one of the most consistent predictors of later failure in life.

Given this tendency, it is not surprising that many parents convince themselves that their troubled children are "just going through a phase." Even when parents notice a problem in the family system, they are likely to bring the child in as the designated patient, while their marital pain stays unacknowledged. This was no different for Ruth, as her mother's denial kept her from sensing the degree of her daughter's pain. Over time Ruth found that connection to her family was too painful because she felt judged and therefore rejected. She, just like the rest of the family, became accustomed to seeing herself as strange.

Validation of her traits outside the family allowed Ruth to see her differences as strengths. While her family was proud of her accomplishments, the fact that her successes reinforced her distance from the family seemed to separate them further and triggered other defenses. Power shifted between Ruth and her mother, Helen. Instead of seeing Ruth merely as strange, Helen began to view her negatively. She saw her daughter as selfish, condescending, and judgmental—common responses to a family member's attempt to become autonomous. Ruth's new power to remain outside the fusion with her mother caused Helen to project onto Ruth many of the attitudes Helen herself had employed to disguise the pain of Ruth's separation: Helen had been condescending and judgmental toward Ruth. In many ways, Helen was correct about Ruth's "selfishness." For Ruth to find the strength to become her authentic self and survive and flourish in her differences, she had to create some comfort using these defenses.

Vaillant is right that defenses are wise, creative, and essential. Without these defenses, Ruth would have been unable to remain in the family. Her sense of self would have been overwhelmed by the dissimilarity of her inner and outer worlds.

People who are completely overwhelmed by this dissimilarity represent the other extreme of the behavioral scale. These people are often disabled by *psychotic* defenses such as paranoid schizophrenia or psychotic denial. They are often as potentially dangerous to themselves as they are to loved ones or even strangers. In families where these "insane" states exist, serious professional help of the highest caliber is required. Preparing someone for engagement with seriously debilitated family members or systems is outside the scope of this book, though many of the same ideas described here about families and the importance of support apply.

While Ruth's case is certainly not psychotic, her family could have been helped by professional intervention to deal with their pain more directly. Many of us would find ourselves swamped were it not for the defenses that protect us. Several paradoxical states occur in most families: feeling alone when we are together with them, being physically present but lost in our own thoughts, loving them for all that they are and hating them for what they are doing or have done to us. Our defenses soothe the feelings attached to these powerful contradictions. They allow us—through fantasy, denial, distraction, rationalization, overcompensation, or focusing those feelings on someone or something other than the person who is causing us pain—to ignore the painful paradox inherent in a flawed intimacy.

When Helen became critically ill with breast cancer, Ruth was at a loss as to how to relate to her. The accumulated pain of their clashing defenses allowed very little genuine positive feeling to remain between them. There was no way to intellectualize the pain she felt about the coming loss of her mother, however. Under the brute force of the impending death, Ruth felt her old defenses crumbling.

Her mother's illness reminded her of the connection they had had when she was a very young child and also allowed her to feel some gratitude for her mother's pride in her accomplishments. At that moment, with the power of transience weighing on her, Ruth needed to find another way to be a member of her family. She had come to a time and a place at which her defenses were now getting in the way of her need to be a good daughter to her dying mother.

In this crisis, Ruth found herself at the place I call the humble tumble. Sometimes fate throws you or a member of your family a curve ball, and all the reasons you've employed and all the methods you've been using to defend yourself against your family suddenly seem absurd. Ruth's mother's projection had rubbed up against Ruth's intellectualization for a decade, making most of their exchanges seem as if they were taking place in a house of mirrors. Now, with Helen at life's end, none of that mattered.

An un-fun fun house of mirrors is probably a better description of this phenomenon in which each member of the family has his or her shape distorted by the wavy effect of defenses. You say something you feel in your heart, and in the mirror of your family's defenses, you're reflected as a misshapen ogre with a narrow torso and a huge head and shoulders. You give a bitter response, and you're a squat fireplug compressed into a tiny, whiny voice, a child pleading not to be abandoned. In these regressive moments, it is only defenses that can restore your fragile ego to its full height.

LISTENING WITHOUT JUDGMENT

When we attempt to reconnect with our family, knowledge of the defense mechanisms—that they exist to protect us and that they can mature over time—can help us separate the man from the mechanism and drop the labels we may have attached to different family members. The goal of this new language of defenses should not be merely a new set of labels through which we can go on judging our families or ourselves, but a new method of disengaging from the larger emotional field. Knowing that what we feel in the fun house of our families of origin is due to the defense mechanisms in play can allow us to find compassion where previously there may not have been any.

For Ruth, learning that persecution was actually a defensive strategy was an eye-opener that helped her accept her mother's confrontational style of communication and the avalanche of judgments that often issued from her mother's fundamentalist religious stance. Understanding these misguided attempts to "save" her children as displacement of her mother's own guilt made Ruth realize that her mother's stinging messages of judgment were, in fact, attempts at staying engaged despite being overwhelmed by fears of ending up alone.

It's important to note that knowing their origin does not lessen the sting of Helen's judgments, but it can help keep Ruth from engaging in a defensive battle that she can never win. *As Ruth ceases to react to her mother's attacks, her mother's attacks actually become less virulent.* While the attacks may never cease altogether, Ruth has become an agent for change within her family by focusing on herself and the true love she has for her mother. This is what is known as focusing on process and not content.

The content of the attack is not the issue, and the more we respond to its specifics, the more the attack escalates. If you can ignore the *content* of the attack—you are a drug addict, a loser, a heathen, a whore, a Democrat, a whatever—and stay focused on remaining out of the battle without defending yourself, the attacks are likely to diminish over time. By refusing to take the bait, you allow the other person to vent without validating their attack. This focus on the process of communication instead of its content can illuminate the defense mechanisms at play. By knowing the ultimate value of our own essential humanity and refusing to be provoked, we are much more likely to diffuse the conflict. *There is no conflict if we do not engage.* (There may be feelings to deal with, however, and exercise, talks with trusted friends, or even prayer may help us to keep our emotional channel clear.)

If you have been able through the exercises and information in the previous chapters to remember the true spirit you share with your family, you have a motivation to attempt to build a new connection to them. In this chapter we want to find a way to make that connection a better one, one that allows you to accept their defenses and be more who you are in the family atmosphere.

Through reflecting and re-framing, you have come to understand, or at least become open to the possibility, that conflict in your family was heavily influenced by forces that the individuals involved could not completely control. In that way you may now appreciate that much of what you felt damaged you in your family was not meant to injure you personally.

When you return to the family with an awareness of the defenses still extant there, you have an opportunity to truly reconnect. Being aware that many irritating actions are merely defenses allows us to be more emotionally authentic with our families and less emotionally reactive, while still keeping a boundary around our identities.

The various defenses your family members employ are for their own protection and not aimed specifically at hurting you. Try to remember that the defensive person may look strong, but, in fact, he feels cornered. He may be flailing internally, grabbing at anything he can to keep others away, but it is only in order to keep himself together. If he happens to strike you, it's most likely out of his weakness rather than personal malice.

Defense mechanisms may, in fact, be alternatives to worse behavior. The troubled cousin who has caused herself and the family a lot of heartache because of her drug problems is seen by them as a weakling, a lunatic, a criminal, or disrespectful. Now include in this assessment of her the lifelong battle she's had with depression. Her drug use may be a defense against more dramatic aberrant behavior, such as suicide or violence against others. Add this information to a family systems analysis of the young drug addict as the identified patient carrying the anxiety for the entire family organism and it becomes much easier to listen to her problems without passing judgment. A family member using this analysis of the drug addicted cousin can actually be a more effective agent for change.

The ability to listen without judgment is, paradoxically, the only real chance we have of helping the cousin get straight. If you want to ensure that your children keep using drugs, just keep demanding that they not do it. Harp on this and you will only strengthen their defenses. However, tell them that you love them and respect them, that they can take all the drugs they want—if they are willing to live elsewhere and risk hunger or worse—and the odds are good that your children will not continue to take drugs for more than a very short time. Listening without judgment means that you remind them that you want to help them succeed, that you will go to a counselor for your own pain and help them find a counselor for theirs, but that you are not going to support them if they make destructive choices.

This same open strategy applies to interpersonal relationships as well: angrily tell your daughter that she cannot marry that man or you will disown her, and you probably ensure that she will. Tell her that you love her and respect her ability to make a choice, while also stating your truth that he seems like a bad match, and she is much more likely to tire of him quickly.

The trick to operating effectively in this arena is to respect the autonomy of the other family member while honoring your own reactions and not activating defenses of your own.

Richard has successfully accomplished this transition from a defensive participant to an agent of change in his family. For many years he was a reactive member of a destructive triangle between his younger brother, Tom, and their father, Gus. When they were children, their father often accused their mother of infidelity. In many of his jealous tirades he humiliated his wife and son by claiming that Tom was not really his son but the son of a neighbor. The pain of these exchanges affected Tom more than Richard, but often made Richard feel guilty that he could not protect his younger brother from his father's confusing words.

Understandably, Tom felt like the illegitimate member of the family and often sabotaged his own success. As a young boy, Tom's shame manifested itself in desperately trying to please his father. He became a star athlete, sublimating his need for paternal affection into performance on the baseball field and as a championship diver. By succeeding in competitive arenas, Tom found a place where his father would appreciate his talent and praise him. His success and his father's expression of approval never fully compensated for Tom's doubts about his paternity. In adolescence, Tom began to self-destruct, acting out his shame by walking away from a major league baseball career and leaving home early to join the Army.

As he fell from grace, Tom learned that another way to engage his father was failure. They began a dance that went on for decades. Over and over Tom would fail at some endeavor, unconsciously using passive aggression to prove his father right. Each time he failed, Tom would ask for help like a small boy who still needed his father to bail him out. This vicious cycle spread to Richard, as their father would complain to Richard about Tom's behavior. Richard, angry but withdrawn, would agree with his father that Tom just "didn't have it together." Richard's participation in this triangle—by accepting his father's labeling of his brother—made Richard feel his own guilt. This led Richard to the same kind of superiority-caretaking-judging-superiority cycle that had colored the family interactions for decades.

Tom's role in the family as the scapegoat solidified. Tom would defend himself with denial in regard to his daily finances and with grandiose fantasies about the success that would rescue his position in the family. Richard's defense mechanisms were projection and intellectualization as he invested his brother with his own feelings of low regard while always believing he knew the *real* way everyone should behave.

As often happens in family dynamics, when Gus stopped bailing out his son in a tough-love stance, Richard stepped in to take up the slack in a displacement of his earlier guilt. Richard's actions only perpetuated his brother's denial and froze them both into roles of overfunctioning and underfunctioning.

In most situations in which defenses are especially strong and active, the defenses barely cover the underlying need for connection—and they often reinforce triangles that are unseen. Tom and Gus did not often seem to have any respect for one another, yet their negative intimacy kept them connected—as demonstrated by their passionate culture of mutual complaint. They each unconsciously settled for a relationship that was conflicted rather than risk no relationship at all.

One day when Gus was complaining about Tom's lack of success, Richard realized his part in the old blame-Tom–blame-Dad dance. Without anger in his voice, Richard said the "unsayable" to his father for the first time: "You know, Dad, all those years you told the family that Tom was not your son really hurt him," Richard said in a non-judgmental voice. "He's never really felt like you loved him."

"Well, that's ridiculous," their father blustered, caught completely off guard. "Of course he's my son. What an idiotic thing to say."

"View it from his eyes, though, Dad," Richard continued, deciding to seize the day. "He's never really felt like he belonged. I think if you wrote him a letter and apologized for how much that hurt him, it could really open things up between you."

There was a long silence on the phone as Gus weighed the decision. While he did not write the letter immediately, he did eventually write his youngest son. Tom, then thirty-eight years old, cried long and hard, and carried the letter around with him for months. In this one change of approach, all three men connected to the emotional truth underneath. Gus has not had anything but loving things to say about Tom for some time now, and Tom has begun making headway on a career that had been a dream only a couple of years ago.

When you take an action such as the one Richard took, it sometimes feels like an out-of-body experience. Could that be *my* voice saying those calm, loving words? Where did I get such wisdom? In the end, though, it is the place all of us would like to be in our families, a position of emotional engagement with the family from which we can appreciate them for who they are with all their strengths, weaknesses, denials, and projections—but in a climate freed from judgment and blame.

THE BEST THEY COULD

While there are a wide range of defensive tactics, probably the most common ones visible in families are projections and denial.

Those nagging criticisms that your parents perpetually make about ways in which you disappointed them are in many cases projections of dreams they had for themselves that they were never able to fulfill or denials about truths that were too painful to bear.

When I was a teenager, I wanted to be a doctor, an ambition my parents heartily endorsed. Life didn't turn out the way I'd hoped at fifteen, but I've still made something of myself. Despite my success, every time I visit my mother she asks me if I'm ever going to go to medical school. This is Codes of Love in action, I've come to understand. I used to take her question as evidence that despite the distance I've traveled to be who I am, I'm still disappointing my mother.

In fact, that's not true. My mother is very proud of me. To her mind and according to her upbringing in a small West Virginia hill town, a doctor was the ultimate in status—a healer, compassionate, of service, and comparatively rich. My mother isn't judging me as a failure; *she's still hoping for the ultimate in success for me.* Before I understood her projection of her ambitions, her comments would cause me to come out swinging verbally to defend myself, and the situation would escalate into an argument or withdrawal.

Misunderstandings like these are often operative in our past dilemmas with our parents. The ways in which they insisted that you participate in activities that you really didn't enjoy frequently were attempts on their part to give you the childhood they wish they had.

Sometimes the conflict and mistrust that ensues from being forced to endure art lessons when you have fundamental problems with spatial relations or from being compelled to participate in Boy Scouts when you are a loner who hates group activities can influence the way you and your parents relate for years to come.

Your parents think you just have a bad attitude, lack talent, or are disobedient, while you wonder if they ever really knew who you were. Often it was all just a terrible mistake.

For Jeffrey, a forty-three-year-old architect, the issue was Little League. From the time he was seven until he reached eleven, his father insisted that Jeffrey participate in Little League, despite Jeffrey's complete lack of skill on the field. His whole family would turn out—aunts, uncles, cousins—to watch Jeffrey strike out time after time or stand perplexed in the outfield as the ball dropped a few feet behind him and he scrambled to throw it to first base, always missing it by a good ten feet.

The family was stoic in the face of Jeffrey's humiliation. His uncle even brought a Super 8 movie camera to every game and recorded these events. Jeffrey, week after week, was anxious because he knew he could never please his father through his efforts on the field. He felt too intimidated to express his own growing lack of interest in the game because he heroically hoped that one day he would improve.

Only at the end of his Little League career did the family realize how incredibly nearsighted Jeffrey was. He was nearly legally blind. The reason he was the strikeout king and such an inept fielder was that he simply couldn't see the ball.

In his twenties, Jeffrey interpreted his entire relationship with his father negatively with this one piece of information in the foreground. Dad wanted so much for Jeffrey to be a ballplayer that he was oblivious to the actual fact of who Jeffrey was and what he needed to succeed in life.

Through re-framing, Jeffrey was able to rehabilitate his attitude toward his father and see his father's insistence that Jeffrey play ball as an expression of affection. Jeffrey's father had been neglected by his own father, who never showed up for his games and never encouraged his interest in sports. Jeffrey's father wanted to provide what he had been craving his entire childhood by making sure his son was not ignored. Frequently when we want to correct an injustice we overcompensate. Jeffrey's dad was projecting onto him his pent-up need for attention and affection. Unfortunately he placed it in an arena in which Jeffrey couldn't appreciate it or have his real talents encouraged.

It often hurts both people when a simple misunderstanding or mistake, like Jeffrey's father not recognizing Jeffrey's myopia, goes undiscussed and becomes a rift.

Stephanie, the woman in the chapter on reflecting who set a healthy boundary with her mother, used a wonderful exercise to handle her problems with projection within her family. Whenever she'd think, "My mother doesn't really understand me," she'd flip that sentence to make herself the subject and her mother the object. "I've never really understood my mother." For Jeffrey, "My father never saw me for who I was" becomes "I never saw my father for who *he* was." "My father wanted me to be someone I wasn't" becomes "I wanted my father to be someone *he* wasn't."

The usefulness of this exercise is to bring you to compassion for the misunderstandings our defenses engender. If you think you are misunderstood, most likely the person who doesn't get you right feels the same way about you. This startling notion forces us to reconsider some of the basic disappointments that color our view of the family. Our father's not understanding us doesn't usually come from some willful ignorance on his part but rather from the fact that he was projecting hopes and dreams onto us that he hadn't had the opportunity to fulfill on his own.

By inhabiting and revisiting his memories related to the dark years he spent failing at Little League, Jeffrey got to the Code of Love underneath. He appreciated his father's stoicism, identical to Jeffrey's, both of them continuing to show up despite the disappointments. His father was there for every game, every strikeout, and every dropped pop fly, not because he wanted to humiliate Jeffrey but because he loved him whether he succeeded or not.

Once again the land-mine–gold-mine paradox is at work. The very source of conflict between Jeffrey and his father is, in fact, a place in which they have the opportunity for the strongest and most understanding connection. Conflict is a place where individuals reveal who they are. Conflicts from the past, such as the one between Jeffrey and his father, or conflicts in present time, such as Ruth's desire to find a way to connect with her ill mother despite their years of distance, are leverage points—points that offer a large payoff for a small investment of self. The humble tumble reveals the leverage points in our family and the opportunities life presents us to make progress in our relationships by finding the courage to engage in conflicts in a new way.

For years, Helen had been telling her distant and dismissive daughter Ruth that during her childhood "I did the best I could." Ruth's reaction to this was a snort. "Yeah, right," Ruth would shoot back. "If that's your best, I think you could have done a little better." When defense clashes against defense, there can be no movement, no intimacy. Each person may feel safer, but they are isolated—from others and the larger truth.

In seeking a better connection with her mother in her mother's last days, Ruth worked through the reflecting and re-framing exercises as a way to get past her defenses and gain a new perspective. Denial is often the disavowal of the good as well as the bad. Looking at her mother with compassion, Ruth could see how her mother had done the best she could: Her mother often drank, yes, but she never fell into the patterns that the rest of the family did and always showed up for Ruth's school events. Although Ruth was in a sophisticated world Helen just barely understood, she was demonstrably proud of her daughter and had worked to maintain a relationship despite Ruth's condescension and hostility.

Ruth came to see the cruelty of her automatic dismissal of her mother's claim that she "did the best she could." It was, in fact, an apology that Ruth was too heavily defended to hear. This realization brought clarity to Ruth but also grief—a humble tumble of her own—for all the years she'd lost with her mom. The next time her mother weakly offered, "I did the best I could," Ruth dropped her tendency to dismiss.

"I know you did the best you could, Mom," Ruth said. "But, do you understand how lonely I was? How abandoned I felt? Knowing who I am now, do you see how hard it was for me to live in that house?"

Her mother reached out to hold Ruth's hand and held it for a long time.

"You were so quiet, Ruth," Helen said with tears in her eyes. "You were in a world of your own. I had no idea. I'm so sorry, honey. I'm so sorry."

Intimacy is a mysterious place, a place where you present yourself open to the world. By sidestepping her defenses, Ruth returned to that place of true connection with her mother, a place she hadn't been able to be in years. Her true need, honestly expressed, welled up and was matched by the true need of her mother, and they stood together again in that truth of the human condition—the need for genuine connection.

This need for intimacy is what keeps us coming back to our families.

In fact, is there anyone anywhere in the world who could understand what Ruth endured better than her mother could? In the intellectual world in which Ruth made her professional life, she'd told the story of her troubled childhood hundreds of times, parceling pieces of it out as the circumstances inspired. The upper-middle-class professionals that were Ruth's peers were shocked by her story and marveled at her for having triumphed over it. In its own way this story, too, was a defense, a way of maintaining Ruth's self-image as a loner, different, and a bit strange. The next place for her to mature was by reconnecting with the parts of her that were most like her family.

You may say to yourself, *"I don't want to go back home. Everyone there is so crazy."* Use the projection exercise to turn this around: "I don't want to go home. I'm so crazy." You shape-shift in the hall of mirrors at the family fun house and come out the other side not sure who you are, but knowing certainly that you're no longer who you were when you entered. You can't blame your family for that, however. *In the end you are the only person who can be responsible for establishing and maintaining your authentic self as an adult.* The place of strength, the place of connection you're hungering for, comes, like so many things, as a paradox. The more you step away from your old patterns within your family, the more connected you will be able to be with your family. The paradox is present because new behavior does not engender the old familiar feelings, the feelings you have come to think of as "family." As my friend Julia Cameron says, "Going sane feels just like going crazy."

When I went first went home that Christmas in my grandiose car, I, too, was sucked into the sane-crazy paradox. I wanted so much to be with my family, yet I also was too fragile to reveal how I really felt. I craved true intimacy, but I struggled with the warring defense mechanisms—my own and my family's. There is something seductive and comforting about old patterns of behavior. In many cases, as confusing as these interlocking defense mechanisms are, they are what we think of as "home."

THE MYTH OF SELF-SUFFICIENCY

The most insidious defense is to live in the myth of self-sufficiency, to pretend that we have no relationship with our families and stay far away. This form of denial—expressed as the refusal to go home at all—relies on a false assumption, the assumption that we do not have a relationship with them because we are not physically present. I have worked with many grown children of divorced families who have not had contact with one or both of their parents for many years. They are often angry and state that "I wouldn't want a relationship with my father, even if he came begging." The sad truth is, they *have* a relationship either way, whether they want to realize it or not—and this relationship is a fantasy, constructed of myths and mirrors, that lives in their head.

From three thousand miles away, we can be anyone we want to be in our family without having to face the messy reality. We can be the savior, sending home money and making a loving phone call. We can be the grandiose intellectual, too smart to need them or too busy with a demanding schedule to take time to just "be" with our family. We can be the lonely martyr—sadly stoic, ultimately heroic—sacrificing precious time with our family for a higher calling.

From that distance, our family can be anything we need them to be as well: a family that fits our fantasized Hollywood version of ourselves. We can imagine environments in which they live, choosing images that let us feel secure. We can imagine them stuck in a time warp, forever lost in some childhood version of themselves, a symbolic shabby house, full of conflicts that justify our continuous absence. Or we can romanticize a simple loving homestead where our absence is noted and we are pined for. Fantasy plus distance is a powerful defense, one that allows for a profound imaginary connection when the *real* connection, as we imagine it, would be too excruciating, too boring, too aggravating, too sad, or too loving, too joyful, to bear.

What makes real connection to our family so full of ambivalence is that intimacy is messy. Life is messy: we get sick, we act stupid, we fail at things, we hurt others, and we get hurt ourselves. Yet, we can't mythologize the traits or responses or emotions we want from our families when we are actually with them. Only in present time can we get the real thing, only in present time can we feel our mother's love as unconditional, as criticizing, or as demanding—or, more likely, as some combination of all three. Embracing the fullness of life—encompassing the completeness, the humanity, the full catastrophe of another—is made possible only by being able to offer a corresponding level of our own complex vulnerability and strength.

If I had been advising the family of those two young mothers in the coffee shop, I would have had them hunt for the points of connection that were so obvious to an outside observer amid their discussion and dismissal. Their ambivalence about their mother symbolizes for me the struggle we all have to be authentic and loving in a world where so many simple miscommunications distract us from the needs and abilities of those we love.

For some of us, separation from our family was a violent event. We stomped off, we left in the night, we didn't call for years, we stayed aloof and judgmental, or we stayed home but withdrew. For so many more of us, like the two young mothers, we hide our true selves from connection with a veil of politeness that demeans the many times our parents have saved us in whatever small ways.

In coming back as adults, from near or from far, and *choosing* to reconnect with the family, we are performing a powerful act. We are choosing to be connected, to be real, and to endure the intensity of authentic engagement, knowing that only by dropping our defenses, revealing our secrets, and having the courage to tell our truth and hear the truth of others will the connection we long for be vibrant. Coming home this time, and in this manner, not only is our past brand new, but so are we.

Codes of Love Exercise: ALL IN THE FAMILY

Are there any parts of my story about going home for the holidays that resonate for you? When you go home

- Do you feel ambivalence about returning?
- Do you make last-minute plans?
- Do you engage with the children?
- Do you struggle not to judge your family?
- Do you struggle to stay engaged?
- What is specific to your story that you don't see in mine?

Codes of Love Exercise: PROJECTION REVISITED

In this exercise, we turn the table on ourselves. Take the phrases that you usually use to refer to the members of your family or to your family as a whole. For example:

- "They just don't understand me."
- "They never really loved me."
- "They are crazy."

Now make a list of these. In each sentence, take the subject and make it the object and the object becomes the subject. For example:

- "They never really loved me" becomes "I never really loved them."

Now reverse all your sentences in this way. Reflect on the relative truth of those new statements.

- Do you really love them?
- Do you really understand them?
- In relation to your family do you feel crazy?

Codes of Love Exercise: THE FAMILY FUN HOUSE

Think about your family's defense mechanisms.

- Which ones can you see them using?
- Under what circumstances?
- What do you think your own are?
- If you can, ask someone else what they think yours are.
- What are you defending?

Codes of Love Exercise: THE MAGIC WAND

If you had a magic wand, what would you change

- In your family?
- In your life?

- Why do you think that change would make you happier? Would it?
- Is the yearning for something different a defense?
- What would your family change about you?
- Are you able to accept them for who they are? Even obsession can serve us: the fantasy of a perfect family keeps us from committing to the one we have.
- Are you able to accept yourself?
- Are you willing to change?
- Do you really need to?

Codes of Love Exercise: THE AWFUL TRUTH

Okay, what is so terrible about your family? List all the terrible qualities, incidents, embarrassments, and jealousies that describe them. How bad is it? Take each quality, incident, and embarrassment and intensify it in your mind or on paper until it is much worse. Expand on the actuality until it is absurd. Does this seem to make it all less dramatic?

Codes of Love Exercise: MOMENTS OF TRUTH

What incidents have taken place in your relationship with your family that have tested your ability to remain detached? Which ones have tested your ability to stand your ground? What special things have happened recently with your family that amused you? That moved you?

Codes of Love Exercise: THE HUMBLE TUMBLE

- What current crises are going on in your family?
- What is the big deal?
- If no one did anything, what would happen? (Are you sure?)
- When have you made judgments about the outcome of an event that did not come true?
- Have you found yourself humbled lately? Why?

Codes of Love Exercise: FINDING THE INSTRUCTION IN THE STORY

Learning about defense mechanisms is not meant to be yet another way to deconstruct and analyze our families. It is a method to help us gain some objective distance in our families as we watch for familiar defensive structures. This notion that we can "see" what is going on in these complex interactions grants us a better balance of feeling and thinking. My mother may be in complete denial about the behavior of one of the kids, but by understanding the defense she is employing as part of her protection for her fragile sense of self, I am much less likely to judge her or to attempt to pressure her to "see" things as I do.

The "instruction in the story" refers to our ability to see what is happening without having to change anything or to run, but this should be a temporary filter on our world. Now this exercise is to stop thinking in terms of defense mechanisms. That lesson has served its purpose.

CHAPTER 6
Codes of Love

All families communicate in codes, a shorthand that bonds the generations through an intimate language of shared meaning. When one family member says cousin Samantha is "pulling a Betsy," the other cousin knows without another word that Samantha acted in an eccentric way similar to the way their cousin Betsy acts. A sister remarks to her brother that her daughter is "discovering her inner Joyce." They both understand the daughter has suddenly become just as particular about grooming and fashion as their mother had been.

These codes can be a shorthand for acceptance too. While Joyce may have caused her daughter enormous grief in her childhood and adolescence, with her strict expectations about appearance, by identifying her daughter's "inner Joyce" she alludes to a struggle that only she and her brother know intimately. Both siblings acknowledge that they've moved beyond the struggle with humor and humanity. In this way, codes close a circle around the family, creating a sense that the family is its own world, with legends, mythologies, enduring traits, and traditions passed generation to generation through oral history. These codes are also hidden in the moments of family conflict as the emotions in the moment cloud the intent or meaning of the messages one family member sends to another. Deciphering these codes means reassessing our resentments.

Another kind of code is a shared set of values or agreed-upon appropriate behaviors, as in a code of conduct, a code of silence, a code of educational excellence, or a code of physical prowess. Families must be clear about the meaning of these codes, however, if there is to be harmony. Just as the meaning of words alters over time, so does what one generation of family members think of as *support* or *success* or any other concept on which a family works toward a shared sense of value.

A family may have a collective culture that emphasizes a particular profession or monetary success, or one that elevates the notion of putting family first. One generation may demonstrate its interpretation of these in a certain manner, but the next generation may experience the code differently because they are different themselves, and so is their world. Despite cohesion and loyalty, a family can seem to lose or distort the meaning of its codes over time. To a man who started in America as an immigrant, owning his own store in a big city might have meant success. To his son, success may mean expanding that store to five locations in the suburbs. To the next son, however, staying in the family business might feel like failure. He may leave the retail world behind and become a lawyer to honor his own code for success.

Each new interpretation of a family's code is an expression of the next generation's quest for self-definition. Each generation must go through its own maturation process, which naturally causes its elders to maneuver to keep the family together, its codes intact. This reinterpretation of values by young adults often causes a crisis between the old society being reevaluated and the new one attempting to prove its superiority. The immigrant father may feel betrayed when his son leaves the old neighborhood for the quiet of the suburbs, feeling that he never would have deserted his own father that way. The son who leaves may feel abandoned when *his* son rejects the family business in favor of becoming a ski instructor.

Parents and children may clash over their different interpretations of *support, loyalty, lifestyle,* or any of a number of concepts that are nurtured in the family experience. Yet through these disputes, each generation in its own way invests the family's codes with new meanings, thereby keeping the value of the codes alive and current. Engaging in these conflicts shows that the family values are worth fighting over, and the conflicts themselves ensure that the values behind the codes can endure. It is the ongoing struggle to decipher the codes underneath that reinforces the family's closed circle and the shared sense of value that binds the generations.

Once when I was down and out in my twenties in Florida, I called my father collect to ask if he'd send me one hundred dollars for food.

"I'm sorry, son." he said. "I can't do that."

"You, what?" I asked, challenging him. I knew he had the money. Was he just going to let his son starve?

"When you get the money, call me and tell me how you got it," my father said, and hung up.

I slammed the receiver down on the hook ten times before I controlled my rage enough to place it properly.

What I wanted from my father, then—my Code of Love—was sympathy for being in a tight spot, and I wanted that sympathy expressed as financial support without question. My father, in his own Code of Love and what I now see as his wisdom, knew I'd been in this particular tight spot more than once and for more than a year. Sending me money would only help keep me there. One of the Bryans' Codes of Love is to be hardy, hardworking, and resourceful. My father saw me not as desperate but as a Bryan, an able-bodied young man perfectly capable of taking care of myself, of getting a day-laborer job if I needed money for food.

My rage at his refusal forced me to look at my life, something I was loath to do, considering how much of a shambles it was. Many of our Codes of Love are amplified in the clash between our desires and our family's refusal to meet those desires. My resentment toward my father became my motivation for change: I would "show" my dad. I'd never be in that humiliating position with him again, I vowed.

I never was.

At the time I saw what my father did as the opposite of a loving act. I saw what he did as cruel, and I saw him as rigid and unfeeling. He saw the truth: I needed to learn to be self-reliant. I was forced, by his refusal to help me, to look at the ways in which I was impeding my own progress. His lesson was invaluable, and the separation that resulted from my reaction was perhaps an unavoidable part of the process. Had I seen the inherent lesson immediately, it would have saved us both a lot of grief and lost time.

The central purpose of family life is to engage in the evolution of its members. For much of our lives this purpose is fulfilled through simple acts of nurturing—food, clothing, shelter. With this as a template, many of us think that what we want from our families is the unconditional support we received as children. We continue to want this unconditional support even when we are asking for things they should no longer provide or could not give in the first place.

Georgia, a thirty-five-year-old cartoonist, was a dreamy introspective child who wanted a demonstratively affectionate family. Yet that was not her family's style. While closely knit, the family culture supported group activity by collectively volunteering in elections and working on environmental causes. Their sense of righteousness was foreign to Georgia, who liked to turn questions over and over in her head for the answer, enjoying exploration more than certainty. Her family, however, fiercely supported individuality, romanticizing the ideal of the lone wolf, the brave individual who stands firm against the tide. Within the family circle, Georgia found only crushing homogeneity. Being a loner against the family tide was debilitating for Georgia's intuitive sensibilities.

Her hunger for intimate contact sent her hungrily out into the world, where her family-bred confidence in the righteousness of a singular perspective helped Georgia develop a unique aesthetic in her artwork. This confidence ultimately led her to great success. Her intimate knowledge of people's need for love and approval— the very things she rarely felt at home—became something she gave off rather than looked to receive. She took tremendous satisfaction from her generosity to colleagues and in trusting her intuition about those she loved. Her trust and generosity came back to her from the circle of people she created around her, and her success gave her a confidence and stature that she was even able to project within her family. What we cannot get from our families, we ultimately must find within ourselves.

For some, trying to find a sunny ending in the painful ways in which families cause trauma and insecurity can seem a glib denial of the damage done. But one thing that has become abundantly clear to me over time is that family events have the meaning we give them. In many cases, what we see is only what we are doing to ourselves. This is, of course, not the case in aggressive forms of abuse and neglect, but for most of us the estrangement from our families is not the result of actual violence. More often than not our anger at our families—or our inability to be authentic—stems from disappointment in them or in ourselves. We often feel that they didn't give us what we needed at some crucial moment or that they didn't see and appreciate us for who we were at the time. But the idea that things should be given to us is a child's view of the world. As adults we know very few things come our way just because we sit passively wanting them.

While some of our family's Codes of Love are easily grasped, other codes are enigmatic and built within layers of meaning and experience often stretching backward and forward through generations. It is always easier to focus on the conflicts within the family than to see through the conflicts to the deeper mystery of what the conflict says *to* you and *about* you.

In most cases it is only later that we realize our disappointment stemmed from what we needed or wanted at that crucial moment. What we needed from the family then is what we need to find for ourselves now. Maturing is or should be the process of transforming from the powerlessness of a child to the power of an adult who understands what he needs and blames no one for his inability to get it. Victimhood keeps us from seizing our fundamental power to make our own destiny.

Choosing to leave victimhood behind, you begin to see your family as the laboratory for a new definition of yourself. This new self is defined through your struggles and through your intimate relationships. To really engage with your family in a struggle for a meaningful relationship requires you to ask yourself some fundamental questions: Why was I put on this earth? What am I here to learn? The answer to those questions is found in the tension between the similarities and differences you have with your family. At no better time than during moments of conflict do we demonstrate character to one and all, including ourselves. The capacity to stay engaged in your struggle—with your family *and* with your autonomy—to continue to try to find the meaning for yourself, as well as to continue to be open to the meaning of another, is the definition of character itself.

Often, the very things our families deny us, the things they do that throw us back on our own resources, produce character-defining lessons in self-definition that force us to evolve. In essence, the Codes of Love in these conflicts release elements of the answer to our fundamental questions by knocking us back on our own resources at crucial junctures in our development. Our struggle with our families helps us identify our central needs and points us toward a quest for meaning that can define the direction of our lives.

June, the woman in the Introduction who wanted empathy from her father, wanted someone who could mirror her pain and soothe her wounds, and received instead her father's logical, solution-oriented columns of pros and cons. Her father was a logical, methodical man who didn't like to dwell on emotions. When he'd lead her through a nonemotional review of all the factors behind her dilemma, she was infuriated. June was annoyed by her father's plodding, deliberate deconstruction of a problem to which she'd attached so much passion. Her father would never understand her, June decided, and so she sought out friends who would empathize with her needs.

As June matured as a writer, she gradually came to appreciate her father's approach. He moved quickly toward finding the solution inherent within the problem without wallowing in the surrounding emotions. June realized that in adopting some of her father's style of rational analysis, she had developed what is called "informed empathy," which forges a strong backbone for her instinctual inquisitiveness. She became a brilliant essayist whose sense of the truth underneath the human dilemma pointed her to the lesson to be learned from every story. She became known through her writing for her deep understanding of human truths, reflected in work that was known for its balance of empathic appeal and logical solution.

When June's father demonstrated his method to his agitated daughter, he was showing a kind of love that June was unable to appreciate at the time. Her frustration distorted what her father was sending her way.

Often, this is the only way messages can be communicated in families. My father was reinforcing a deep-seated family code when he asked me to call him back and tell him how I got the money for food. He was saying—although I was too angry to hear it—"Add to the Bryan legend of self-reliance by solving your own problems with your skill and wit."

In order to decipher your family's codes, you've got to be able to receive the signals as they were sent by placing them in the larger context of your life and that of your family. Your first impulse will always be to refuse the coded expression. The heat you generate around that refusal and the anger your family may feel about their disappointment in you will also get in the way of those signals coming through. The signals are significant as the coded expressions of love, and your work in recognizing your own signal anxiety will help you see through to the deeper messages.

RECOGNIZING THE SIGNALS

People send out signals with every gesture they make. Watch a woman seated at a restaurant table place the fingers of one hand lightly across her lips. Is she holding in her words? Is she pensive? Is she shy? Is she flirting? Only if we know the context could we guess her mental state with any hope of accuracy. Even then, it would be at best a guess and probably a projection. Depending on how our own day has gone and what we are looking for in life at that moment, we might ascribe a meaning to her behavior that would more closely reflect our desires, not hers.

We all give off signals that are open to interpretation. Our downcast eyes when someone tells us a story can hide the shameful admission that we've done the same thing or an unwillingness to meet the speaker's eyes because we don't want to betray our doubts or our boredom. The step back when someone enters the room can announce our respect for this person or our fear. These signals we send out into the world with our unconscious movements are received by those around us through their particular filters of experience, temperament, and inference.

Say, for example, a man tells me the story of a painful episode from his past in a manner that is designed to shock me. As the tale unfolds, I place my palm across the top of my chest just below my neck. The speaker interprets this gesture as evidence he's succeeded in shocking me. To me, this is a pose of modesty, not the body-language equivalent of a gasp. I am humbled that this person chose to share this part of his life with me, and I am grounding myself in my body to honor the intimacy of the exchange. With the multitude of interpretations possible in the hundreds of signals we send out each day, it is no wonder intimacy can be so complicated.

Family emotional fields further complicate the transmission of signals. At a family gathering, each person's emotional field is charged with the atmospheric pressure that comes from the clash of the different energies family members bring with them into the room. When you walk into such a room, you can almost feel the mood; it is as palpable as the weather. Grandma Minnie's kitchen was always warm, but my family's house had frequent storms and periods of that sweet-smelling air just after the rain. We've all been in houses where the air is dry as a dusty sandal or the atmosphere is as chilly as a snowfall. Individual energies swirl and blend. Storms build and disperse. Low-level depressions and cold fronts separate us from each other.

Communicating through this is often as difficult as trying to get a clear signal from one cell phone to another. There is no way to change the interference. It exists to some degree or other everywhere. There is a way, however, to best receive what's being sent to you and to best ensure *your* communications are getting through.

Examine the way you listen to others. For many of us, myself included, the mind seems to operate on a minimum of two channels. I hear some of what the person who is speaking to me says while my mind churns away on a different subject. I take in some of what my companion is offering, but I also think about something someone said earlier and what I have to do tomorrow, and am further distracted by the sensory input of everything in my surroundings. If I'm in a defensive state of mind, I may just wait for the speaker to stop, not hearing a thing he said, while I formulate my next speech, which in no way could be characterized as a response under such circumstances. My mind is so crowded with my own concerns and perceptions that I'm most likely only receiving fifty percent or less of what my companion is offering me. In a family situation, cut that fifty percent in half.

LISTENING TO YOUR FAMILY

To understand your family's Codes of Love you must listen to what they are telling you, but you must listen to them in a new way. Listening to your family is a revolutionary idea in and of itself. For many of us, the only way to survive in the family was to withdraw and go deaf or employ some form of selective hearing. In our childhoods and as adolescents the messages we found in what was sent our way were too jarring to absorb. In the complex family atmosphere, the static of so much that is unsaid often crowds out actual information that could be useful to us. Each time we walk into a family event, our minds become overloaded with signals sent, signals garbled, and signals received.

When you enter that family event, you often have no clue

what has transpired in the lives of your family members that may influence their moods and reactions. But unlike observing strangers at a restaurant, we have a long history with our family members, and we often assume that we know their minds. Nevertheless, each member of the family has his own view of history and her own separate meaning, and often we know little or nothing about what influences their moods and behaviors.

In many instances you may be so focused on the event itself that you ignore the extrafamily dramas in your own life that affect your capacity to receive the signals from your family: Are you anticipating the worst? Are you seeking approval from others? Are you feeling accepted or rejected? Are you worried about what should be happening instead of what is happening? Are you feeling inadequate or overwhelmed? All of these can affect your ability to clearly receive messages sent by similarly conflicted family members.

If you have been doing the work of this book, your ability to listen in the family context may be hampered by what philosopher Bill Isaacs calls the "crisis of emptiness": Will I fit in? Can I be truthful? Having started to question the way you've viewed your family in the past may be exhilarating in private, but when you are actually among them, the fact that they may not be exactly as you previously believed can be disturbing. Blame and judgment was the way you ordered your reality and defended yourself against harm from your family. Dropping blame and releasing judgment may make you feel vulnerable.

Remember: *Memory is not gospel.* If you allow for this, you may begin to question the fractious interactions you've had in the past and begin to wonder

- How should I treat them now?
- What can we say to each other?

- Who am I with my family if I no longer despise them?
- How do I show them I love them?

You do not need to have the answers to those questions. The only thing you need to have is curiosity. Curiosity can give you a powerful perspective on the world. The power of a question can invest you in its answer, which gives you the motivation to really listen.

Curiosity can empower you to find a new way to view your family with compassion and love. There may be questions about the family history that you couldn't answer or episodes you've re-examined that you'd like a fresh perspective on. All of these questions are answerable if you ask a question candidly and listen to the answer with care.

A NEW KIND OF REVOLUTION

This is not to say that if you return home with a big bunch of questions for everyone to answer, suddenly the family conflict will dissolve in an ocean of love. All change engenders resistance. Whenever we try to change, forces both internal and external will always rise up to support the status quo. Only by embracing the resistance do we gain the power to actually change. This paradox is the reason that many efforts to change fail. It is not necessary to do away with the status quo to change it—in fact, it is imperative that we embrace the status quo as a necessary condition for change. Therefore in order to change as people, we need to embrace our family, not abandon them.

Some in the family will not take kindly to being questioned or will be disturbed and defensive rather than encouraged by your new attitude—they are expressing their natural resistance to change. The key to remaining your authentic self is to stay emotionally present and engaged, while remaining out of the emotional turmoil. In this case that means to risk what organizational consultant Otto Scharmer calls "revolution."

There are many different styles of listening. The way a mother listens to a child she suspects of lying is distinct from the way a hunter listens to the forest for the sound of prey. Both listen with an objective—a search for something specific—rather than an openness to whatever might be offered up. Your partner in a conversation will pick up the way you cock your head and the searching or bored look that tells him you are close-minded. If he senses that he must defend himself, that your mind is made up, the exchange you have will not be as honest as you might like.

By employing curiosity we can change the interaction from one of advocacy to one of inquiry. When you are advocating your position—persuading, arguing, blaming, defending—you are not listening. To be attentive and relaxed while listening will allow for the possibility of fresh meanings to appear between you and the person with whom you are speaking, even if the other person is defending herself. Through curiosity you can communicate trust and comfort and love. You can honor the experience of another in a way that expresses a willingness to learn.

So little silence hangs in the air between people. Many feel they aren't doing their part as a conversational partner if they allow even a few seconds of dead air. It is in this very hesitation, this moment of present-time reflection, that the creative possibilities of listening can free up both the speaker and the listener for a new perspective. Most of what we know about life in the family can have several different meanings: if you truly listen to your family, you can find that meaning everywhere, including within yourself.

PAYING ATTENTION TO FILTERS

Abby sought her meaning through connection. At first she was disappointed by the kind of communication she had with her mother. While Abby wanted hand-holding and heart-to-heart talks, her mother was a woman of few words who liked to share activities instead of emotions. Forced to hunt elsewhere for the intimacy she craved, Abby opened herself up to others outside the family. This ability to share innermost reality is a prerequisite for intimacy. When she found people who fulfilled this need, she was unfailingly loyal.

Abby formed deep and sustaining friendships because she gave so freely of herself. She has kept her close friends from college for more than thirty years, keeping in touch with them regularly by phone and mail, and more than yearly visits. With her need for explicit communication met by others in her life, Abby was able to see an elegance in the way her mother expressed love for Abby, a love that was deep even if it was communicated in gestures and shared activities. Learning to make the space for her mom's sparse words taught her even more about how to listen to others and value what they bring.

But, first, Abby had to learn to listen to herself. Knowing what you yourself really think and feel is the key to intimate exchange. As you enter a conversation with family members, you must first establish your personal weather report:

- Are you feeling dark or depressed?
- Are you brooding about some other problem?
- Are you feeling playful or sunny?
- Are you experiencing the world as full of hope?
- If there is something you have been rehearsing in your

mind, a point you want to get across, are you feeling a certain pressure to explain building in your head?

These are the filters that will color the meaning of the dialogue to take place.

Understanding your own state of mind compels you to maintain the common space, to honor it with thoughtful hesitation before you speak. It's unwise to say the first thing that comes to mind to fill that space; it's often wiser to honor that intimacy by saying the true thing that comes to you a few seconds later. If you are relaxed and attentive despite the interference from your filters, you can be mindful of the reactions you have to what your companion says. Being truly attentive can surprise you, in that the parts of the conversation you respond to may be different from what you expect.

If your nephew has launched into a diatribe against his father—your brother—your first instinct might be to defend your brother against unfair accusations of neglect. This reaction is one of loyalty to your brother and to your generation of the family, which is just now beginning to take the leadership role. You may feel an urge to build solidarity against the young. But if you allow yourself to be quiet in the common space between you and notice the response you are having to what your nephew is saying, you can create new meaning between you and your nephew. If your nephew complains that your brother is forgetful and disorganized—and he is—denying it to form solidarity with your brother will only undercut your credibility with your nephew.

If instead you pause, reflect, and then tell a story about your brother's disorganization and how you handled it when you were teenagers, you will validate your nephew and lend him a tool he can use in dealing with his dad, without your being disloyal or being drawn into a triangle. At any rate you will demonstrate a different kind of solidarity with your brother by signaling that when your generation is in charge of the family, there will be more honesty and discussion and less reflexive defensiveness. Listening and responding and staying engaged with the search for truth can be revolutionary behavior in a family.

Martin worked alongside his father in the family business, hoping to learn his father's secrets of success. Each time he'd ask his father's advice or opinion, his father would respond, "Do whatever you think is right. You have good judgment." This only infuriated Martin, who felt his father was entrapping and sabotaging him. Martin also suspected that his father secretly gloried in his failures. Even if Martin begged or got angry with his father, the answer and attitude was always the same.

When Martin held the common space between them and listened to his father's real message, he got the Code of Love underneath: Martin was listening for specific guidance but instead was being directed back to his own resources. His father had nothing he needed to prove to Martin. He was secure in his own being and wanted to make Martin the same way.

As Martin reflected on the silence between them instead of filling it up with his longing for something that would never be forthcoming, he saw the wisdom of his father's reticence. His father never criticized Martin's decisions, allowing Martin to make his own mistakes. What Martin heard—once he was able to truly listen—was that he needed to rely on himself. In reality, this failure to direct Martin was stronger support than if his father had shown him the method and logic behind all his decisions, and left him incapable of making his own.

RISKING REVOLUTION

Part of the dread we may feel when the family is coming together is the weight of all the slights and insults, arguments and withdrawals, that have colored events in the past. We often arrive hunting for an apology for some big hurt from the past. Our resentment renders us powerless to talk about the subject, which can spiral us further away from honest communication. If, instead, we "risk revolution," we say the unsayable and engage with an open mind, we gain respect for the possibility that an answer may surprise us. A revolutionary way to engage the family is give of yourself through honesty and curiosity, which is the more efficient way to effect a change because you are introducing new behavior into the old dynamic.

Connie's mother interrupted one Thanksgiving dinner with the unprompted declaration that Connie was a drug addict, which was something that her mother had done from time to time over the years, to Connie's embarrassment. Connie had had her problems with substance abuse, but those years were a long time behind her. This time, she saw her mother's strange outburst as a desperate attempt to gain attention and draw Connie into a fight, a fight that Connie would lose, as always.

In previous years, Connie had taken the bait. Her response had been to withdraw or to slam her fist down on the table and battle back. Certainly she had the same inclination this Thanksgiving. But on this evening she suppressed her rage and gave her mother what she wanted—attention. She said to her mother, "Mom, you know that was fifteen years ago. Why would you bring it up now?" The simple act of engaging her mother on the motivation behind her insult—and not on the content of the insult itself—diffused the situation instantly.

In responding with a question instead of trying to rebut the content, Connie exercised in that instant a revolutionary skill—separating feeling from thinking. Feelings should not be ignored, but used instead as a stimulus for a quick check-in to discover the real conflict: I'm feeling angry at my mother for bringing up my youthful drug use. Why? She is projecting her own fear of being addicted onto me, and that's unfair. She undercuts the career I've built, doesn't see me for who I am today, and wants to make herself the center of a drama that I don't want to be in. I don't have to be in that drama, so I'm not.

I know my mother loves me, Connie thought, attempting to encompass all of her feelings, her love and compassion as well as her shame and anger. *I also know she gets nervous on holidays and has had two glasses of wine, which always sets her off. Maybe I should ask her why she brought this up out of the blue. It's a mystery to me, when you come right down to it.*

In asking the question, Connie wasn't seeking a final answer but actually got across the message that was most important to her: she reminded the rest of the family that she was no longer on drugs. By engaging with her mother in this revolutionary fashion, she built a new common space between them. She attended to her mother's desperate need to be noticed and, in doing so, allowed the absurdity and childishness of her mom's remark to hang in the air. The contrast between her mother's insult and Connie's mature response silenced her mother on the subject, at least for that evening. From that point forward, a line in the sand was drawn: I will not go with you into that space that makes me feel bad.

When you risk revolution by being curious about the family's patterns and habits, you risk real intimacy. If Connie had raged back at her mother, as she always had in the past, they would simply have played out an old drama on the stage of the Thanksgiving dinner table, demonstrating a flawed relationship and tension that would be registered once again in family history as the "thing that ruined Thanksgiving."

In fact, Connie and her mother have a cordial relationship that is marred only by brief storms, but most of them have taken place at family gatherings when stress is high. Connie broke through this pattern by bringing her mother back into that intimate space between them, where Connie could be calm and they both could be held responsible for their comments and behavior.

BREAKING DOWN DENIAL

You cannot know what others will say when you openly address a family secret. But replacing a widespread denial is a powerful way to risk revolution and create intimacy.

Everyone in Caroline's family was very proud when her mom quit smoking after thirty years when she started having bronchial difficulties. She got a lot of pats on the back and support for her struggle. Caroline went home for a visit and observed that her mom frequently disappeared for a few minutes. One time when she came back Caroline distinctly smelled tobacco on her clothes. When she brought this up to her father, he denied it was true. "Your mother quit smoking two years ago," he said. "I don't know what you're talking about."

This left Caroline in a quandary. Her family was collectively denying something that could end up killing her mother. On the other hand, she didn't want to disturb or disrespect her parents by confrontation. Family secrets are poison, even those as relatively benign as Mom sneaking a cigarette. Secrets create emotional estrangement and distort reality by keeping anxiety at a higher level.

When Mom showed up at the dinner table reeking of tobacco, Caroline fought the urge to stand up and say, "You're all fooling yourself if you think I don't see that Mom's still smoking." Had she done that, the drama would be about Caroline and what they'd been hiding from her rather than about seeking a solution to the problem.

Caroline took her mother aside in the kitchen and created a common space of intimacy and curiosity in which Caroline could seek answers in a loving and concerned fashion. She asked her mother if she'd ever tried the nicotine patch or some of the other antismoking therapies and offered to take her to a doctor for a consultation. At first her mother was defensive and denied that she was smoking, but Caroline maintained her curiosity and refrained from engaging in battle. Finally, her mother softened, happy to be able to discuss the situation once she was sure she was not going to be blamed. Guilt and denial lie at different ends of a continuum, and we must try to find the middle ground—the place where we are not in denial, yet also not guilty for pushing our own agenda. Asking the question of her mom broke through the family denial in a way that said, "I love you, I want to help, and it is your decision. "

Everyone brings their particular blend of denial and guilt into the room—the images of your most glaring mistakes; the forgotten strengths and basic traits, gleaned from the great chain of generations; the attempts to protect family members from their failures; the mental snapshots of your family engaged in activities in the past. The static created by these layers of emotions and memories makes it that much harder to receive what's really being sent in present time.

A sister and brother—one successful and one struggling—attended a Fourth of July picnic. Andrea, the successful sister, met up with Dan at the drink cooler. While Dan told Andrea about his new prospect of making a killing in business, Andrea saw images from the past of Dan asking her for money when a deal fell through. This history also included Dan writing bad checks on Andrea's account and apologizing for it afterward in a way that was unsatisfactory to Andrea.

Both the blessing and the curse of their family life were compressed into this exchange. Part of what we love about being in a family is the depth of interaction, but it can also be what we hate about the family if we are trying to leave some of the past behind. The avoidance of the truth in an effort to protect our family members from their reality doesn't serve either party well when trying to bring our relationship into present time.

Typically what would have gone on in Andrea's head as Dan detailed his grandiose scheme would have been a soundtrack best characterized by the sarcastic phrase "Yeah right!" To really listen to Dan, Andrea had to put aside the emotions and images of the past and ask the questions she was always longing to ask, risk the revolution of intimacy by saying, in a loving way, what she really felt, but saying it in a way that might actually help her brother.

Choosing revolution over rhetoric, Andrea said, "You sound very excited by this idea, Dan, but you spend so much time telling me how easy it's going to be. I expect you'll have to work very hard too." This in itself was a revolutionary attitude to take toward her brother's grandiose plans.

"It's simple," Dan replied. "You buy that first building and fix it up, then you buy another, and another and pretty soon you're managing your empire by cell phone from your box at Yankee Stadium." Despite Andrea's new attitude, Dan responded as he always had in the past. Yet this time, Andrea did not resent his hopes, or buy into the scheme—it was not her job to finance his life.

"I love you and I can't give you the money, but it sounds like a great place to run a business if you can get away with it," Andrea said. "But for me, I've always found you have to love the work itself, not just the fantasy of what happens after you succeed. It takes a lot more hard work to realize that fantasy than you anticipate going in."

In this exchange Andrea did not throw negative pictures of buffoonery at Dan, but she also didn't support his delusions. She registered her opinion and gently advised him, in a way that honored her sadness at how often her brother had been bamboozled by get-rich-quick fantasies. Previously, she would have undercut him, tuned him out, rolled her eyes, or changed the subject—all of which would have dodged the real issue. This time Andrea was authentic and truthful without being sucked into the age-old paradox of families: Is it love or codependency? Am I being truly supportive or am I enabling someone to avoid the responsibility for their actions? Am I being false to myself or true?

In a family the conflict between wanting to support your family members in their endeavors and knowing when they need to be left alone to solve their own problems is a source of constant tension. A sister may think that her parents are being heartless when they refuse to put up the deposit for her brother's apartment so he can get a new start after losing his job. The parents may know how careless the brother has been with money and irresponsible with his job and want him to feel the consequences of his actions, hoping this will motivate him to mature. The children may think that the parents don't love their son, while the parents, who are pained by having to seem so stingy, know that sometimes refusal to help is the most loving act of all. Truly this situation is a Code of Love, a moment when meaning clashes with meaning and the resentments, not the message of love, get through.

Barry made a tidy fortune in telecommunications, surprising everyone who knew the grinding poverty he came from. He felt it was his duty as the successful one to help the rest of his family out. He set up an account and transferred money into it monthly, enough to cover his mother's basic living expenses. He also sent a check for one thousand dollars each month to his single-mother sister to help her defray the cost of raising three kids.

Despite this generosity, the amount he sent was never enough for them. Each time he upped the contribution, his mother or sister would say they needed more or plead for him to cover a specific expense, such as a computer or a new dress for the high school dance.

This left Barry agitated. He had money, to be sure, but not an endless amount. He felt as though his relatives weren't using the money wisely, just expanding their lifestyle with the expectation that he'd come through when the money ran short. His initial generous impulse had created a depleting codependency that left him resentful and actually threatened him with financial ruin. There would never be enough money, he realized, if they were drunk with it. He also realized he was sending them money instead of sending them love. Yet, Barry didn't want to cut his family off completely, and each time he wanted to refuse a request for help he found himself feeling guilty.

Between adults, resentment is often a sign that you're enabling a dependency. If you are trying to save someone with your actions, if you cannot discuss the matter openly, if you are providing goods to keep the peace, or if you have an outcome attached to your generosity, you are in a state of codependency. In certain cases, enabling a relative can be the right thing to do: If your brother is trying to get his business started and he needs a couch to crash on while he works for the first check, you are being helpful, not codependent. If he's borrowing your extra car until he scrapes up the down payment so he can lease one on his own, it's fine, as long as he's still working every day to get off your couch and it doesn't go on too long.

Often the most we can hope for is to stay engaged with our family despite our conflicts and miscues. Even when we can decipher our family's Codes of Love, the progress toward falling in love with our family may seem (and be) gradual. All they need to see is our continued interest in the struggle. Isn't that all we really need to see from them too? That they are trying? Perhaps we may never actually have the kind of relationship where the bond goes beyond words and the love is present in the air around us—our love and respect communicated in signals clearly sent and always received. Yet if we can learn to stay engaged and speak our truth without anger, and hear their truth and not judge them—then in our own way we are much closer to unraveling our families' personal Codes of Love.

Codes of Love Exercise: THE CODES

- What were your family's signals of affection?
  - Of disappointment?
  - Of anger?
  - Of joy?

- What kind of weather does your family usually experience?
- How well do you listen?
- Who is the best listener in your family? The worst?
- Are you waiting for the big apology from someone in your family? From a friend?
- Have you risked revolution lately? If you could, what would you say? To whom?
- Can you hold the common space of inquiry with that person? If not, why not?
- Do you notice any signal anxiety as you answer these questions?
- What new love have you found that was coded?
- What are your family's Codes of Love?

CHAPTER 7

Falling in Love with Your Family

As the holidays approached the year I was writing this book, I decided I couldn't go home for Christmas. Although I was now connected to my family and we had regular contact, it had been three years since I'd been home for the holidays. The tendency to postpone the visit was almost automatic. While I was in graduate school and teaching, it seemed like an awfully long trip to make, and I had such important work to do. With the book, I was on a tight deadline. Taking three or four days off to fly to North Carolina seemed like too much of an interruption.

I didn't intend to ignore my family. I was sending money so my sister and mother could buy presents for themselves and the kids. I had bought a plane ticket home for my nephew Matt, who was living with me and going to college here in Los Angeles. I intended to call them on Christmas Eve or Christmas Day, between sessions of research and reviewing assignments from the Codes of Love workshop I was teaching.

At the end of the final workshop before the holiday break, just as everyone was filing out, two of the students innocently asked where I was going for the holidays. Before the question was out of their mouths, I could hear in my mind what I had told them about the importance of holiday observances and the need for ritual. As I described my plans—reading, studying, and writing—I realized that I, too, needed to go home.

I made last-minute reservations for airplane tickets, a hotel, and a car. I would have to fly in without telling them because they had no phone. At once, I felt the thrill of making a surprise visit.

On Christmas Eve, I flew across country and then drove an hour in an ice storm, nervous on the slippery, now unfamiliar roads. As I approached their town, I realized that, since they had recently moved, I didn't know exactly where their new house was. I bought a map at the Mini Mart and drove around in circles, my frustration increasing as I was unable to find them. I had to surrender the first part of my reunion fantasy of a home-cooked Christmas Eve dinner when hunger forced me to stop at a Waffle House to eat.

Back in the car after dinner, I jabbed at the radio trying to find a station that wasn't playing Christmas carols. My reaction to carols is a good barometer of my holiday mood. I'm usually a big softy, and carols such as "O Come All Ye Faithful" can bring a tear to my eye. This Christmas Eve, as my frustration and anxiety grew, the carols reflected a sentiment I barely remembered having. Minutes before I found their neighborhood, I came across Handel's *Messiah*. My spirits were lifted by the majesty of the music. Its elegant simplicity and the power of the voices soaring together made life seem hopeful and worthwhile.

My frustration had diminished and my holiday joy and anticipation had returned by the time I finally found their street. Most of the houses had no numbers, so, it came down to a choice between two. My eyes roamed between them: one decorated with lights and tinsel and the other dark and deserted.

The dark one must be it, I thought. As kids, none of us ever liked putting up the Christmas lights, especially because that meant spending an afternoon squabbling. Suddenly my nieces and nephew came bursting out of the brightly decorated house—not the dark one after all. I rushed up to greet them, and we all hugged, laughing in the cold North Carolina night. I was home.

Inside the house, there were more surprises. Heaped on the living room floor—in fact, covering the living room floor—was a mountain of presents. There was only a path through the presents to the television, and the tree was barely visible. My mom and my sister were on the couch watching the tube. I hugged them and sat beside them, determined to stay put and examine my feelings, just as I had instructed my students to do.

Slowly I gained perspective on my surroundings. There were nine people living in this three-bedroom house: my mom, Paula, her three daughters, and April's (the oldest daughter's) three children, plus April's boyfriend. It was like a gigantic slumber party. The noise level contributed to my escalating anxiety. The television, a stereo somewhere in a bedroom, and the constant hubbub of three children under the age of five and several barking dogs in the backyard made for a decibel level somewhere between a rock concert and a limited wartime engagement.

As I drank in the scene, the weight of what Mark Twain jokingly called "the full catastrophe" began to sink in: I noticed a broken doorknob on the back door, the bathroom door wobbling on one hinge, and a pile of kids' clothes in the kitchen. The old sense of too much to do and too little time returned to me from my past. I felt myself beginning to go somewhere far away inside.

In my past, this is the point where I would have started judging everyone for the mess, or cleaning up, or slumping into the couch and burying my mind in the television. Instead, I told Mom and Paula how great it was to see them and how happy I was that theirs was the jolly house twinkling with holiday lights.

I was cheered when I heard that my niece April had a steady job and had bought most of the mound of presents under the tree. April had also put up the Christmas lights. I remembered the Christmas fifteen years ago, when I'd loaded up the Lincoln with presents I couldn't afford to make a show of holiday cheer, when I felt I didn't measure up. I decided not to mention that obvious parallel to April: it would have seemed like a judgment disguised as a reminiscence. Instead, I simply congratulated April on her job and cooed over her newest child, a beautiful year-old daughter.

April smiled at the compliment as if to confirm my approval, and said, "Aren't I doing well, Uncle Mark?" I told April how proud I was of her, and the compliment was genuine. As had happened to me in my adolescence, her problems put her in the position of being the family's designated patient. The fact that she had a steady job was all that mattered, and my approval was all that was required. She deserved it, and I told her so.

Suddenly the exhaustion I'd been fighting swept over me in a wave. I said it was probably time for me to get to my hotel room and promised to return for breakfast.

"I never heard of such a thing. Sleeping in some old hotel when you could be with your family," my mother chided. "Why don't you just stay here? Curl up on the couch or on the floor with a blanket?"

I dodged my impetus to defend my decision.

"Mom, I need my own space to think and to sleep. I'm not going anywhere but to bed," I replied lovingly. "I will return in the morning."

"Paula, can't you make him stay?" she pleaded.

"I love you," I said gently as I hugged Paula. "I am so glad I am here and we can visit."

"I love you, big brother," she said, as she always does.

"I love you, sis," I replied as we revived the little "I love you" dance we've been doing since childhood. I hugged all the kids, who weren't in bed yet even though it was almost midnight, and I headed out the door.

The forty-two-dollar-a-night hotel room was far from quiet—the unintelligible murmur of the television next door overlaid by the hum of the heater—but it was a sanctuary. Despite my exhaustion, thoughts filled my head, preventing me from falling asleep.

I have often been upset by the choices my sister, mother, and even April have made. I have had to struggle with the frustration this causes me, and I did again that night. My inner critic tossed and turned in bed. Damn these women! Can't they take better care of their futures? What kind of life can they provide for these children?

Whose voice was that? Where was my compassion? I counsel men and women in situations identical to this every month in my Prodigal Father work, but when it comes to *my* family, that loving, understanding self steps out of the room. In the not-so-distant past, thoughts just like these and a tendency to lose my sense of humor had kept me distant from the members of my family. I had assumed at times that *I* knew best how they should live their lives and care for their children, and I had told them so in no uncertain terms. As I fell into a restless sleep, I dreamed that I lived on one planet and they lived on another. I refused to visit their planet because it was too noisy there and no one ever went to bed.

I slept in and missed breakfast at the house. As I drove over at ten to see what Santa brought the kids, I felt guilty. I thought the guilt was inspired by being late, but it was more an artifact of my restless night of judgments against my family. I hoped I would be able to maintain the loving, detached posture I had achieved the night before, but I wasn't sure. Suddenly on the radio came Handel's *Messiah* again, and I was once again swept away from myself by the beauty of the music. The music brought tears to my eyes as

I was reminded that perhaps there was a God who had a plan smarter and certainly bigger than mine.

Many hours later, after the presents and the dinner, everyone's patience began to fray. The two boys—Aaron, five, and Andrew, two—were fighting and fussing. At first I thought, This is Paula's problem and April's problem, not mine. Why can't they get these kids under control? Then I realized the little boys had not been outside all day.

I started to suggest that someone take them out when I realized there *was* no one else: April was working, Paula was cooking, and Mom's hip was too bad for her to keep up with them. Reluctantly at first, I pried myself off the living room sofa and began the hunt for their hats, coats, and gloves. They insisted on taking their lanterns, and after a brief battle about missing batteries, we headed out.

The boys burst out of the front door screaming in delight, and my nephew Matt and I had to jog to keep up with them. They ran in circles and at each other, their faces glowing with joy in the lantern light. Standing in the cold with these little lives buzzing around me, I was brought away from myself and into the reality of their world and the hard life my mom and my sister have to live. It takes so much work to keep a family together. That afternoon I'd helped Paula fold thirteen loads of laundry she'd brought home from the Laundromat: piles of little T-shirts and a tower of tiny jeans and miniature socks, which when heaped on the table came up to my chest. What a huge job parenting is, I remembered, a job that is never really finished.

Aaron was shouting and running. He ran away as fast as his legs could carry him, looking back to make sure his two-year-old brother was all right. Then he'd take off in another direction, but he never strayed far. Andrew, not quite three, was scared and frozen in the middle of the street clutching his lantern. I knelt beside him and drew him to me to comfort him.

Matt and I helped him decipher each faraway sound: the barking of a dog, a holiday party, the sudden honk of a distant car horn. My face beside his in the darkness, I appreciated how enormous the world outside his halo of light seemed to him. Having names for the sounds didn't seem to assure him as much as the presence of someone whose side he could burrow into. He'd only known me for a few hours of his life, but I was there beside him. I was family.

In that moment, the question of whether these kids would be all right someday no longer seemed relevant. What was relevant was how they were *right now*. For right now, they were having a good time, burning some energy and making some noise. For right now they were surrounded by family and by love. Children give and receive love so easily. All I had to do was be kind. The innocent seriousness of his face, as he struggled in these dark surroundings, transformed seamlessly to radiance as the sounds repeated and he began to trust his world. I hugged him tighter as his confidence grew, to acknowledge the gift his joy gave me. Then, with a spark of independence, he wriggled free and went off to chase his big brother.

We returned home, and after a brief skirmish over which toys would accompany them to bed, they fell into that hard sleep reserved for children.

Sitting back on the living room couch with the children asleep in the next room, I was reminded of something I have heard a hundred times: Eighty percent of life is showing up. Even though this was not my perfect house or my perfect kids, they were nonetheless God's children and deserved what attention I had to give them. As Andrew had done in the lantern-lit night, we are all doing the best we can with the light we have to see by. We cannot wait for the future to arrive and then say I told you so, which is the coward's way. The hard way, the *real* way, is to face the reality of another's life—the mediocrity, the despair, and the glory—and find the love in the commonplace. The true hero's way is not so much a battle but a surrender to the truth: I will answer when called, I will sit and listen, I will hear what they need, I will let the adults bear the results of their own decisions, I will contribute what I can, and I will stay engaged with them, and I will remember to love them without judgment.

"Uncle Mark, you seem different this year," April said.

"Different how?" I asked.

"Nicer, I guess," she said.

I realized then, that I had stopped wishing things were different and fallen in love with my family.

UNCONDITIONAL LOVE VERSUS UNCONDITIONAL APPROVAL

When you lead with your heart, not with your head, you can get to a place beyond words, a place of true connection. In those moments with Andrew, I was no longer judging his chances in the world, no longer concerned about what his future might bring. What was important was the lesson in the moment—the fundamental promise of safety and concern—that I could guarantee only for that short time. Immediately following moments of deep connection, doubts often rush up to protect us from the fear of disconnection: I'm feeling love, but what's the price? This is good, but is it enough? He is okay now, but what about tomorrow?

Some of us know the instant we fell out of love with our family, but for many of us the process was gradual. Others of us, are still in denial. The relationship continues in a superficial fashion, although we are emotionally absent, our emotions dulled—even while sometimes living in the same house. Luckily, evolution has helped us by building love into our genetic code—those early humans who protected their young and each other allowed the species to flourish. This love exists and still subtly drives many of our human interactions. The point of doing the Codes of Love work is to transform your love for your family into an active love that is satisfying and sustainable.

How, then, do you fall in love with your family?

When you think of being in love, the last people who come into your head are your family. The songs and movies of popular culture celebrate romantic love, the kind that people hope for and dream about, the kind that is supported by ancient myths. In romantic love, you are attracted to someone who matches your interests, values, and tastes. In this style of love you orchestrate the interaction with active pursuit, fantasy, and, if it is to succeed long-term, working to maintain the relationship. When it is working, particularly in the beginning, you feel known, seen, and understood. With many love affairs, when you break up, it's over. With families it never ends.

Love in the family is less specific. If asked, most people would likely say, of course I love my family. In most cases, it would be embarrassing to admit anything short of love for them unless they are dangerous or destructive people. But family love is frequently reflexive, inactive, and extremely conflicted. For many this kind of being in love is mostly driven by a sense of obligation. Most people don't work on their love with their families; they accept it for what it is, the hand that was dealt them. There was a time as a child when the opposite was true; love for your family had all the qualities of a romance.

As children, our parents were like Macy's Thanksgiving Day balloons: figures much larger than life, who loomed over every aspect of the day, casting enormous shadows. Each action we took, each decision we made, had greater meaning when described to our parents, just as we feel as adults with our beloved when we are in a state of romantic love.

One has only to observe the way a little boy looks up to his father, as if he were the most powerful and intelligent creature ever born, to recognize a sense of adoration mixed with complete trust. One has only to read the astonishing things little girls write to their mothers on handmade cards every Mother's Day to appreciate the delirious quality of the love a little girl can have for her mom. I once saw one from a seven-year-old girl that ended with the line "I love you, Mommy, because you are the most beautiful and the kindest and greatest mommy that was ever born and because you love me." We have all seen those cards. Most of us have written them.

This love, released by complete surrender, becomes the template for our later romantic love affairs. The object of our romantic love is an enormous figure to us for whom we are capable of extraordinary feats of self-sacrifice. When people fall in love, they work toward a form of blindness, worshiping the ideal, wishing that no annoying complexities interfere with the attachment. Each time we begin a romantic love affair, our family—our mother, our father, and our siblings—are all present, influencing our images of what we expect from love and how much we are willing to sacrifice to get it.

Although you have developed a new perspective on your family dynamics through reading this book, remember that every time you are in the room with your family, the emotional field will act as a powerful gravitational pull, trying to draw you back into the old patterns. It will take vigilance to keep from activating the protection of the old defenses. Sometimes, nothing seems to work.

What, then, you may think, is the point of doing this work if I can't change my family? If I can't change them and I can't stop them from making me crazy, how can I ever find a way to truly love them?

In fact, the only part of the family you have the power to change is yourself. By changing the way in which you express love to and experience love from your family, you will have a starting point to influence the other love relationships in your life. Falling in love with your family as an adult will allow you to establish a satisfying and rewarding person-to-person relationship with them that will be your new model for love in the world.

In his classic exploration of love, *The Art of Loving*, Erich Fromm examines the unique nature of love between a parent and child and advocates that it mature into a more active state. Born into a state of perfect fusion with the mother, the child comes to know love as a passive state. "I am loved because I am my mother's child," Fromm writes. "I am loved because I am helpless. I am loved because I am beautiful, admirable. I am loved because mother needs me. To put it in a more general formula: *I am loved for what I am,* or perhaps more accurately, *I am loved because I am.*"

For many of us, this infantile version of being in love with the family persists. This passive attitude is framed through questions: "Why don't they love me?" Or it is explained in declarations: "I've never really felt loved." "They don't understand me." Fromm says, and I agree, that mature love is an act of potency: "Infantile love follows the principle: *'I love because I am loved.'* Mature love follows the principle: *'I am loved because I love.'* Immature love says: *'I love you because I need you.'* Mature love says: *'I need you because I love you.'*"

Many times I've heard people complain that what they want from their parents is unconditional love. When they describe the content of their interactions with their parents, I come to understand that what they want is unconditional approval, much like the women in the beginning of the previous chapter. Though they dismissed their mother's observations as annoying and unnecessary critiques, in fact they wanted continual expressions of approval from her. These continual expressions of approval are the *child's* conditions for love, the way in which a *child* experiences being.

The person who squawks about wanting to be loved unconditionally typically places plenty of conditions on the love they offer in return.

THE NEED FOR LOVE VERSUS THE NEED TO LOVE

The idea of falling in love with our families often conjures images of sitting around holding hands and having heart-to-heart talks. Yet, there are many ways that people share love, just as people grieve and express joy in a wide variety of ways. Finding authentic love for our family often begins by our growing up to love's many faces.

According to Fromm's characterization of it, in immature love, the beloved object sees himself reflected in the eyes of his beloved. The point of the interaction is to always be seen as beautiful, perfect even in the smallest and excusable flaws. Truly intimate love has its eyes wide open to the many flaws of the beloved and accepts them, even loves them, as all too human aspects of that person's whole character.

Abby always felt distanced and detached from her mother. They never had long cozy chats about their lives the way Abby and her girlfriends did. Whenever Abby tried to turn to her mother with a marital problem, her mother would say vaguely, "I am sure it will be fine," and proceed to change the subject. When Abby heard other women talking about the loving and complex ties that bind mother and daughter, she felt sad for what she and her mom had missed.

Abby decided to try to understand her mother better by asking about her mother's childhood. Although Abby knew that her grandmother had been aloof, she had not realized that her grandmother was often depressed. Abby's mother, normally so emotionally closed down, cried when she told Abby about her own mother's threats of suicide. With this new information, Abby began to forgive her mother's emotional distance. She understood the history behind her mother's attitude that "If you don't talk about it, it isn't a problem."

Trying to decipher her mother's Codes of Love, Abby remembered how hard her mother had worked raising a family on a low budget. She realized that her mother, like so many of her generation, showed her love by doing not by talking. Abby remembered how excited her mother had been whenever she sewed a new dress for Abby.

Armed with this new knowledge, Abby stopped trying to discuss subjects that made her mother uncomfortable and began to ask her mother for help with household projects. Abby had been dying to decorate her new house but couldn't afford most of the things she had in mind—especially a particular kind of blue floral drapes for her living room windows. Sewing the drapes would be a big job, but Abby's mom was happy, even eager, to help.

As they worked, Abby's gratitude grew. Her mother never complained and continued to work happily long after Abby gave up in exhaustion. Finally, the curtains were complete and the living room was transformed. Abby realized there wasn't another person she knew who would have worked so diligently and shared so thoroughly in the joy of the completed project. Abby's mother may not have known how to talk to her and may have found Abby's career and marital problems too confusing to discuss, but she enjoyed being part of Abby's life and was happy to show it through her actions, if not through words. Now, every time Abby looks at the beautiful living room, she marvels at the mother's gift of love.

When Abby stopped blaming her mother for not being a sympathetic ear, she found other things to admire. Abby's mother was independent and resourceful, and she did not criticize her daughter, as many of Abby's friends' mothers did. Her mother had many friends and interests and was determined not to be a burden on her children. Looking at her friends' mothers, Abby realized how fortunate she actually was. As she focused on her mother's strengths, Abby began to delight in her mom.

To turn our need *for* love into a need *to* love is a powerful act of maturity, an act of a mature self who understands his or her own limits and capacities and through them forges an active state of love. This kind of love is a gift both to yourself and to others.

Many people who have trouble loving their family have complained that part of the problem is that the members of their family are people they wouldn't choose to speak to under everyday life circumstances. Only because these flawed human beings are members of their family are they forced to interact with them. This is the land-mine–gold-mine paradox of love: the family's mix of characters—ranging from repugnant to heroic—is a laboratory for personal growth in your capacity to receive and give love.

As a child, Amanda's whole world revolved around her love for her father. One of her earliest childhood memories was of waiting by the gate for her dad to come home. Instead of taking up dolls and ballet as a child, Amanda learned to trout fish. As she said, "My world was perfect when I was with him."

Yet her parents' marriage was troubled. As a little girl lying in her bed at night, she often overheard her mother yelling at her father about his involvement with other women. So complete was Amanda's love for her father that her response to this was to wonder why her mother was making up stories about Dad. The only other woman in his life, as far as Amanda was concerned, was Amanda.

Her parents' marriage struggled forward. Amanda became the A student and star athlete, maintaining her position as her father's favorite as the family grew. She attended her father's alma mater and continued her academic success. One day, she decided to surprise her dad by showing up at his favorite restaurant. When she arrived, she saw her father engrossed in an intimate conversation with a woman roughly her own age. As she neared the table, it was clear to Amanda that her father and the woman were having an affair. She backed out of the restaurant—and out of her father's life—in shock.

Her glimpse of her father and his mistress destroyed Amanda's heroic vision of him. Her father had been her hero and now suddenly tumbled from his pedestal. Amanda's world order was destroyed, and her "Daddy's girl" identity shattered in pieces on the floor along with the fallen icon of her father. She felt that her father had cheated not only on her mother but on the whole family. Amanda reinterpreted each loving memory as a betrayal as the lens of suspicion reorganized her past.

The despair Amanda felt was overwhelming. Her judgment of her father was, in fact, a judgment of herself. If he was so bad, wasn't she bad also? She sublimated her self-doubt by becoming a hero child, earning the highest grade-point average in her college class, becoming valedictorian and embarking on a promising professional career. She deliberately married a man unlike her father, one to whom she was well-suited and, most important, a man who would never cheat on her.

When Amanda began her Codes of Love work, her motivation was to find a way to love her father. Despite her successes, personal and professional, the rift with her father marred her general feelings of contentment. Her parents had divorced when Amanda was newly married and over time had developed a friendship stronger than when they were married. If her mother was able to forgive her father, Amanda believed she should be able to find a way to do it too.

Discussing her feelings openly with her family, Amanda learned much. When her parents had married, they were passionately in love and her father was completely fulfilled by the marriage. As that passion ebbed to the more commonplace kind of intimacy, her father cheated on her mother seeking that passion again, a feeling that took him out of his depression and feelings of worthlessness.

Amanda had so idealized her father she had no idea that he had such low self-regard and might be capable of such basic acting out. Amanda realized that the real man who is her father is neither a hero nor a villain but a simple man who had struggled in his own way to get things right. In freeing her view of her father from extremes, Amanda began to see him in human terms. The person she adored as a child really did exist, but so did the man who made mistakes and lost his family in the process.

By no longer seeing him as either the shining prince or the family saboteur, Amanda was able to fall in love with her father all over again. She was able to regain sight of his good points when she no longer needed to see him in black-and-white terms. She was able to appreciate his ability to live in the moment and his sense of the right way to pace life and how to play, qualities that Amanda had lost in her own life when she disowned her father. In rediscovering her love for him, she was also able to love the more ordinary aspects of herself, slowing down enough to spend more time with her children and regain her sense of play. She had spent so much of her adult life in a tiring pursuit of perfection that the frenzy and drive had sapped much of her joy.

When we fall in love with our family, we engage them as characters with their own idiosyncrasies, viewing them in a completely new way: from a strong sense of self and an even stronger curiosity about who they truly are. Once we clear away the need to hunt for causality and place blame, we can return to the family spirit.

The first step on this new path home is to understand and then put aside the theories in this book so that you can look for the laughter and the joy in your family.

The forces that you now understand to be at work in the family are implicit. Making them explicit or confronting family members with this new analysis will only continue to keep you at an emotional remove. Do not arrive dispensing information about who carries the "anxiety for the family system" or "triangles" or "defense mechanisms." That would only be using the insight you've gained as yet another defense mechanism—intellectualization. It's just a new set of labels and a different language for blame.

THE PATH OF MOST RESISTANCE

During one visit home when I was newly therapized, I lined my family members up in the living room and said, "There is a fatal flaw in this family, and I'm going to find it." You can imagine how well this went over. I blush with shame and laugh when I recall that scene today.

Imagine if I had sat Grandma Minnie down to discuss the emotional triangle between Paula, my mom, and her or tried to explain how her agoraphobia might be an expression of the anxiety in the family system. She would have wondered why I was having such a hard time in life. Grandma Minnie understood family love in a way that I did not fully appreciate until after her funeral. Hers was a simple love—food and shelter and shared resources. I hope she would have heard my explanation of the family systems view of her world as my attempt to love her. But thinking back to Minnie's Codes of Love, I probably should have gone to her house and hoed her garden to show her I loved her.

The act of love, the act of potency, here, is to jettison the baggage of the past and simultaneously honor your own grandmother for her gifts, her role in the community, her humanity, and her sustaining position in the family, without wasting a single breath on trying to change her. This is a sign of respect as well as love.

The respect you offer her (and your other family members) is a measure of the new respect that you will have for yourself. You demonstrate and experience this new respect for your authentic self when you begin to have the strength to show your family the love they deserve.

The intimacy you crave, which is the reason you want to find a way to love your family, is difficult to experience at a distance. To fall in love with your family, as I said at the beginning of this book, you must go home. The real laboratory test for your newfound perspective is to expose yourself to all the messy frayed connections and misstatements of person-to-person contact.

The decision about whether you are strong enough, prepared enough, and compassionate enough to be a loving and authentic presence in your family is one only you can make. I urge you to reflect carefully on this decision and discuss it with the person with whom you've been doing your Codes of Love work.

Perhaps your resistance to going home is, as mine was the Christmas I was writing this book, reflexive. I talked about leverage points in the previous chapter, moments of weakness that are in fact potential moments of awareness, when defenses are down and real growth can take place quickly.

We are all aware of the path of *least* resistance. When you are stuck in a traffic jam, you can see how the drivers naturally gravitate toward the opening point in the bottleneck where the cars escape from the blockage. In emotional conflict, however, the path of *least* resistance is often the addictive path, the one we know best, the place of reaction not proaction. In returning to our family, we must remember that signal anxiety is addictive, and many of our actions in response to it disguise the feelings that motivate change.

This path of *most* resistance is frequently the fastest way out of a jam. Counterintuitive action is often extremely effective for subverting the status quo: telling people what you really think and feel instead of just going along, staying away from mood-altering substances, inquiring with someone about the very conflict that you have been avoiding, telling someone the secret you have been keeping.

Paul, whose conflicted relationship with his father we discussed in the chapter on remembering, took the path of most resistance to fall in love with his father. Paul's hatred of his father stemmed from the adolescent fistfights he'd had with his father and the drunken tirades of verbal abuse that ring in his ears to this day. A man like Paul, one would think, would have no motivation to find a way to actively love his father. Through years of psychotherapy, Paul has become accustomed to the idea that his social isolation, his problems succeeding at work, and his own former drinking and violent behavior were essentially his father's doing.

Yet even people from violent and conflicted pasts have a hunger for something better with their family. Paul's mother and sister both died early of disease, and now his family consisted of only his dad and his aunt. Each time Paul contacted his father, once a month or so, the calls were gruff, as Paul didn't really know what to say to his dad. He didn't want to abuse him, although sometimes the conversations became hostile. There were even times when Paul, lost in his own pain, prayed for his father to die, so he wouldn't have to deal with him anymore and so he could be relieved of the pain he carried around about his wounded relationship with his dad—and therefore himself.

Through his Codes of Love work, Paul began to understand that even if he didn't really speak with his father or if his father died, they would *still* be locked in battle until Paul found a way to respect his dad. So Paul chose the path of most resistance. Instead of ducking his father, he walked into the fear and the pain. He began to engage with his father. He started calling him every week or so. He asked his dad about his wartime service. They talked about all his father had hoped for and survived. Through these talks, his father became more human to Paul, and the fear began to subside.

For Paul, these conversations were profound, as the feelings of isolation his father described were identical to the isolation Paul felt. He began to see his life dilemmas as a reflection of his father's life dilemmas. "I started to feel sorry for him," Paul said. "Before this I had never felt anything but anger."

When his father told Paul that he had slipped on the ice during a snowstorm, Paul had a genuine feeling of concern for him. This was something that Paul never expected to feel, but suddenly their drinking, their rages, their struggles not to be violent with their intimates became points of mutual understanding rather than places of conflict. The counterintuitive action of expressing curiosity about the man who had "caused him so much pain" led Paul another step down the path of most resistance: in a move that surprised everyone, including Paul, he asked his father to move out to California so that they could be together in his declining years.

Slowly, Paul redeemed his own capacity for love. "I'd spent a lot of energy keeping that anger going," Paul said. "If I don't focus so much on the anger, it is easier on me and on him."

Falling in love with your family should not have to happen at a deathbed. It is possible that Paul and his father may never sit down and talk like figures in a Hallmark-card image of the family. But when you consider where they started, this new connection is nothing short of amazing. Sometimes just learning to be civil and respectful is as far as a person can go, but it is progress. For Paul, being able to drop the anger he has always carried is, in his world, equivalent to falling in love with his family.

We will all face limits as we begin to find the love we have for our family. You may have to try hard not to compare your family with others or with some idealized image of the happy family. As Tolstoy said in the famous opening line to *Anna Karenina*, "Happy families are all alike; every unhappy family is unhappy in its own way." Yet, even happy families have some conflicts, and all families have strengths.

For Emil exploring family photographs with his aunts and uncles was a transforming experience. In his Armenian family, Emil had always felt like the oddball, the kid who asked a lot of questions and wasn't satisfied by the cursory and frequently dismissive answers offered by the adults. This led to his being labeled a brat, a damaging appellation that stuck with him for years. In fact, when he sat down to look at old family photographs with his aunts and uncles after a Mother's Day dinner, his first question to them was, "Did you hate me?"

The projection exercise works beautifully in a situation like this. Emil's real questions might have been "Didn't I hate you? Didn't I hate myself?"

As an adult, Emil has been perpetually on a quest for happiness. He often jokes that the travel brochure he was handed about the way life was supposed to be—with its pictures of beautiful houses, financial security, and friendly, loving people—was a "snow job." When he was a boy, he was always comparing his family to other families. He idealized these other families, imagining them as happy and uncritical, with no major problems, a fantasy that kept him from appreciating his own.

In therapy, he'd picked apart his parents' relationship for clues as to the roots of his own low-level depression. His father was a cabinet maker who enjoyed the craft of woodworking but was never much of a businessman. Although the family lived comfortably in the suburbs, his mother had always wanted more. She was merciless, in Emil's memory, in her criticisms of the family's lifestyle. She always wanted a better house or car or more money for clothes. His father, who seemed content with things as they were, was removed from the marriage. After the kids left the house, Dad started living at his cabinet shop while building a new house to please his wife. A few weeks before the house was completed, Emil's dad died.

Emil's professional success slowly ebbed away after his father's death, which was an emotional shock wave that continued to shake the family for a decade. His brother started drinking heavily and was never able to hold a job for long. He lived with their mother, who frequently slept in the car to avoid the rampages of her drunken son. Emil's attempts to help them only met with vociferous rejection. The family shattered.

Sitting with his relatives on Mother's Day, Emil opened himself up to intimacy by asking the question whose answer he most feared, "Did you hate me?" The look of shock and puzzlement on his relatives' faces was the only answer he needed, but still he misinterpreted them. "No! You were a great kid," his uncle responded incredulously. Emil's suspicious mind-set immediately discounted this answer. Of course his relatives would say that. He remembered differently.

The relatives started producing photographs from his childhood: pictures of his parents in their twenties romping on the beach, joyful birthday parties, Emil with his prized train set. As image after image reawakened his stored memories, they began to describe a youth that had also been lost to him.

His relatives reminded him how proud his trumpet-playing father had been of Emil's teenage rock band and the way his mother had served as manager and promoter, getting the kids gigs in local clubs. His aunt recalled how his mother had invested so much of her own time and energy in his elaborate train set with villages and mountains that nearly filled a whole room. The elders also had amazing heroic tales of the family's journey here from Armenia and their struggles to get established.

As the memories piled on top of each other, Emil felt a long-forgotten emotion welling up inside of him—family pride. Through the pictures he embraced all that he had neglected, and through the history he found strength and heroism he'd never known. In a sense, he had to own his inner brat and realize that the distance created was as much his fault as it was his family's. He had to face the fact that as a child he had been embarrassed by his noisy, demonstrative Armenian family, so different from those more sedate families of his American peers.

As he entered the forgotten world portrayed in the family photographs, Emil could feel his view of his parents expanding. In isolation from our families, we isolate character traits of our relatives as well, turning a negative eye on aspects of them that could be seen as positive. At a distance, Emil had seen his father as incompetent, unambitious, and dreamy, essentially through the eyes of his hypercritical mother. He'd also been enraged by his grasping, perpetually unsatisfied mom, whom he blamed for killing off his dad with her bitter harangues. As with most things we hate in our family, these critical voices were actually holding Emil back, reinforcing his apathy about financial woes of his and his sense of never having or being enough.

Once he decided to turn his view of his family around, he was able to reenergize these same traits he loathed and use them to aid his own rehabilitation. His father had been, in fact, a happy man with a strong visual sense, who found pleasure in the joys of everyday life. Emil was able to do the same, once he dropped his critical voice. His mother's hunger for something more made her an uncanny businesswoman who knew how to manage debt and get good prices for her work as well as the best price for things she bought. Emil strengthened his attachment to the positive sides of these traits and, in doing so, began to fall in love with his family all over again. This newfound family pride gave Emil the self-respect to disperse the dark clouds of pessimism that had hung around him for years.

Emil now says, "If I was asked to choose a family to belong to at this point today, I could say, yes, I would choose mine." In declaring that, Emil is also saying, "If I were to choose a life to lead today, I would say, yes, I choose mine."

Falling in love with your family is falling in love with yourself.

FAMILY COURTSHIP

Reconnecting with your family is a process, not a single act. We have to invest the same amount of time and energy in courting our families as we would in courting a spouse. We have to want to do the things they do, we have to be curious about their interests, we have to be interested in their goals and dreams, and we have to be concerned about their welfare and happiness.

For many years, whenever I went home for a visit, my mother urged me to attend services at her fundamentalist church. Since my adolescence, Mom's religious beliefs have been a source of friction between us—just as they were between my father and her, and between my father's father and my grandmother Elizabeth. As a result of this, I've always felt ambivalence about going to services with her, because I didn't want to endorse a religious viewpoint that I found repressive.

One Christmas, a more mature Mark came to visit. When my mother asked me to go to the Christmas Eve service, my inner response was, It's only an hour of my life. After all, over the years, my mother has had an earful of what I believe about her particular religion. That year, I had a strong enough sense of self to realize that attending this one church service was not going to compromise my identity.

As it turned out, that service in the small white wooden church was one of the highlights of my visit that year. I got to see my mother's joy at the service, as well as her strong bond with the other members of the church, where she is a loved and respected person. During the candlelight service itself, I cried so hard I couldn't sing along to "Silent Night."

Many of us create false separations from our families by remaining aloof from their everyday lives. There are so many little moments of connection available to us if we decide to be curious about our family.

Janice, a thirty-five-year-old advertising executive from Manhattan, refused to visit a Wal-Mart with her mother. Year after year, she considered it beneath her sophisticated urban tastes. Her mother, in turn, thought her daughter a spendthrift, throwing her money away in fancy New York boutiques. One year Janice decided, "What the hell. Who's going to see me, anyway?" She called her mother and suggested they go to Wal-Mart. They went and had a blast.

Janice bought a disposable camera and photographed the entire journey to prove to her friends she had done it. She shot photos of her mother in the parking lot, shaking hands with the greeter at the front of the store, and trying to decide between one laughable Christmas figurine and another. This episode helped Janice drop some of her pretensions and enjoy her mother's frugality. "I realized it is the ordinary stuff that I really love," Janice says, "because it reminds me of when I was a kid and went everywhere my mother went—to the hairdresser, the grocery store, the gas station. I realized that I miss that."

You do not need to share all the tastes, opinions, and interests of your family in order to be in love with them. In fact, it is probably a healthier and less fused family in which individuals are allowed to have and share their differences. The one thing you need most in order to fall deeper in love with them is curiosity. A simple question such as, "Why do you do it that way?" or "How does that make you feel?" shows respect, interest, and humility.

Inquiring with an open mind allows for intimacy, since it is a discovery that happens together. It is also often a surprise that preconceived notions disappear once you start to inquire. Curiosity is a great way of testing out the authentic self in the family dynamic: if you are inquiring, you are engaged emotionally with the person you are asking questions of, but your true self is still present.

A breakthrough in my relationship with my father came through just such a shift to curiosity. I realized one day that I was asking a lot of my older male friends for advice, but not my father. The absurdity of this was profound. My father has lived a rich and varied life and is as qualified to speak to me about car transmissions and mortgage rates as any other person in my life. Yet somehow it made me uncomfortable to ask his opinion. I was held back by the adolescent idea that I shouldn't need my father's advice anymore. I had to be on my own. Besides, if your father gives you advice, aren't you supposed to follow it?

This hang-up, I realized, was my own. My father was just pleased to be asked. I was buying my first house, and I asked him about mortgage rates, fixed versus adjustable, and he was pleased to give me his point of view. Since I am no longer a teenager bound to his opinion, I added his advice to the other advice I had been collecting and made my own decision. Instead of being upset that I hadn't followed his advice to the letter, my father was interested in what I had decided and how it had worked out. He respected my choice and my autonomy, partially because I respected him.

This is what we are working toward in falling in love with our families—a person-to-person connection of mutual affection and respect.

During that journey home to North Carolina that began that this chapter, there were many moments when I fought the impulse to turn around and go back to California—the place I have come to think of as *my* home. There were also moments when I was so excited to be with my family that I wanted to buy a house in North Carolina and move my life across country. Falling in love with your family will always bring up contradictions.

Crouching next to two-year-old Andrew, trying to make sense of the darkness that surrounded us, was a moment of connection, the kind that kept me on that road to home. Watching him grow from timidity to courage and feeling his body transform from shaking to confident was a powerful experience for me. He gave as much to me as I got from him. Alongside him, I could feel myself growing stronger too, with something to give that I barely knew I had—until I began to share it.

In that instant we didn't need to talk about the exchange, nor could words really describe what was transpiring. Our spirits intersected, and then he was gone, leaving me behind in the darkness, knowing that for the rest of his life, I would keep coming back.

Codes of Love Exercise: THE HOMECOMING

Go home.
You know what to do.
Good luck.

CHAPTER 8

Friends, Lovers, and the World at Large

In the introduction to the book we raised the question: *What if you were loved more than you know?* Now, here at the close, the question has transformed: *What if you can love more than you know?*

There's an old Persian folktale in which an aging grandfather went to live with his son's family because he's getting old and frail. After a time, the son decided it was too difficult to keep his father in the house. The quarters were cramped, and the old man was interfering with the family's routine. One day the son decided to take action. He told his young son to move the grandfather into new accommodations.

"Make room for him in the barn," he instructed his son. "But be sure that he's comfortable. Make him a bed on the softest pile of hay, and give him one of our best blankets. Make sure that he's covered and warm."

The next day when he went to check on the arrangements, he saw the grandfather asleep on a bed of hay covered by only half a blanket and ran to find his son.

"I thought I told you to cover your grandfather with our best blanket," he said angrily.

"I did," the son responded.

"But why did you give him only half a blanket?" the father asked.

"Because, Father," the son replied, "I am saving the other half for you."

How we treat our elders suggests to our children how we ourselves should be treated. Previously in this book, we have looked to the past. Now we turn our eyes forward. Feel your connection to the generations stretching backward and then envision this same chain stretching forward, with you as the pivot point. What we do today, how we behave toward others, and how we behave toward our children, will be reflected back to us—and through us—into future generations. Your capacity to provide for your own authentic happiness and share it with others will be a marker for all the members of your family who follow.

Authentic happiness is not a giddy one-time experience: it is not a ride on a roller coaster or a trip to Disneyland. This is a kind of happiness that radiates out from a profound contentment and strength of character—sustained by a deeper level of intimacy with those we love than we have previously experienced. Accepting our heritage, its struggles along with its strengths, allows us to accept and love ourselves, which in turn enables us to accept and love another: our spouses, our children, even our friends and neighbors. Freed from our old need for defenses and dramas, we are free to participate more fully in the relationships we have formed, and often for the first time in our lives, we can have compassion for another person's struggles without losing our independence and integrity.

Compassion is a position of strength because it allows the most flexibility in the give and take of intimacy. This strength—which is made up of the ability to be aware of emotional triangles, the ability to conduct ourselves according to our sense of value and worth, and the ability to demonstrate the trust we have for others—this strength is what gives us the wisdom to make the world a better place and make our lives more meaningful.

Through compassion, we become better sons and daughters; better husbands, wives, and parents; and better intimates. The legacy we can leave to all the generations of our families is the honor we choose to demonstrate or not.

We cannot repair every damaged link in the chain of generations, but we can mend those damaged links closest to us. The hardest part, I've found, in coming to grips with damaged links is to accept the responsibility that enables us to change. When people first begin to accept responsibility for their part in the conflicts that have marred their lives, they usually fall into the trap of saying, "Now that I take responsibility for my actions, I get to do whatever I want." Accepting responsibility means understanding the impact your actions have on the world around you and choosing to be responsible, not just for yourself but for the well-being of others.

If you frequently go through periods of a month or longer during which you refuse to speak to your mother, expect that your children will do the same to you when they reach maturity. If you find yourself raging through the house, screaming at your family because you just came home from work and the place is a mess, bets are your daughter will battle the same rage herself someday—unless you decide to put a stop to it.

The purpose of this chapter is to help us start examining our actions, not only with our family but with our friends and lovers, with a look forward into our future and the legacy we will leave to the generations to come.

The place to start using this forward-thinking approach is in your decisions with those members of your family who have been resistant to your efforts to spread peace. These are the people who, no matter how hard you try, sabotage your best efforts with their inability to let go of the past. The points of greatest conflict for us can often be the leverage points for the most powerful change.

ANNE AND BARBARA

From Anne's perspective, her mother, Barbara, was a monster, a woman who had done everything in her power to sow dissension in the family. Barbara, Anne believed, had positioned relative against relative and her children against her husband, while Barbara was always in the middle as the arbiter of the dispute—and as the hub of all the nasty gossip. Barbara had strictly controlled every detail of Anne's life and had been highly critical of Anne, even undercutting Anne to her own children. When Anne attended night school, Barbara pulled Anne's children aside to tell them their mother didn't care about them because she was away from home so often. Barbara always demanded one hundred percent loyalty and was brutal at the slightest hint of betrayal.

In her adult life, Anne was seen as courageous by her friends and her peers in the family because she refused to play into Barbara's power struggles. After one particularly bruising argument, Anne cut her mother off for good. Even though it was painful to maintain the breech, Anne remained adamant. She cut her children off from their grandmother. Several years later, when Barbara entered a nursing home after a stroke, the distance weighed heavily on Anne's shoulders. But after so many years of stoically maintaining her resentment—and feeling that separation was necessary to her mental health—she could not imagine repairing her relationship with her mother. Even though Barbara was now weak and incapable of divisiveness, Anne saw her mother as still manipulating, still finding a way to demand loyalty, and still in control. "A woman like that," Anne told her friends and cousins, "doesn't deserve to be forgiven." Ann even told her children that.

With Barbara so debilitated, it was soon Anne who looked like the mean-spirited one. Anne refused to visit her mother in the nursing home and denied her teenage children the chance to make their last few memories with their grandmother. At this final opportunity for peace in the family, it was Anne whose anger seemed cruel. Her actions reflected poorly on herself, not on her mother. Those actions signaled to Anne's children that if she was to fall into dependency in her old age, the family culture approved of carrying a grudge to the grave and on into eternity.

What they say about apples not falling far from trees is usually true. Anne has much of the stubbornness and many of the manipulative skills of her mother, as demonstrated by her actions and her demand for unquestioning loyalty on the part of her children. And like her mother, she is unwilling to accept her part in it. She believes that there is no reason for her to drop the attitude of blame concerning the past and demonstrate simple acts of forgiveness and kindness to a dying woman. Nor can she see that this stubbornness will undoubtedly affect her relationship with her children, who will resent Anne's strict control, in precisely the same manner that Anne resented Barbara's.

I have compassion for Anne's struggle. Not many of us are big enough to drop long-held resentments. The order seems too tall. But most of the time the door to the soul opens slowly. At first being kind to her mother would seem like a weak act to Anne, an admission that her mother was right all along. The process of remembering, reflecting, and re-framing could benefit both Anne and her children—and may give Barbara some peace.

If Anne does not find the strength to be her better self, this dispute with her mother will color her relationships in the family and in the world for the rest of her life. She'll remain bitter about her mother long after Barbara dies, when Anne herself is in her senior years. The bitterness of this relationship will continue forward as a legacy for her children in the way they treat Anne and perhaps in the way their children ultimately treat them. The intensity of the emotion Anne feels around her relationship with her mother is a sign that it is her leverage point, and her mother's illness is the moment at which she has the choice before her to make her legacy one of hope, maturity, and forgiveness or one of bitterness and isolation.

The defining characteristic of a hero is that he or she *acts*. The hero may not get it right in one action but struggles on, defining character through his or her journey. In fact, character is usually made up of what we do on the fourth and fifth try. Anne's refusal to reconcile with her mother is not an act. It is, in fact, a lack of action, a position taken long ago and now made rigid by stubbornness. The heroic act would be for Anne to break the chain: if she were to remember, reflect, and re-frame her choices, she might understand why she and her mother are so similar and caught in such a painful situation. When you learn to rethink your family in multigenerational terms, forgiveness become irrelevant. The goal becomes to accept and make peace with the family, and thereby define a standard of behavior, without having to make speeches and proclamations about change. The only person you can change, should ever change, or can expect to change—is yourself. This is not leadership by commanding and cajoling or withdrawing; this is leadership through self-definition.

CHOOSING CHANGE

We carry the lessons of the past with us in aspects of nearly every decision we make. We can *choose* not to carry forward the blame and shame of our family conflicts. All of us want to be bigger, stronger, smarter in the future. We want to be more connected, more loving, more emotionally intact and capable as well. We also want to be grateful and understand who we are now, and we want to be appreciative of who we are becoming. "Holding the dialectic of the self" means embracing this paradox: The self is constant, but always evolving. We have a core self that is the "I" we experience as "me." I am me, and I will still be me when I change; in fact, I will be more me. This core self has needs and a need for expression that changes across the life span.

By maintaining a more authentic relationship with your family, you will be able to participate in their evolution—positive and negative—as you celebrate your own evolution. Maintaining this relationship with your family reacquaints you with *their* paradox—that they are the same and ever changing. Loving them in their imperfections as they age, laugh, lust, lose their way, succeed, and eventually die teaches us to love ourselves in our own imperfections. Embracing our own imperfection means that we will no longer reject love because we feel unworthy of being loved. Embracing the challenge of change, accepting and understanding things as they are, and observing the evolution around us means that we can remain a positive and loving force in that change. Then, in ever widening circles of influence, we can apply our new perspective to the evolution of our friends, family, our work environments, our communities, and the world at large. We will be able to give because we will be whole.

People often ask me how to get a loved one to stop a compulsive behavior, such as drinking too much or too frequently, overeating, or workaholically avoiding their family. In feeling powerless to help a loved one change, people frequently blame the loved one. I tell them that paradoxically we always have a part, however small, in the health of the extended family system. We must be willing to look for the answers and show up and be counted: we must stay engaged in order to help ourselves and everyone else in the process. Staying engaged is different from wanting to change someone.

Sally's a twenty-nine-year-old woman without the resources for therapy, came to me to help her mother stop drinking. I suggested Sally join a support group like Al-Anon, instead of just pointing fingers, if she wanted her mother to get sober. Taking action to help *herself* learn boundaries and emotional balance is the one thing Sally can do that will really help, not only her, but her mother.

If a wife wants a husband to stop cheating, she needs to find help for *herself* so that she disengages from the dance. If a single woman thinks that all men are jerks, she needs to examine her role in allowing them to walk all over her. The only person we can truly change is ourself, but the good news is that changing *ourself* changes *everything*. If we cannot influence a loved one to stop the destructive behavior, we can at least understand that behavior better and define our role in his or her life in a way that allows us peace.

In much smaller ways there are opportunities for these kind of changes every day. In fact, small changes really matter more than grand gestures. Harassed as we are by the annoyances and stress of our daily lives, it is nearly impossible to appreciate the impact our actions have on the future or to place those around us in a broader context. Someone cuts us off in traffic, and road rage makes us want to tail them and flip them off. A bank clerk is condescending to us, and we snipe right back and end up stalking out of the bank, coloring our day and everyone else's with our suddenly foul mood.

If we do not try to place these irritating people in a larger context, if we have no curiosity about what it might be in their lives that caused them to be this way on this day when you interact with them, if we forget that their actions are probably not personal to us, we will forever be at their mercy. Our annoyance at these events is understandable, but how we express our reaction to these irritations is the difference between becoming part of the generalized annoyance and having power over it. It is the same with our family.

FAMILY SCULPTING

While my initial impulse for writing this book was personal, working with these ideas in Codes of Love workshops has shown me they lend an important flexibility to our interactions with others. This flexibility is often immediately apparent in people who have worked with these ideas and stems from what appears to be immediate and very positive changes in their attitude when they frame their history in the Codes of Love approach. Since the early Codes of Love workshops grew out of my teaching style and intuition developed with the early Artist's Way and Prodigal Father workshops, I felt that I needed an experiential doorway, a hole for the imagination to go through, that might give workshop participants an external process to mirror their internal change. I found what I was looking for in an old gestalt game. This particular tool, developed by Virginia Satir, is called "family sculpting," and the process is described beautifully in Satir's student Bill Nerin's book, *Long Day's Journey into Light*.

In family sculpting, a group of strangers assembles to role-play the important moments in a family's past. The person whose family is being reconstructed—whom Satir called the star, usually much to the delight of the participant—chooses an alter ego to play himself and casts the others as the relatives. The star positions or sculpts the players in poses that he or she believes reflect the attitudes family members took during an important transition in the family's history.

As I said, I began to use a version of this technique as a way of showing my students what the internal process of re-framing their family would look like in three dimensions. Enacting the important moments from each of the students' family story lines gave us a dramatic entry point that provided a shortcut to the heart of that family's Codes of Love. The sculptures illustrated the forces that shaped family patterns in visceral images that might have taken workshop members months to come to through talk therapy.

As we experimented with this technique, the results were profound, not only for the individual exploring his past and for me as a teacher, but also for all the players participating in the tableau. Despite the fact that the players receive little or no information about the person whose pose they are adopting, from the pose itself they get an intuitive sense of the personalities at play and the effect of the sculpture on the sculptor.

The poses reflect the sculptor's attitude as much as that of the relatives who are being sculpted. For example, one workshop participant sculpted a family fight beginning with his father slouched back against a wall stirring a drink in a highball glass with his index finger. The sculptor posed his mother with her hands clasped demurely across the front of her body and with her head looking over her shoulder as she whispered dry criticisms. It is possible his parents never assumed these postures during this particular incident, but the poses were symbolic of their attitudes during a large part of his adolescence. His choices for how to position them were more about how he viewed their relationship to him and to the world than about the specific incident being sculpted.

We typically started with the subject's parents and sculpted their meeting and romance until the time the star entered the picture. Depending on my sense of what needed to be expanded upon, we either went forward into the star's life or went backward into the world of the parents' parents. Although the sequence was improvised, typically we visited all these parts of the past in one session.

After a tableau was complete, I walked through the players placing my hand on their sternums and asked them what they felt in the pose. Quietly and lovingly, they would describe the emotional significance of the position they had been placed in. This, too, resulted in a deeper understanding on the part of the star, but what was consistently amazing was how accurately the role players were able to intuit the responses of the role they were in. These were not performers; they were just people with families of their own. We all know much more than we know.

As we learned from family-systems research, a problem that affects us today frequently has its roots in the lives of our grandparents or the way our parents were raised. By making the world of the star's grandparents come alive, the star frequently gained a wealth of insight into the forces that shaped his parents and the way patterns of behavior transform yet persist across the generations. Sculpting some of the big moments or family legends from the star's parents' lives built compassion and understanding for the parent with whom he or she struggled. Once that compassion was in place, the same compassionate attitude traveled outside the family dynamic, to be reflected in the star's and the role player's interactions in the world at large.

Some participants had the impulse to dismiss this as improvised melodrama—a bunch of strangers playing your aunt Sarah and uncle Jerry and everyone in between, announcing their own feelings as they "channel" your relatives. There is a certain expectation about the appropriate emotion for an event, such as the death of a loved one or a child leaving home, and sometimes the results were banal. After a death scene, when I would put my hand on the sternum of, for example, the dead person's "daughter," she would invariably say, "I feel sad." Or the man playing a father whose daughter left home would say, "I'm so alone. My baby's gone."

Yet, the group frequently uncovered insights that were surprising, counterintuitive, and often eerily inexplicable—what one member of my first group finally labeled "big juju." In one reconstruction, the star was posing the players in scenes from her teenage years. She chose to move from a happy scene that took place when she was thirteen directly to a skiing accident that took place when she was seventeen. As she started to position the players in the poses they would have been in during the time of the accident, the woman who was playing the star as a teenager burst into tears. "I don't know what's happening," the player said, "but suddenly I feel as though I'm in a really dark place." She sank to the floor.

The star had wanted to skip over a sexual molestation incident from her early teens, but something subtle in the star's demeanor must have cued the woman who was playing the star to experience the sorrow, isolation, and shame of that incident. We ended up sculpting that scene to examine the dark feelings. The perspective the star got on her family dynamic from this exercise helped her greatly in moving forward from this incident and making peace with the person who had caused her so much heartache.

These odd intuitions are gratifying to the group, shoring up their confidence in what is admittedly a fairly unusual way to spend the day. The most gratifying aspect of the process is the effect it has on the person whose life we sculpted. Without fail, the star comes away from the session changed.

One woman looked visibly lighter after a session in which we spent much of our time trying to understand her mother's grasping bitterness. Through sculpting, we explored her mother's hopes and dreams as a child and came to see how an early bad marriage and poverty shook her fragile sense of optimism and crushed her resilience. Understanding this relieved the star of the feeling of responsibility for her mother's happiness she'd carried with her since she was a little girl.

Paul, the man who hated his violent father, began communicating with his father weekly instead of once every couple of months. He eventually started arranging for his father to move to California to live nearer to him. Nancy, the woman who found out at age sixteen she was adopted, suddenly got a call from her brother to whom she hadn't spoken in five years. They are now back in regular contact.

While the effect of the work is most powerful on the person whose family is being sculpted, the players report back that the work affects them in their daily lives. One of the best examples of this is the sculpting we did of Wallace's family.

Wallace, a forty-six-year-old college professor and artist, is a joyful, soft-spoken Chinese American man. He came from a close family but always felt estranged from his father, George, a man who, though a loyal and constant presence, was emotionally removed and withdrawn. George spent most of his time and energy with Wallace's mother, May, running a souvenir shop. George never spoke much and seemed to experience little happiness in life. Wallace and his father were sometimes close, but Wallace often felt his father didn't seem to be close to anyone. Wallace used his sculpting to satisfy his hunger to better understand his dad.

We started at the dance where his mother and father met. George was a dashing bombardier, a Chinese national, who had been recruited to join in the effort against the Japanese in World War II.

Shortly after they met, George went off to training camp. May and he kept in touch through letters and phone calls, marrying just before he shipped off to bomb Japan. After the war was over, he remained in Asia. His family was fiercely anti-Communist. He signed up to be a bombardier in Chiang Kai-shek's army. George, loyal to his family and his native land, was assigned to drop bombs on his own country.

Wounded in battle, he ended up in a hospital in Shanghai while the Communist forces were marching on the city. A friendly doctor warned him that if he ever wanted to see his family again, he should flee immediately, because when the Communists arrived, they would surely kill him. He was smuggled out on a boat to the United States. The family George left behind in China were all killed in battle or ended up serving lengthy jail terms for espionage once the Communists took power. To his sorrow, Wallace couldn't really tell us what had happened to his relations back in China. Not only had his father been a man of very few words, there was a lot about what had happened to his own family that he just didn't know.

When George arrived in Los Angeles, the immigration authorities detained this decorated war hero who had served his adopted country proudly in battle. As he was coming from Communist China, he was deemed a suspicious character. After his frightening epic journey from China to the United States, he withstood two weeks of interrogation before he could see his American family. When they were finally reunited, George opened an Oriental curio shop and spent most of the rest of his life there.

Time and again in the Codes of Love work we touch upon these family legends, the stories that the family tells over and over again when discussing the life of one of its members. These tales are often told without a real understanding of the historic or cultural realities that made them so captivating in the first place. There is often no way to comprehend the personal impact of wartime, or poverty, or the immigrant experience, or a cultural revolution, whether here or abroad, unless we ourselves experienced it. Yet knowing these difficulties exist in our family's past can open the door to understanding.

Through sculpting, George's agonizing journey from country to country in search of home demonstrated to Wallace in a three-dimensional, highly emotional fashion the reason why his father had been so removed: he'd been a war hero, he had sacrificed for his adopted country, he had bombed his homeland in the name of a cause, and he had lost all of his family. Through much of his life, Wallace had defined his dad within the confines of his experience of him—a quiet and unemotional man who ran a souvenir shop. After viewing his father within his cultural milieu and family history, George's reticence and withdrawal no longer seemed so incomprehensible to Wallace. The depth of his father's feelings and his heroism came through.

For the rest of the workshop participants, the effects of working on Wallace's story were also powerful. As we went around the room at the close of Wallace's story, the group, mostly middle-class well-educated humanists, was in a state of shock. The story exposed a more subtle form of prejudice and ignorance than they had thought about. Most of them were completely unaware of the history of China during World War II or the lives of Chinese Americans at the turn of the century. By seeing it in the personal record of Wallace's family, they began to understand the price of that ignorance. Several realized they'd actually been customers at George's shop.

"He was just the man behind the counter to me," one woman said. "I didn't even think about him. I had no idea he had such an incredible story."

"How many people in the world do we do that to every day?" another workshop member asked. In the weeks that followed, she said, she began to notice the people who worked behind the sales counters where she shopped, imagining for the first time what their lives might be like, what special qualities might be hidden by their role as a clerk or bag boy or cashier. She began engaging them in conversation and found to her surprise that almost everyone has an interesting story to tell.

The four postulates of how you make meaning in the world apply equally to the circumstances you find yourself in and to the attitude you spread into the world:

- Are you benevolent or malevolent?
- Do others see you as safe or threatening?
- Is your life meaningful or meaningless?
- Are you worthy or unworthy?

After sculpting Wallace's family, members of the group reported back at the next session that their attitudes toward strangers they came across in the world had changed. One man said when he was cut off in traffic, his first thought was, I wonder what's going on in that woman's life that's making her so pushy? A man who was being treated rudely by a bank teller simply expressed his displeasure with the treatment and called the manager over to discuss it in front of the teller. Another participant went bike riding with a group of former racers that weekend. They were cycling down a city street and a car cut through their line, nearly knocking several of them over. She raced up alongside the car to tell the driver what she thought of him, as she had often done in the past. When she saw he had two young daughters sitting in the backseat, she said "Hey, mister. What if that was one of your daughters on this bike?"

Had she sworn at him and flipped him off, as was her first impulse, the driver might have easily dismissed her as a militant cyclist or an angry young woman and soothed himself by explaining how he had been driving safely and the nutty bicyclists were in the wrong. Instead our rider chose to close the space between the two of them with a personal observation of shared experience. With the rude bank teller, the dynamic was similar. The workshop member decided to make the teller responsible for his behavior and risk taking a little blame for the conflict by insisting it be discussed. Once again, had he returned a rude response, both of them could have dismissed the interaction with: *Some people are just jerks.* Yet, Jay, this workshop member, stayed engaged with the problem and was able to leave the bank without carrying his outrage with him. The bicyclist called the negligent driver on his actions in a way that most likely ensures he'll be more careful around bicyclists in the future. Both thereby increased the chances that something positive could come out of an everyday unpleasant episode.

FAMILY SCULPTING EXERCISES

- Stand in front of a mirror and look at your face. What do the lines in your face mean? How would you describe this person to someone else? Is the person happy or sad? What do you think would make this person feel better about herself or himself?

- Ask a friend or two to help you with this exercise. Pretend that one of your friends is you. Now, using your friend as if he or she were a mannequin, position the friend as you feel yourself to be in relation to your parents. Do not tell the person what you are trying to portray. Do not explain in words; do this silently. Use the person's arms, legs, head, eyes. Is the head turned toward your parents or away? Is the face smiling or not? Is the body standing or sitting or kneeling or exalting, with arms raised? There is no right or wrong way. Don't feel as if you have to be politically correct; just let your imagination take over and sculpt yourself—go with your gut. Now, stand back and look to see if the pose looks right. Does it? If not, change it. It is okay to try several times. This is just an exercise.

- Now, examine how you feel about what you see. Does this give you any new information about the person you are trying to portray? Check in with your own body reactions. What memories come back?
- Ask your friend what he or she is feeling as you. Tell your friend to let the answer come from the physical position itself; in other words, the person should not tell you what *he or she* thinks or feels, but try to feel the answer come from the body, and not censor the answer.
- Now sculpt your friend who is playing you as if a miracle has happened and he or she has discovered they were loved more than they knew. How does that feel? Ask your friend to tell you.

Working through the Codes of Love, workshop participants often discover that their intimate relationships with friends and lovers are also affected.

AUTHENTIC FRIENDSHIPS

For many of us, particularly those with difficult relations with our family, our circle of friends has become a voluntary form of family. Fifty years ago if you got in a jam, you'd call the family, because you wouldn't want the rest of the world to know your plight. Many people I know today, when they find themselves in a rough spot, call their friends, because they don't want to have to answer for their plight to their family. Despite this phenomenon, friendship is an elective state of association, not a permanent bond like family. Even though you have years of history with a friend, sometimes you don't want to say what you really think and risk alienating or even losing him or her. Yet, as you know from the family, everything in the relationship suffers from the things that go unsaid. If you cannot speak candidly with your friend, what is the point of maintaining the friendship? However, there is a difference between candor and cruelty.

David had a difficult friendship issue he had to raise with his friend Bert. The two men, friends for twenty years, attended regular meetings of their political club. Recently, some of the other members of the club had complained to David about Bert's strong body odor, which had been noticed recently and persisted over several months. None of the others wanted to sit next to him or be on committees with Bert because of the smell and how awkward it made them feel. David felt it was his responsibility as a friend to raise the issue with Bert, but it was so personal and so delicate that he didn't know where to start off. Most of us face similar difficult conversations at times.

He called Bert and started to chat about common interests. David could have taken the easy way out by triangulating Bert, being the messenger for the other members of the group. Instead he decided to do it bravely, and personally, by *inquiring*. David told Bert he'd noticed that Bert seemed a little down lately and asked if anything was bothering him. Bert confessed that since he'd lost his job the year before, he'd been depressed. David matched that declaration with empathy, recalling a time when he was depressed for months at the end of a relationship.

Bert then opened up further on the subject of his low mood. He said his apartment was a mess and his car was a trash receptacle on wheels. He needed some way to get out of his funk. David matched Bert again by offering that after that same breakup he didn't make his bed or put away his clothes for months. David then said he'd noticed that this depression was affecting Bert's personal appearance and self-care, too, and mentioned the body odor issue.

"That is hard to hear, but I am glad you told me," Bert said, to

David's relief, adding, "What do you think I could do to get out of this funk?"

"What I did was to start with the things I could change," David recommended. "Take a shower. Throw your clothes in the laundry. Clean out your car. Throw away the junk in your apartment. That's what started me out of my depression, doing the small things. When I was cleaner and more organized, things seemed more hopeful."

The next time the club met Bert was sparkling clean and odor free.

By approaching his friend from a basis of inquiry, seeing his friend's condition as merely a behavior and not a character flaw, David was able to communicate with his friend on an emotional level. Had he avoided the issue, his friend would have lost a chance to benefit from David's friendship. Had he said, "Hey, buddy. Take a shower. Everyone's talking about how bad you stink," David would have just added to Bert's depression. By being secure enough to identify with his friend's plight, David performed a service, something any true friend would do. This is risking revolution. We have all had to hear things we would rather not; we have all had our days of despair or embarrassment. The effectiveness of David's approach comes from the compassion he demonstrated and the trust his friend Bert showed in him. As Harvard psychiatrist Les Havens says, "If we want to teach a man something, we must first join him where he is."

Being secure in our position as compassionate citizens in the world makes us secure enough to risk justice. The security comes from knowing yourself and knowing that your only motive in raising the issue is to help your friend. When our relationships are important enough to us, even if the response to an unpleasant truth is hostile, we will stay engaged in the discussion. We will pause before we speak and make sure that we are honoring the space between us, the space that contains our deep feelings for each other as well as the underlying human frailty that unites us.

If we're ever going to have a real lover or a real friend, we have to have a real self to offer them. As psychiatrist James Masterson says, this self must be able to do the following:

- experience a wide range of emotions
- know his or her worth
- be truly intimate without fear of engulfment or abandonment
- make and stick to commitments
- know how to soothe painful feelings
- be alone

If you examine your role in your love relationships through this definition of the real self, you will know how much of your true spirit is present with your loved ones, family or otherwise.

Once we establish better boundaries with our family, we become more able to maintain them in our other relationships. We learn how to reject fusion with a lover or a friend and how to remain engaged without loss of self. In an authentic friendship, if we are unable to speak the truth, we will be aware of the loss of self that implies—and we will be able to take the difficult step of speaking up, one scary sentence at a time.

AUTHENTIC PARTNERSHIP

To be truly in love with another, we must be able to "hold the dialectic," not only for ourselves but also for our lover. We must love them for who they are today, with their flaws and frustrating habits, and also love their fantasy of whom they are becoming. The more dreams and visions that we share, the more tenable is the friendship that supports the love. So many relationships fall apart on one partner's inability to encompass the totality of the other. Perhaps your lover ignores the less savory aspects of your personality, or perhaps he or she belittles your dreams in the here and now, or perhaps he or she chooses to see you for only that which you wish to become, or perhaps he or she is afraid of change and scared to lose you. Unable to embrace the complexity of our lovers, we often unwittingly hamper each other's progress in the world and lose sight of our own.

The reason to right the relationships of our past is so that we don't have to relive the negative aspects of them over and over. We each have a positive internal engine that seeks resolution of our internal dilemmas. Instead of waking up to realize that we are involved in yet another failed relationship and then judging ourselves for our inability to find the right kind of mate, we are much better served by assuming that whatever forces are at work in the universe have brought us this situation again as an opportunity to wonder

- Why am I here again?
- What am I meant to learn this time around?
- How can I have a *new* kind of relationship with the same kind of person this time?
- What can I do this time that will make us both happy?

Refraining from judging ourselves, just as we refrain from judging others, can be liberating. Suddenly the curiosity that we have learned to show others grants us insight and compassion for ourselves and our struggles. Now we can enter into the arena of intimacy once again, this time with renewed optimism and a respect for the mystery, because we are not trying to find the right mate or change someone else, because we are more secure in our own capacity to love. Losing the old sense of self-judgment lifts the fear of failure that keeps many of us from even attempting the dance again, even with new shoes.

Many years ago, I carried a card with me that said, "I am never angry for the reason I think." I looked at this card several times a day as I taught myself to reflect before I spoke in haste. Now, many years later, that lesson comes back to me as I watch couple after couple argue about the dry cleaning or the carpool or the money he or she is spending. These reasons are not the real issues, as people rarely argue about the things that are very difficult to face directly, let alone articulate.

I knew a couple who used to always fight on the way to the airport when one or the other of them was traveling on business. The issue in play was always different, but the pattern was predictable. One day they realized that they weren't really fighting about the dog or the cleanliness of the house but about their fear of separation. The fight on the way to the airport was a way of replacing the pain of being alone with anger and emotional distance. Watching for factors outside our relationship that are creating the conflict can give us hope because they shift the focus from each other to the stressors in the system.

When Henry and Margaret would argue during their marriage, Henry would declare, "That's it. I'm leaving." To which Margaret would always respond, "Go ahead, then. Go." It was many years after their divorce that they realized that when Henry announced, "I am leaving," he was, in fact, hoping that Margaret would say, "Darling, don't go." Henry wanted to be implored to stay, and Margaret was terrified of being left. In their anger, each said the opposite of what they wanted. Finally, never having heard the true need underneath their anger, the marriage dissolved.

When you look back on your failed relationships, you can see aspects of the difficulty of honest self-expression in each one.

Looking at a wedding photograph from her first marriage, which had ended ten years earlier, Dahlia, a fifty-five-year-old librarian, stopped in wonder and remarked, "Who was that woman who married that man?" Dahlia remembered she seemed to be always in tears in that marriage. Each time the couple would discuss a vital issue in their relationship, she would battle sheepishly for a while and then burst into tears. Her predictable catharsis was not based in insight, and it did not move the discussion forward. Her tears were simply a way to avoid change. Many of us spend hours crying in some therapist's office in a similar avoidance maneuver.

Many men, such as Dahlia's then husband, are destabilized by a woman's tears. So whenever the discussion got too close to something of real value, Dahlia used her tears as a defense to dissolve and end the dialogue. This is something that she'd never do nor allow in a friendship or in a work situation, but it was an unexamined part of her dynamic with her husband. Now, in her second marriage, in which she has resolved her concerns about autonomy, she is able to use humor and candor to discuss her concerns with her new husband. It's no wonder that she looks back on her wedding photograph as a mysterious artifact from someone else's life. By being brave enough to express herself honestly in her new marriage, Dahlia shows that she was able to see the lesson inherent in her first divorce, and she can work to change her part in the dance.

We almost always play a part in our own victimization. In order to discover the Codes of Love within our love relationships, we need to examine the part we play in how things go awry. This is true even in the case of an infidelity. In many relationships one partner is almost relieved to discover the other one is having an affair. The relationship had been limping along for some time, and with the infidelity, the couple has an acceptable reason to declare it ended. The one who was cheated on may be the "designated victim," yet the larger truth is that he or she had some part in whatever went wrong between them. When Sandy's marriage broke up, the couple hadn't had sex in six months. When her husband would reach out to touch her in bed, her body would stiffen and she would shrink away. Her revulsion at her husband's touch shriveled his self-esteem, but it went undiscussed. It was too painful a subject to broach because it might lead to a discussion of divorce.

For the two months before her husband began his affair, it had become uncomfortable for Sandy and her husband to be in the same hallway together, even though, or perhaps especially because, they had been married ten years and had two children. To share that much with someone and to end up so brittle and withdrawn is a painful turn of events that now happens one million times a year in America, to half of each year's group of newly married couples. Though the majority of these struggles will not include adultery as Sandy's did, many will, and the loss of such an intimate friend is painful no matter how it happens. The chance to reawaken these friendships with the respect and love we once held for our former partner is one of the most important payoffs of this Codes of Love work.

When conflict breaks out between intimates, the qualities one party loves about the other person still exist. They've just become dormant in the fraught dynamic of the relationship. You can spend evening after evening arguing about intimacy issues, dredging up conflicts from ten years ago, but you know from the work you've done through this book that the past has precisely the power you decide to give it. My advice is: Don't talk the relationship to death.

Go dancing.

Bring the relationship into present time and take it out of the past and out of the gloomy predictions of the future. Being secure enough to risk justice is also being secure enough to risk gratitude, humor, and joy. This kind of enlightened pride is not a saintly position in the world, not a superior position through which you retain your analytical distance. It is a comic position, a lightheartedness that finds joy in the discovery or is energized by the struggle and greets each day with the hope of progress not the requirement of victory. Relationships never benefit from one partner telling the other all the things he or she needs to change. The people we love don't need to be fixed; they need to be *adored*. Through knowing they are loved truly and accepted completely just as they are, they themselves will become secure enough to risk change, knowing that you will still love them if they fail.

Would learning the Codes of Love have saved Sandy's marriage? It might have. But not all of us are prepared to give up our victimhood and our need to be right. Too many of us are willing to blame only ourselves or place it all on our loved ones. But for Sandy and her husband, and their two children and those children's aunts and uncles and grandparents, the Codes of Love might help them transcend blame and find hope, give up victimhood and discover strength, bury resentment and resurrect love.

Perhaps by Remembering what it is they loved about one another, Reflecting on their own part in the good times and the bad times, Re-framing their problems as part of a larger family system and the anxiety that moves through it, and Reconnecting with each other without blame and judgment will help that family, both blended and extended, look forward into the future with an eye to how their children and grandchildren might someday sculpt them.

Epilogue
Why We Do This Work

In the summer of 1994, during a late-night car ride I took with my then fourteen-year-old nephew Matt, this book began. We were driving from my father's—his grandfather's—in West Virginia, to take him back home to his mother's house in North Carolina. Matt had been quiet for many miles. When I glanced over at him, his hands clasped tightly on his lap, his shoulders hunched forward, his head angled to the floor. In the dim light he looked like a boy half his age. There was a sadness about him that was so deep that it seemed to have become a part of him. I got the feeling that he was struggling to find a reason to go on.

"How come nothing ever changes in our family?" he asked. "How come everything bad always happens to us?"

This conversation with Matt cast me back twenty-five years to a conversation I'd had with my aunt Marcella when I was sixteen. I hadn't asked her the same questions because I thought *I* had the answers. I thought nothing in my family could change and nothing ever would. The sadness behind my certainty mirrored Matt's despair.

I feared for him. I had left my family early and stayed away long. I learned as a grown-up what it was to distrust love and had become used to being alone. I always felt an inner distance from people, but this distance was really inside me—the distance between the young man I once was and the man I could've been. I knew what Matt was afraid of that night—that this tight isolation that contained him was his lot in life.

In too many families children are forced to hunt for answers in a world that seems inexplicable. They believe they are powerful enough to be the cause of their parents troubles, or to solve them. Children often think they know the answers, but they do not. They hope that someone else will notice what they suffer, but no one does. They hope the cavalry will come to rescue them, but it does not. Finally, they leave, hoping someone will notice their absence or someone will ask them to stay, but no one does. Then, they lose connection with the people who love them most. The fact that I was now the adult on the ride, and the situation was so much the same, twenty-five years and thousands of miles later, shook me to my core.

The person who heard Matt was the fourteen-year-old Mark, not this Mark who had learned to soldier on. It was all I could do to keep driving in spite of my tears, feeling afresh that teenage fear that no one really loved anyone. I knew what Matt wanted to know: *Why wasn't anyone there to protect me? Why didn't anyone notice my pain? Why wasn't there anyone to comfort me?*

These questions were really pleas for help from the child I had tried so hard to leave behind, the child who, when he found that he couldn't change the family or change the world, for a time gave up trying to change himself. Years later, when I had moved those same questions from the realm of self-pity to the realm of curiosity, my perspective on my childhood was transformed: my family was not full of blind or crazy people, just people coping with stresses and struggles I had no way of understanding. By that night, I was old enough to know that the adults couldn't offer me this comfort because they still longed for comfort they had not received.

After I dropped Matt off at his mother's, the image of him and the questions he raised stuck with me and became my call to arms. Comfort could begin with me. Love, tolerance, understanding, compassion, and acceptance could all begin with *me*. I would have to search in my heart to find a better me to generate the love I had craved. The place to start to find that better self was among the memories, both good and bad, of my life in my family.

I tell you Matt's story and mine because I know that in some small way it is yours also. You and I know that it doesn't have to be this way. We know that things can be different if only we choose to make them so. I know this is why you chose to read this book. You hope, as I did, that things can change in families. Things *do* change in families, and they change when we change ourselves. Things have changed in mine—and in Matt's.

Matt has become more loving of his mother as he has found the space he needed to become himself. He is twenty years old now, living with me in Los Angeles, and just completed his first year of college on the honor roll. He carries himself with a kind of courage and self-confidence that I longed for as a youth. He radiates the optimism of a man who, even at his young age, understands the power of hunting for the solution instead of lingering in the problem. Even in his short life, he has traveled a great distance to get to where he is today.

I have come to a place and a time in my life when I am surrounded by an extended and blended family, and the joy it gives me is constant and surprising. To go from being a man who believed he hated his family to one who is delighted at the daily tumult they create is something I never could have hoped for and feel honored to have achieved. Divorces and estrangement have transformed to loving friendships and the use of shared resources, food, and lodging—the simple laws of my grandmother Minnie live on today.

My son Scott's mother and her husband had not been comfortable or accepting of my presence in his life as little as five years ago. But we stayed engaged and kept working on trying to form a relationship that would be comfortable for us as well as supportive for Scott. I expressed my gratitude to them for doing the heavy lifting of parenthood over the years of my absence, and at last, through letters and visits, we've built a friendship. Scott and I talk several times a week as he continues to succeed in his education and his own fathering of his daughters.

My former wife Julia and I have healed the rift that led to our divorce in 1993. We remain part of each other's inner circle. I am in her army and she is in mine, and I love her in that respectful, special, and sometimes frustrated way reserved for family. When someone is in your army, it means that they will come to the rescue no matter when or where. When Julia was briefly sick overseas in 1995, I was the first friend there. I wanted to make sure she saw a familiar face in a strange land. She once cleared her calendar for several weeks to help me edit *The Prodigal Father* when I was behind schedule.

Part of the reason we remain close is our love for her daughter, Domenica, whose adventures and successes give both of us great joy. Although we have not lived together since she was sixteen years old, Domenica still calls me her stepdad. I have been on the sidelines of her high school and college graduations and had the most fun outfitting her college jeep with a great stereo. Now that she lives in Los Angeles, I hear it frequently pounding around the corner as she pulls up in front of my house for a visit. I hope someday soon I'll get my Chris Isaaks CD back.

Had I remained stuck in the same old shame, sadness, or resentment of these two divorces and various estrangements, I would not be able to enjoy being the hub of summer activity for my extended family the way that I am. My dad and Jan, my stepmom, are driving their motor home across America this summer to camp in the yard. I am taking my vacation this August to visit my brother Jim and his family, Mom and Paula, April and her kids. Matt's sisters, Sarah and Mandy, and my brother Jon's children, Brandi and Little Jon, are coming out to visit our house in Los Angeles for summer vacation—I think they like the pool. I learned my lessons along the road home that resulted in this book. I take the kids to video arcades instead of threatening to take them to therapy. My job is to provide the quarters and try to beat them at the new Star Wars game.

Life, all in all, is good. I wish the same for you.

Going Home for the Holidays
A Checklist

Remember that even in the most loving of families holidays can be stressful due to our expectations. There is no perfect holiday for anyone. We all deal with it one day at time—progress not perfection. If it is the first time home for you in a long time, try to do it by yourself, or if you have a mate, be sure to spend some alone time with your relatives without your spouse, and *if* you are a father or mother visiting a child, be sure to consider the child's age, and the people who have been raising that child. Try hard not to exclude any family in your old home town, and resist the temptation to spend all the time with high school buddies— they will be proud of your interest in spending time with your family. Do not bring them along if they were a sore spot—don't bring your old hoodlum buddy home. Do not stay too late or expect too much.

1. **Try to make contact before the holiday.** Holidays are so weighted with expectations that the potential for emotional eruptions is higher, particularly if this is the first visit after a long period of estrangement. Everyone may be trying so hard to be nice that it can seem surreal. It's better to begin speaking with the family before the holiday so that you can feel an affinity before the big day and get a sense of what is going on in their lives.

2. **Stay in a hotel or with a friend**. You may need space for yourself. Many families expect that you will stay with them, but a place of your own allows you to recharge your energies in solitude. It also allows you to stay less reactive to the emotions that will well up during the holiday. Remember your family may need breaks from you as well. Try to be conscious of their need for space and solitude too. Don't take their need for autonomy personally.

3. **Plan to do something specific with family members**. We get into trouble when we sit in the house and try to communicate. By doing something together, you let the activity be the focus and a forum for communication. Go to a favorite restaurant; take a favorite walk from your childhood. Pitch in with the mundane chores—but do not try to take over the kitchen. Just offer to help and pitch in— grab the dish towel and start drying. Do not ask them, "Can I help?" from in front of the television. They will be less inclined to accept your offer if you are otherwise engaged, and they will notice if you do not really help.

4. **Ask questions about the past**. Asking about the past can be a non-conflictual point of contact. Ask about any people you remember. Ask how they are doing. Revive a favorite memory and ask their perspective on the event.

5. **Have curiosity about their lives in the present—their world**. Ask them about hobbies. Keep a spirit of inquiry. Go to their beauty parlor. Go to their church, synagogue, or mosque. Explore their favorite restaurants, supermarket, and so forth, so you get to know the ordinary aspects of their world.

6. **Bring a camera**. Having a camera creates that millimeter of distance that helps to preserve your sanity. It allows you to participate and observe at the same time. This permits you to reflect in present time with a bit of safe space around you. It also becomes a source of joy as you take pictures that you will send back to them as a gift of your trip and can use to continue to build the relationship.

7. **Have an ally**. Recruit a friend, family member, therapist, someone who is aware of the feelings you have about being in the family. This is someone you can check in with about what you are experiencing. Make a commitment to yourself that you will not do anything rash—

such as go to a bar and get trashed, stomp out because of a small argument—without checking in with your ally. You need a reality check. You should make an appointment to check in with your ally in any case, as you may not realize what is happening to you until you talk to someone else.

8. **Watch for signs of signal anxiety.** Are you eating or drinking too much? Withdrawn? Grandiose? Promising too much? Exaggerating your current life? Take a minute and stop to breathe. Take three deep breaths—these are signs that you may need to check in with your ally.

9. **Monitor your body signals.** Are you flushed? Sluggish? Claustrophobic? Fidgety? These are all signs of nervousness, not cause for alarm. Be aware. Are you able to sleep? Get exercise to help handle these signs of anxiety.

10. **Don't force them to talk about their feelings.** The need to have them express their feelings says more about your anxiety level than it says about them. Let them tell you what they want to tell you, when they want to tell it.

11. **There is no need to buy them anything ostentatious.** Money cannot buy love, but thoughtful gifts go a long way toward making someone feel that you *see* them. Don't expect gifts from them, though accept them graciously if they are given. By all means, do not promise anything you cannot deliver, and try to stay away from the grandiose gesture—love is most easily found in small, intimate exchanges.

12. **Manage your expectations.** Keep it lighthearted. There is no need to make up for lost time. Just work to stay emotionally present without being swamped by feelings. No need to keep yourself to some ideal standard that cannot be met or to hold them up to it either. Let go of the need for an apology for some past hurt. If it has been a long time, just listen. Just tell the facts of your life when asked in the best way you know how.

APPENDIX II
The Codes of Love Rules of Engagement

1. **No kicking, biting, or gouging.** We can choose to stay out of conflict by simply not engaging in the old battles. I no longer need to defend myself about the lost years because they are over. People make mistakes, and we have to keep our focus on the positive, not on the old resentments. Take a time-out if things get rocky.

2. **Let sleeping dogs lie.** This is not meant to be a permanent form of denial. There is a time and place for going over tough subjects, but they should be planned and thought out. No need to wake the dog in public, when you are surrounded or tired. If someone else wakes the old dog—that is, brings up a difficult subject from the past (such as: "Are you still living in that horrible place?" "Are you still broke?" "You owe me money." "Are you still sleeping with that terrible boyfriend?")—then try to answer bluntly, "Yes, and I do not want to discuss it now," and change the subject. A simple question such as "And how are *you* doing?" will often suffice. Know that many people who bring up difficult subjects and "throw them in your face" are often not conscious of how difficult the subject is for you. We often bring up our most painful past mistakes, even when we don't mean to, for the same reason. There will be a time to discuss "issues," but at first, let the old dog sleep. Stay in the present.

3. **Don't make promises you cannot keep.** This is particularly good advice if you have been away for any length of time. Many of us have a tendency to want to do more for our family members than we can. This is natural, but it can get us into a lot of trouble when we let our insecurity guide our giving. It is much better, for example, to engage with your nieces about their hopes for college than to promise to pay their tuition when you are not able to do so.

4. **Don't try to fix anybody.** The world is doing okay without me running it. Try to accept what is happening as part of the big picture and do not try and fix anybody. The best way to help someone is by example, so rather than nag your daughter about going to college, sign up and go yourself. Let your self-definition advise and inspire her.

5. **Don't try to save anybody.** Most of the actions we can take to try and save someone from the consequences of their own actions just end up hurting them. Giving an adult child money instead of love just enables them to stay dependent and you to stay in control. (Except in situations of abuse or neglect, in which case you owe it to yourself to call social services to help get the family the assistance they need, do not try to save anybody else.) Efforts to keep bankrupt kids afloat, to keep fighting parents together, or to force someone to lose weight are probably doomed to failure.

6. **Listen more than you speak.** This is my toughest one. I talk when I am nervous or when I want to show someone I love them by trying to inspire them. Listening is one of the greatest gifts we can give anyone, especially old people and children. Give them a good hearing—ask questions about their current list of friends, neighbors, their hobbies, television. Any good memories of the past are good to talk about because it can help unlock buried love.

7. **Stay in touch with your feelings.** This is easier said than done. Monitor your body and your breathing; they are the first place that changes in emotions register. The red face, the quickening pulse of anger or shame, are experienced differently than the numbness or tiredness of depression. Listen to your body for how you are feeling, and act to protect it. There is no need to be afraid of tears; they are one group of colors in our emotional paint box. The more we learn

to acknowledge what we are feeling, the more subtle we will be able to be. If you get overwhelmed emotionally, take a time-out—a walk around the block, a spell in your room. Do not let your emotions run away with you.

8. **Use curiosity as a strategy.** Curiosity is one of the most important skills that we learn in life. Try to remain open to new information both intellectually and emotionally. Do not defend when challenged. Instead try to ask relevant questions about why someone thinks, feels, or acts the way they do. This is really listening.

9. **Don't use triangles.** Many of us have grown skilled at communicating through others instead of person to person. Don't tell John something about Mary you hope John will tell her instead of you. Also if John has information that comes from Mary, speak directly to her about it.

10. **Don't punish someone for telling the truth.** Whether it is in families or corporations, we often try and "kill the messenger." To keep an open system of communication requires that we reward people for the truth, not punish them. When information is hard to hear, try to reflect on it for a day or so before reacting. Let the messenger go free.

11. **Make apologies when necessary.** If only we never made mistakes or said things we regretted, but we all do make mistakes. Be quick to admit when you are wrong, and follow through with an apology and a change in behavior. A true apology comes with a renewed promise to do things differently.

12. **Practice loving candor.** Some subjects are too painful to talk about, but when asked a tough question, be willing to give the tough answer that really speaks your truth. This is not an easy skill to use and gets more difficult as the risk of embarrassment, shame, or financial risk increase. Remember that the more authentic you can be the more you allow someone else the space to reach closer to their own truth. The ability to say, "This is how I feel, think, behave," is a place of great spiritual power. We have no one's expectations to live up to but our own.

13. **Release the need to be right.** You can talk about anything as long as your remember to frame any conflict as a clash between ideas and

not individuals. Someone else's belief may be just as valid as yours, so don't get immediately wrapped up in convincing someone you are right. What if you were both right? Either way, their answer probably isn't meant as a personal affront—don't take it personally.

14. **Focus on the process—not the content.** The content of a discussion is much less relevant for our purposes than is the process of communication. Are you able to keep discussion open and have many opinions heard? Are you able to keep secrets to a minimum, since they harm communication on every level? How another person converses (or doesn't) with us says much more about the level of our intimacy than does what is specifically said.

15. **Make love a priority.** It is so easy in today's world to look for the problem instead of the solution. Make an active decision to find the love in every exchange, to focus on the good times and feelings you have shared with your family. Love is not just hugs—it's respect. Look for the love and you will find it. It's there.

Teaching and Traveling with Codes of Love

A Guide to Starting Study Groups

GUIDELINES FOR ALL PARTICIPANTS,
INCLUDING FACILITATORS

1. Gather weekly for two hours or so.
2. Avoid self-appointed gurus.
3. Listen. Do not "fix" each other in group.
4. Respect each other.
5. Expect change in the group makeup.
6. Be autonomous.
7. Be self-loving.
8. A word to therapists.
9. Thank you.
10. Pass it on.

Gather weekly for two hours or so. The exercises are done in order, in the group, with everyone, including the facilitator, answering the questions and then sharing the answers with the group. It's recommended that no one new join the group once it has been in session for three weeks, because it may interrupt the trust and bonding that will have been established during that time. Because of the emotional nature of this work, it's important not to go beyond meeting for two hours or so.

Avoid self-appointed gurus. There are no *Codes of Love* gurus. Each person is an equal part of the collective, no one more than another. There may be "teachers," or facilitators, who are relied on to guide others down the path. These facilitators should be prepared to share their own material and take their own emotional risks along with the group. This is a dialectic rather than a monologue—an egalitarian group process rather than a hierarchical one.

Listen. We each get all we need from the group process by *listening*. We do not need to comment on another person's sharing in order to help them. We must refrain from trying to "fix" someone else. When listening, go around the circle without commenting unduly upon what is heard. The circle, as a shape, is very important. We are intended to witness, not control, each other.

Respect each other. Be certain that respect and compassion are equally afforded to every member. Each person is to be able to speak their own truth and dreams. No one is to be "fixed" by another member of the group. This is a deep and powerful internal process. There is no one "right" way to do this. Love is important. Be kind to yourself. Be kind to each other.

Expect change in the group makeup. Know that many people will—and some will not—stay committed to the group process. We wish to note that many groups have a tendency to drift apart because of the feelings associated with the emotional depth of the material. Face that truth as a group; it may help you stay together.

Be autonomous. Know that you cannot control your own process, let alone anyone else's process. Know that you will feel rebellious at times—that you won't want to do all of the exercises from time to time. You *cannot* do this process perfectly, so relax, be kind to yourself, and hold on to your hat. This is meant to be a gradual deepening of your understanding of yourself.

Be self-loving. If the facilitator feels toxic or somehow "wrong" to you, change clusters or start your own. Continually seek your own inner guidance as well as outer guidance. Keep the gurus at bay. You have your own answers within you.

A word to therapists, members of the clergy, and social workers. Thank you for the wonderful work you do in an important and often difficult profession. Although many of you may use *Codes of Love* to run groups, it's expected that you will go on to explore *your* own *Codes of Love* process also.

Thank you. It is wonderful that *Codes of Love* is used in the many contexts it is (such as colleges and universities, by therapists, and by peer-run circles or clusters). Please remember that *Codes of Love* is intended to be a source of gratitude and an exploration of the hidden love within your family and yourself. Please keep the word *love* in the forefront of your mind. This work takes personal courage, and I thank you for taking the journey with me.

Pass it on. To those forming a peer-run circle or cluster: You do not need to make *Codes of Love* a money-making venture for us. If you follow the spiritual practice of tithing, we recommend buying the book and passing it on.

Bibliography

American Psychiatric Association. *DSM-IV: Diagnostic and Statistical Manual of Mental Disorders.* 4th ed. Washington, D.C.: American Psychiatric Association, 1994.

Basch, Michael Franz. Understanding Psychotherapy: *The Science Behind the Art.* New York: Basic Books, 1988.

Bowen, Murray. *Family Therapy in Clinical Practice.* Northvale, N.J.: Jason Aronson, 1994.

Bowlby, John. *A Secure Base: Parent-Child Attachment and Healthy Human Development.* New York: Basic Books, 1988.

Brown, Lyn Mikel, and Carol Gilligan. *Meeting at the Crossroads: Women's Psychology and Girls' Development.* New York: Ballantine Books, 1992.

Bryan, Mark. *The Prodigal Father: Reuniting Fathers and Their Children.* New York: Clarkson Potter Publishers, 1997.

Burns, E. Timothy. *From Risk to Resilience: A Journey with Heart for Our Children, Our Future.* Dallas, Tex.: Marco Polo Publishers, 1994.

Coles, Robert. *Doing Documentary Work.* New York: Oxford University Press, 1997.

Darnall, Douglas, Ph.D. *Divorce Casualties: Protecting Your Children From Parental Alienation.* Dallas, Tex.: Taylor Publishing Company, 1998.

Etzioni, Amitai. *The Spirit of Community: The Reinvention of American Society.* New York: Simon & Schuster, 1993.

277

Fisher, Helen E. *Anatomy of Love: The Natural History of Monogamy, Adultery, and Divorce.* New York: W. W. Norton Company, 1992.

Freire, Paulo. *Pedagogy of the Oppressed.* New York: Continuum Publishing Company, 1997.

Friedman, Edwin H. *Generation to Generation: Family Process in Church and Synagogue.* New York: Guilford Press, 1985.

Gardner, Richard A., M.D. *The Parental Alienation Syndrome.* Cresskill, N.J.: Creative Therapeutics, 1992.

Gilligan, Carol. *In A Different Voice: Psychological Theory and Women's Development.* Cambridge, Mass.: Harvard University Press, 1982.

Gomes, Peter J. *The Good Book.* New York: William Morrow and Company, 1996.

Gomes, Peter J. *Sermons: Biblical Wisdom for Daily Living.* New York: Avon Books, 1998.

Harris, Judith Rich. *The Nurture Assumption.* New York: Free Press, 1998.

Havens, Leston. *A Safe Place: Laying the Groundwork of Psychotherapy.* Cambridge, Mass.: Harvard University Press, 1996.

Havens, Leston. *Making Contact: Uses of Language in Psychotherapy.* Cambridge, Mass.: Harvard University Press, 1988.

Hoffman, Richard. *Half the House: A Memoir.* New York: Harcourt Brace & Company, 1995.

Hunter, Mic. *Abused Boys: The Neglected Victims of Sexual Abuse.* New York: Fawcett Columbine, 1990.

James, John W., and Russell Friedman. *The Grief Recovery Handbook.* New York: HarperCollins, 1998.

Kagan, Jerome. *Galen's Prophecy.* New York: Basic Books, 1994.

Kegan, Robert. *The Evolving Self: Problem and Process in Human Development.* Cambridge, Mass.: Harvard University Press, 1982.

Kernberg, Otto F., M.D. *Love Relations: Normality and Pathology.* New York: Yale University Press, 1995.

Kerr, Michael, and Murray Bowen. *Family Evaluation.* New York: W. W. Norton & Company, 1988.

Kozol, Jonathan. *Savage Inequalities.* New York: Crown Publishers, 1991.

Lee, Ronald R., and J. Colby Martin. *Psychotherapy After Kohut.* Hillsdale, N.J.: Analytic Press, 1991.

Loftus, Elisabeth, and Katherine Ketcham. *The Myth of Repressed Memory.* New York: St. Martin's Press, 1994.

Malan, David H. *Individual Psychotherapy and the Science of Psychodynamics.* Oxford: Butterworth-Heinmann, 1995.

Masterson, James F., M.D. *The Search for the Real Self: Unmasking the Personality Disorders of Our Age.* New York: Free Press, 1988.

Merton, Thomas. *No Man Is an Island.* New York: Harcourt Brace & Company, 1955.

Miller, Alice. *Banished Knowledge: Facing Childhood Injuries.* New York: Doubleday, 1988.

Miller, Alice. *The Drama of the Gifted Child.* New York: Basic Books, 1994.

Miller, Alice. *The Untouched Key.* New York: Doubleday, 1988.

Miller, Fred L. *How to Calm Down Even If You're Absolutely, Totally Nuts.* Burbank, Calif.: Namaste Press, 1999.

Minuchin, Salvador, and H. Charles Fishman. *Family Therapy Techniques.* Cambridge, Mass.: Harvard University Press, 1981.

Moore, Thomas. *Care of the Soul: A Guide for Cultivating Depth and Sacredness in Everyday Life.* New York: HarperCollins, 1992.

Nerin, William. *Family Reconstruction.* New York: W. W. Norton & Company, 1986.

Nerin, William. *You Can't Grow Up Till You Go Back Home.* Magic Mountain Publishing, 1993.

Neubauer, Peter B., M.D., and Alexander Neubauer. *Nature's Thumbprint: The New Genetics of Personality.* Reading, Mass.: Addison-Wesley Publishing Company, 1990.

O'Hagan, Kieran. *Emotional and Psychological Abuse of Children.* Toronto: University of Toronto Press, 1993.

Peck, M. Scott, M.D., *The Road Less Traveled.* New York: Simon & Schuster, 1978.

Pendergrast, Mark. *Victims of Memory: Sex Abuse Accusations and Shattered Lives.* Hinesburg, VT.: Upper Access, 1995.

Pervin, Lawrence A. *Handbook of Personality: Theory and Research.* New York: Guilford Press, 1990.

Pierrakos, John C., M.D. *Eros, Love & Sexuality: The Forces That Unify Man and Woman.* Mendocino, Calif.: LifeRhythm, 1997.

Rawls, John. *The Theory of Justice.* Cambridge, Mass.: Harvard University Press, 1971.

Ricci, Isolina, Ph.D. *Mom's House, Dad's House.* New York: Macmillan, 1980.

Seligman, Martin F. P., Ph.D. *Learned Optimism: How to Change Your Mind and Your Life.* New York: Simon & Schuster, 1990.

Shapiro, Edward R., and A. Wesley Carr. *Lost in Familiar Places: Creating New Connections Between the Individual and Society.* New Haven, Conn.: Yale University Press, 1991.

Smith, Huston. *The World's Religions.* New York: HarperCollins, 1991.

Smith, Kenwyn K., and David N. Berg. *Paradoxes of Group Life.* San Francisco: Jossey-Bass, 1987.

Stettbacher, J. Konrad. *Making Sense of Suffering: The Healing Confrontation with Your Own Past.* New York: Dutton, 1991.

Tangney, June Price, and Kurt W. Fischer. *Self-Conscious Emotions: The Psychology of Shame, Guilt, Embarrassment, and Pride.* New York: Guilford Press, 1995.

Vaillant, George E. *The Wisdom of the Ego.* Cambridge, Mass.: Harvard University Press, 1993.

Wallerstein, Judith S., and Sandra Blakeslee. *Second Changes: Men, Women, and Children a Decade After Divorce.* New York: Ticknor & Fields, 1989.

Weissbourd, Richard. *The Vulnerable Child: What Really Hurts America's Children and What We Can Do About It.* Reading, Mass.: Addison-Wesley Publishing Company, 1996.

Whitehead, Barbara Dafoe. *The Divorce Culture.* New York: Alfred A. Knopf, 1996.

Wright, Robert. *The Moral Animal: Why We Are the Way We Are: The New Science of Evolutionary Psychology.* New York: Vintage Books, 1993.

Zimberg, Sheldon, John Wallace, and Sheila B. Blume. *Practical Approaches to Alcoholism Psychotherapy.* New York: Plenum Press, 1985.

Zukav, Gary. *The Seat of the Soul.* New York: Simon & Schuster, 1989.

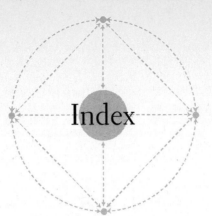

Index

Self *(cont.)*
  steps to shed false self and find authentic self, 91–103
Self-sufficiency, myth of, 174–77
Shakespeare: The Invention of the Human (Bloom), 37
Shakespeare, William, view of family, 36–37
Shame-blame paralysis, 10, 74, 118
Sibling relationships, 200–202
Signal anxiety, 57–60, 79–80
  example, 57–59
  exercises, 136–37, 138
  holidays, going home for and, 267
  symptoms of, 79–80, 267
Somewhere in the Night: Film Noir and the American City (Christopher), 35
Storyline exercise, 20–22
  emotional shockwaves and, 135–36
Stress, positive, exercise, 138–39
Study groups, guide to, 273–75
Support, therapeutic, 19–20
Suspicion, 28, 150, 226
  Carla, writer returning home and career conflicts, 45–47
  death, and motivation to eliminate, 44–47
  family and, 35–36, 105

  humor to combat, 47–49
  mislabeling of, 31
  need to eliminate, 40
  never or *always* as signaling, 60–62
  poisonous effect of, 30–34
  removing, 63
  schema or gestalt, 28

Temperament, 101–02, 116
Triangles, 125–32, 271
  example, two brothers and father, 166–68
  exercise, building triangles, 143
  exercise, 141
  fantasy, memory, object or behavior as, 141
  idealized version of life as, 143
  negative responses to fear of, 141
  processes as, 142–43
  Rose and Max, 128–31
Triggers, 141–42

Vaillant, George, 152, 156, 161
Vengeance, 85
Vicious or virtuous cycles, 145
Victimhood, 186, 256–57
Violent families, 33, 223

Wisdom of the Ego, The (Vaillant), 152

ACKNOWLEDGMENTS

First and foremost, thank you to Mitchell Ivers, my editor, for his faith in me, in the project, and for his inspired guidance.

Jack Romanos, Judith Curr, and the whole team at Pocket Books—Pam Duevel, Laurie Cotumaccio, Laura Ross and David Savaterri, Amanda Ayers, and Paolo Pepe.

David Vigliano, my agent and guru.

Deborah Blackwell for her wise and loving support, her brains and her beauty.

A very special thank-you to Danelle Morton, my collaborator: a great writer, reporter, courageous spirit, and friend, who rolled up her sleeves and helped me find the emotional heart of this book. It would not exist without her insight and extraordinary intellectual honesty. She worked day and night and was the best.

Gracie Hollombe for impulse control, grace under fire, and her loving support.

Oprah Winfrey, Dianne Hudson, Ellen Rakieten, Lisa Morin, Lisa Minor, Rita Thompson, Jenna Kostelnik, and Martha Hernandez for making me look good and fighting the good fight. Jeff Jacobs for remembering.

My friends and traveling companions: Lisa Bashor, Richard Clar, Jane Clark, Jan Gealer, Jim Hagopian, Barbara Kosoff, Jayson Kritch, Brian Leng, Suzan Lozano, Ed Madison, Ricia Quintana,

Debi Stambaugh, Shayla Waite, Jeff Whitley, Sandra Wyman. Jim Woods for the use of his house for the early Codes work. Julia Cameron, Jamie Frankfurt, Sheila Flaherty, Carl Fritz, Jim Miller, Bob Earl, Gavin de Becker, Michelle Lowrance, Fred Miller, Larry Sugar, Shelley Scott, Carolyn and Louis, and Teresa DeLucio, for being the kind of friends who are always there.

Mom and Dad, Jan, Jon, Emma, Les, Little Jon, Brandi, Paula, the memory of Nick Vladimery, Matt, Sara, Mandy, April, Aaron and Andrew, Sherry Runge, Dakota, Christin Ballenger, Blake, Aunt Marcella and Uncle Tom, Brenda, Sandy, Kimberly and the memory of Dickie Bird, Jim, Tammy, Emee, Gail, the memory of Aunt Norma, David, Karen, Bill and Brenda, Todd, James and the memory of Steven, the memory of Uncle Harry, Uncle Glen and Barbara, Ruth, Phil, Grandma Minnie, Grandpa Arnie, Grandpa Frank, Grandma Elizabeth, my son, Scott Graham, Caroline, Madison, Peake Graham, Bill Lobeck and Cathy Taylor, Lee and David Marks, Molly and Hank Pelligrini, Patty and Glenn Graham, and Domenica Cameron-Scorsese.

Jeff Crosthwaite, Patrick Dragon, Dan and Linda Craig, Mark and Shirley Booth, Babette Ison, Betty Rice, Monique Guild, Freebo and Laurie, Randy Robinson, Jody Brockway, Arnold Orgilini, Wally and Laurie, Debbie Reinisch, Rita Hayward, Joan Harrison, Jean Blackwell, Bo and Zorianna, Richard Hoffman, Neil Romanek, Matthew Brandebur, Maureen and Fritz Mueller, Mike Cotter, Dan McNamara, Gordon and Melody Diachenko, Gabe Hollombe (computer genius), Yale Kozinski (computer genius #2), Ben Morton, Marissa Morton, Megan Wright, Stephanie Voss, Carol Shaw, Kristin Spear, Katie Hemmeter, Leslie Fleming, Whitney Post, Lauren Costine, Eric Lerner, Wyatt Earp, Elizabeth McLeod, Karen V., Nancy F. K., Dave Heyward, Kellan Flanigan, David Seligman, Jerome Ferguson, Betty Elkins Rice, Nate and Carolyn, Todd Shapiro, Mitch, Danny and Donny, Stephanie Luxton and Grace, Charlene, Marlene and Darlene, Deborah Morgan-Peters, Gary Solomon, Dina Petrakis Solomon, Doug and Jody O'Donahue, Billy Jones, Marvin Richardson, Dan Pomerantz, Mark Pearson, Bob Skeens, Keith Rudman, Tim Collins, Deborah Blando, and Maureen Miller.

Sandy Mendelson and Judy Hilsinger for publicity, and Evelyn Kunstler, Barbara Carswell, and William Greenfield for their enlightened management. Phil Hanrahan for helping forge the initial theoretical arguments.

The many clinicians whose work I have found invaluable: Linda Powell, Richard Rosen, Michael Kerr, George Vailliant, Carol Gilligan, Rick Weissbourd, Les Havens, Ron David, and Kurt Fisher.

Jack Miller at the Children's Trust Fund, Ron Galbraith at ISA, Bill Isaacs and Otto Scharmer at the Dialogue Project at MIT, Kate Pugh, Catherine Allen, Camillo Gomez and the men and women of Casa, John Davies, the Country Music Association, Mike Parfett and the AT&T team, Peggy Griffin at Lucent Technologies, Julie Anxiter, Paul Sanders, Norman and Marybeth Klotz, June Brickman, Dini Petty, Emily, Lucinda and Daniel, Judy Long, Daneen Skube, Mark and Kristin in David Vigliano's office for putting up with my impatience, Jean Carow at Harpo, Doug SuSu Mago, Holly Strool, Vilma, and Luis Nieto.

The Artist's Way and *Artist's Way at Work* students around the world.